The Best Of *The Mailbox* 2

Primary Edition

Our favorite ideas from the 1988–1992 issues of the Primary edition of *The Mailbox*® magazine

Editor in Chief
Margaret Michel

Manager of Product Development
Charlotte Perkins

Editor
Diane Badden

Contributing Editor
Becky Andrews

Copy Editors
Grace Buonocore
Christine A. Thuman

Artists
Jennifer Bennett, Pam Crane, Teresa Davidson, Susan Hodnett, Becky Saunders, Barry Slate

Cover Artist
Pam Crane

Typographer
Lynette Maxwell

About This Book

Since its publication in 1988, the first **Best Of *The Mailbox*®—Primary** book has become one of the most popular titles available to teachers of grades 1–3 today. Now we're proud to present the second **Best Of *The Mailbox*®** book for primary teachers. Inside these covers, you'll find many of the best teacher-tested ideas published in the 1988–1992 issues of ***The* Primary *Mailbox*®**. These practical ideas were selected from those sent to us by teachers across the United States. We've included many of our regularly featured sections of the magazine plus special teaching units and reproducibles.

ISBN# 1-56234-099-9

Manufactured in the United States
10 9 8 7 6 5

Table Of Contents

Bulletin
Boards

This first-day activity makes a "sun-sational" display! Have each student draw half of a pair of sunglasses on a sheet of folded paper, positioning the nosepiece on the fold. After the student cuts out and unfolds the shape, he draws a picture or writes a sentence in each lens to tell about his summer, then colors the remainder of his cutout as desired. Mount the surfer cutout (pattern on page 23), title, and completed cutouts as shown. What a great way to "ease" into the new school year!

Diane Afferton, Morrisville, PA

Put the polish on a great school year with this scrumptious display! Cut a large basket shape from bulletin board paper. To make a woven basket, fold the cutout in half and cut several horizontal slits on the fold; then weave paper strips through the slits. Attach the ends of each strip to the back of the cutout. Mount the cutout and a title appropriate to your grade level. Label an assortment of apple cutouts with exciting topics and events planned for the school year. Mmmm! Good!

Connie Stark—Gr. 2, Jenkintown Elementary, Jenkintown, PA

Spotlight your new student lineup with this eye-catching diisplay. Have each student cut out, personalize and decorate a construction paper T-shirt (pattern on page 24). Use a permanent marker or a Paint Writer (available at craft stores) to label a white, cotton T-shirt as shown. Display the T-shirts using clothespins and lengths of heavy string or plastic clothesline. What a team!

Sandra Taylor—Gr. 2, Sterling Park Elementary, Casselberry, FL

Students work as a team to piece together this eye-catching display. On bulletin board paper cut to the desired size, draw one interlocking puzzle piece per student. (To assure that student work is positioned correctly, indicate the lower edge of each piece.) Cut apart and distribute the pieces. Have students personalize their pieces using crayons or markers; then have the students work together to reassemble the puzzle. Attach the reassembled puzzle to the display. A perfect fit!

Trisha Klakamp—Gr. 2, Hawkes Bluff Elementary, Davie, FL

Hand over this bulletin board to your students! To create the border have students trace their hands atop sheets of colorful construction paper and cut out the resulting shapes. Then have students draw and color posters showing ways they can work together toward a successful school year. Mount the border, posters, and title as shown. No doubt about it! This display will be a hands-down favorite!

Marge Westrich—Gr. 2, Colby Elementary School, Colby, WI

This spooky display of student work is terrifyingly terrific! Use the mask pattern on page 25 to make several tagboard tracers. Have students trace and cut out construction paper masks, then decorate their cutouts using construction paper scraps, glitter, pipe cleaners, feathers, and other arts-and-crafts materials. Mount each student's resulting three-dimensional creation atop the outstanding paper of his choice. "Spooktacular!"

 Janine Sutko, Rockwell Elementary, Omaha, NE

Welcome open house guests to your classroom with this seasonal display. Enlarge the ghost pattern on page 25; then duplicate student copies on white construction paper. Have students personalize, decorate, and cut out the ghost shapes; then mount as shown. Or display each teacher's name and room number on a ghost cutout for an attractive hallway or media center display.

Kathy Hislop, Walnut Hill Elementary, Omaha, NE

Study-habit tips and perfect papers bubble over from this good work display. Enlarge, color, cut out, and mount the witch pattern on page 26. Attach the title and several bubble cutouts labeled with study-habit tips. Have students cut out black construction paper bats using the pattern on page 26 as a tracer. Attach one bat cutout to each perfect paper displayed. Reward students collecting ten bat cutouts (ten perfect papers) with a coupon (page 27) to be used in place of one assignment.

Pat Garton—Gr. 3, Fairbury, NE

Petunia, the silly goose, will bring lots of reading motivation to National Children's Book Week! Refer to the diagram on page 27 to label one paper plate per student. Read aloud *Petunia* by Roger Duvoisin; then have each youngster cut out and assemble a paper plate goose. Attach orange construction paper feet and add desired decorations. Next have each student decorate a small, folded construction-paper sheet to resemble his favorite book. Glue the "books" under the goose wings; then mount the geese as shown. Now that's a flock of great books!

Beth Besley—Gr. 1, Bethel Christian School, Hudson, NH

Reap a crop of favorite family times with this eye-catching display. On a corncob cutout have each student draw and color a picture which shows a fun time he shared with his family. Then have him copy and complete the following sentences, each on a corn husk cutout: I am thankful for the time my family..., It was really fun for me because.... Glue the husks to the corncob and display as shown. Let the harvest begin!

Ana Wilson—Gr. 2, Ames School, Riverside, IL

Here's a manipulative display that will have students gobbling up an assortment of sorting skills! Cut out and decorate three construction paper turkey faces. Have students decorate feather cutouts for the display. Mount the feathers and faces and three haystacks cut from yellow paper. Attach a pocket to each haystack by folding and stapling a laminated sheet of 12" x 18" construction paper. Program a set of cards for sorting (and self-checking if desired). Use a wipe-off marker to program the pockets. Store the cards in a Ziploc bag attached to the display.

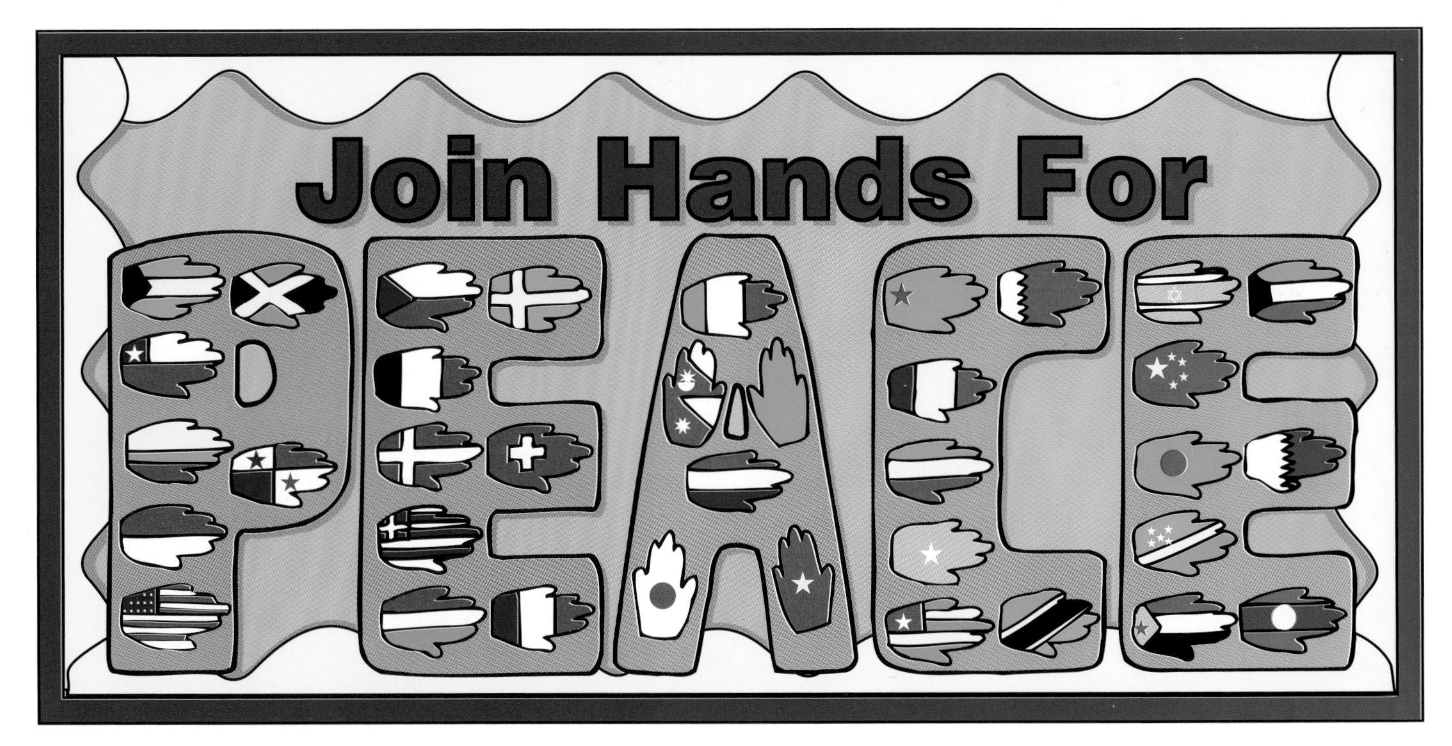

Rally your students together to send a message of peace. Have each student trace one hand atop a sheet of drawing paper and cut out the resulting shape. Next have him color the inside of his cutout to resemble a flag of a different country. Display the completed cutouts atop giant letter cutouts.

Judy Holmes—Gr. 3, Gladstone Elementary School, Gladstone, OR

Focus on the joy of giving with this seasonal display. Each student folds a sheet of white construction paper into fourths. Next he unfolds the paper and illustrates a gift in each section for one of the following: the world, his family, his school, himself. Mount each paper on a length of holiday gift wrap. Mount the completed projects with student-drawn self-portrait and hand cutouts as shown. Happy holidays!

Diane Afferton, Morrisville, PA

Deck your door or display area with this personalized wreath. Cut a large doughnut shape from green paper. Have students mount holly leaf cutouts atop the shape. For a three-dimensional effect, loosely curl the outer edges of the cutouts before mounting. Attach a photocopy of each student's school picture atop a red circle cut from construction paper; then display the cutouts as berries atop the wreath.

Karen Schoenberger, Emporia, KS

Shed light on the joys of giving with this eye-catching display. Mount a reindeer cutout (pattern on page 28), a yarn length, and a title. Duplicate two white construction-paper light patterns (page 28) per student. Have each youngster write how he could brighten the holiday season of a person older or less fortunate than himself on one pattern. Then have him personalize and color his second pattern before cutting out both shapes. Staple each cut-out pair atop the yarn length as shown. Joy to all!

Cindy Fischer—Gr. 1, St. Mary's, Bismarck, ND

Happy holidays! To create one of these three-dimensional displays, have students draw the outlines of seasonal shapes on 10-inch pizza rounds or poster-board circles. Have each student fill his outline with balled-up, one-inch squares of colored tissue paper that have been dipped in glue. Attach a border of garland around each completed project; then mount the projects in the desired shape.

Sara G. McGee, Bel Air Elementary, Evans, GA

Frosty and his snow buddies are a great enticement for practicing word categorization. Mount three snowman cutouts; then label and attach a pocket to each as shown. Adorn the snowmen with buttons, tree-branch arms, and fabric or wallpaper cutouts. Add a title and a dusting of snowflakes cut from white doilies. Place word cards programmed for sorting in a large black hat near the display. Thumpity, thump thump! Look what Frosty knows!

Vickie Simpson—Gr. 1, Eastwood Elementary School, Big Rapids, MI

Students can snuggle up to this cozy, wintertime display. Have each student illustrate a winter scene on a square of light, medium, or dark blue construction paper. If desired, have students embellish their projects with cotton, hole reinforcers, or other "snow" media. Mount the projects atop a bulletin board covered with white paper. Using a blue marker, draw "stitches" around the projects. Attach gathered crepe paper to the outer edges for a quilt border. Let it snow!

Jean Garza—Gr. 2, Country Club Elementary, Farmington, NM

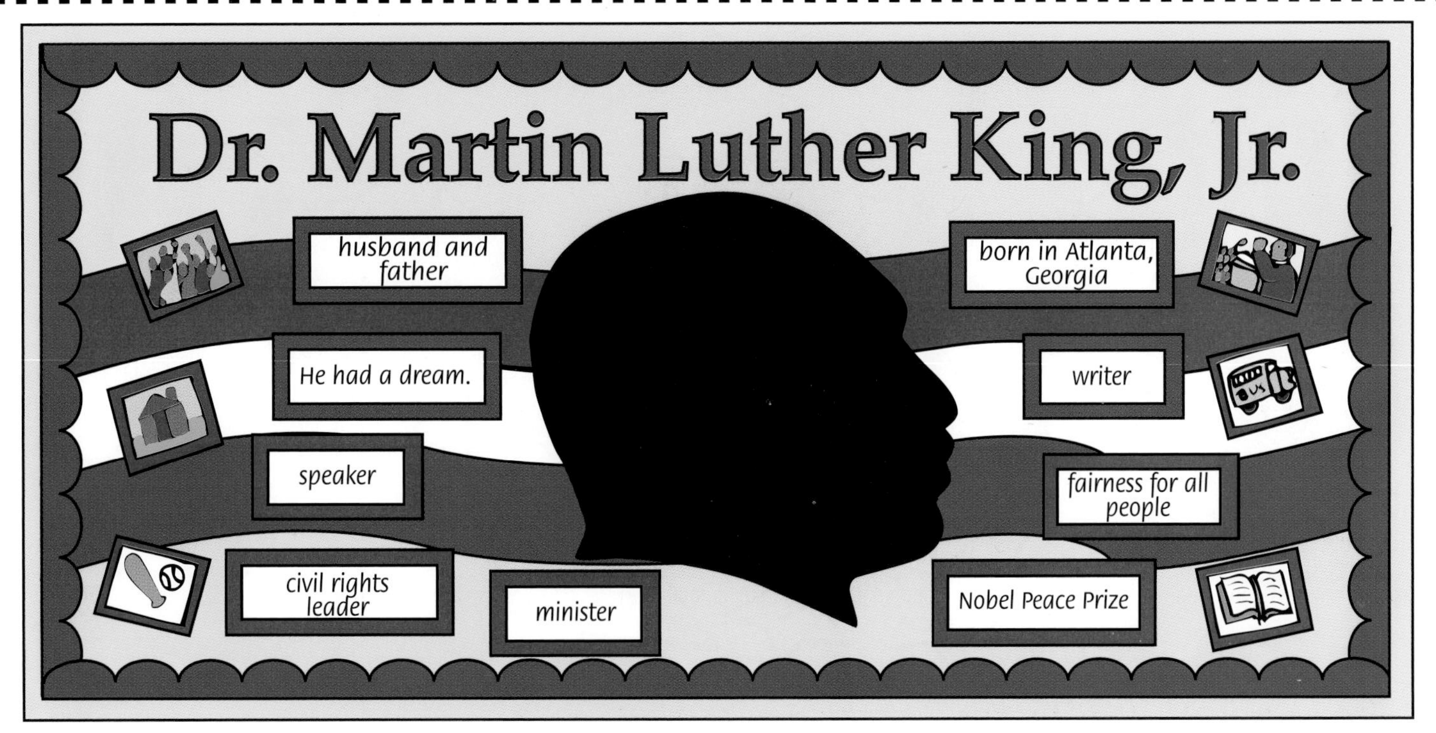

Students uncover facts about Martin Luther King, Jr., to complete this eye-catching display. Using the pattern on page 29, enlarge, cut out, and mount a large silhouette as shown. After his fact has been verified, a student writes or illustrates it on white construction paper. He then mounts his fact atop a slightly larger piece of red or blue construction paper before attaching it to the display. Culminate your students' efforts with a birthday celebration in honor of Dr. King.

Jane Miles—Gr. 2, Greenacres Elementary, Pocatello, ID

What could be more fun than bundling up for a snowstorm? Have each student create and cut out a "chilly" self-portrait, then mount his cutout atop a large half-oval shape cut from construction paper. Using markers or crayons, students draw arms and decorations on the ovals before cutting out and attaching colorful construction paper mittens and hats as shown (patterns on page 29). For those of you who wish for but rarely receive snow, use the title "Dressed For Snow And No Place To Go!"

Mary Moratto, Dallas, TX

Salute the presidents of the United States with this patriotic display. Using the patterns on page 30, enlarge and cut out silhouettes of Lincoln and Washington. Mount the title, cutouts, and border as shown. Then challenge your youngsters to uncover a collection of interesting facts about United States presidents. Have students write verified facts on star cutouts; then attach the cutouts as shown. Now that's a star-spangled display!

Stephanie Bonnivier—Gr. 2, Burt School, Waterford, MI

Nothing could be sweeter than this hearty display of outstanding student work! Have each youngster personalize one side of a heart cutout, then decorate the remaining side as desired. Weekly mount each student's heart creation atop the outstanding paper of his choice. Sweet success will be enjoyed by all!

Get to the heart of the matter with this student-created display. Cut a sheet of bulletin board paper equal to the size of your display area. Invite students to write words and phrases containing the word *heart* on the paper by omitting the *heart* in each word or phrase and replacing it with a heart cutout. In no time at all you'll have a hearty display of heart-warming words!

Isobel L. Livingstone, Rahway, NJ

Watch students sink their teeth into this dental health activity! Have each student cut out a tooth shape (pattern on page 31) and label the lower portion with a dental health reminder. Then, using markers and construction paper scraps, have students personalize and decorate their cutouts in attire suitable for physical fitness activities. There will be tons of grins when the completed projects are put on display.

Diane Vogel—Grs. 2–3, W.B. Redding School, Macon, GA

Let this unbearably cute wizard introduce youngsters to new themes and study topics year-round. Mount a paper strip labeled with the desired topic or theme; then challenge youngsters to brainstorm a list of related words. Write the words on a length of bulletin board paper. Attach the word list to the display and encourage students to refer to it as they complete assignments related to the topic or theme. Abracadabra!

Nancy Glover—Speech/Language Specialist, Alfred Reed School, Trenton, NJ

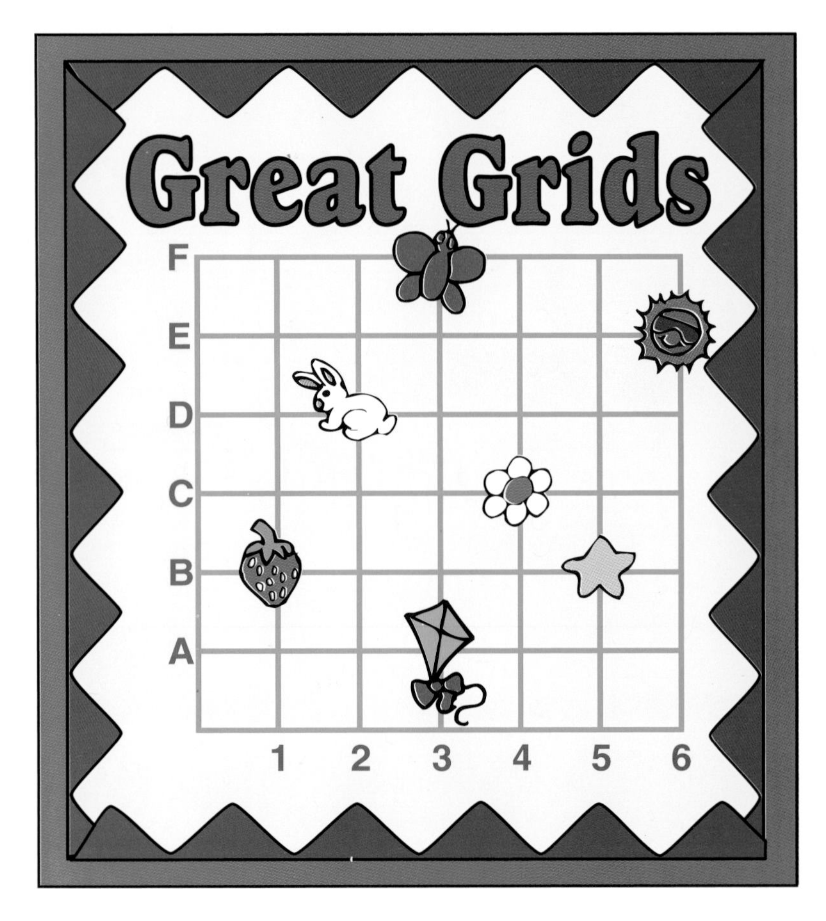

Here's an instructional display that's easy to make and simple to reprogram. Position and staple yarn in place to form a grid. Label the grid using precut letters and numerals. Attach magazine pictures mounted on construction paper or small bulletin board pieces at various coordinates on the grid. In turn, student pairs ask each other to identify a picture at a specific set of coordinates or to give the coordinates for a specific picture. Keep student interest high by frequently changing the pictures and their locations.

Diane Vogel—Gr. 2
Redding School
Macon, GA

Students leave a trail of good work at this bunny bulletin board! To make the border, have students finger paint orange designs; then cut the designs into carrot shapes and attach green construction paper stalks. For bunny, cut a head and two ears from construction paper. Use construction paper scraps, a large pink pom-pom, black pipe cleaners, and markers to add details. Attach a bow tie fashioned from wallpaper.

Sarah McCutcheon, Allendale, SC

Have this token of appreciation ready to display in a snap! Using tempera or poster paint, paint a fence and message on a sheet of brown wrapping paper as shown. Trim the fence to the desired size; then have students use markers to sign the cutout. Mount as shown, adding a character if desired. Surprise a student teacher, teacher's assistant, or principal today!

Dianne Krieser—Gr. 3, Hamlow Elementary School, Waverly, NE

If your literature activities need a new twist, try branching out into poetry. Make a collection of numbered poetry cutouts such as the one shown. (The upper portion of each cutout must be wider than its "tab." For easy implementation, standardize the tab widths.) Mount a tree cutout. Cut a slit in the tree for each poetry cutout; then insert the cutouts. Each day, let one youngster "pick a poem." Read the poem aloud several times and invite students to "say it along" with you. Youngsters will soon have the poetry selections memorized and be reciting them on their own!

Michelle S. Bourlet, Clayton, GA

This hands-on display will make a splash! Mount three student-colored umbrella shapes as shown. Atop the shapes, display number cutouts representing multiplication products (or other math answers). Program raindrop cutouts (pattern on page 32) with corresponding problems. Program the back of each cutout for self-checking if desired; then punch a hole in the top of each and place the cutouts in a bucket. A student suspends the raindrops on pushpins above the corresponding umbrellas.

Mary K. Good, Seaford Christian Academy, Seaford, DE

Here's a "dino-mite" way to motivate your little sluggers! Each week choose seven "team" goals. Write each goal on a sheet of construction paper. Mount the goals and attach a laminated baseball cutout (pattern on page 34) near each one. At a designated time on Friday, evaluate each goal. If the goal has been met, use a wipe-off marker to write the appropriate letter from "HOME RUN" on the corresponding baseball. If "HOME RUN" is spelled, reward students with a few extra minutes of recess. What a team!

adapted from an idea by Colleen Tendall—Gr. 1, St. Pius X, Urbandale, IA

HATS OFF TO YOU!

Zannon is a great buddy.

Dylan tells funny stories.

Randy is so helpful. He helps me when I'm confused.

Maria sings pretty.

Presley has pretty cursive writing.

Yvonne is a great kickball player!

Mr. R.'s class walks very quietly in the hallways.

I wish I could draw like Beth!

I like Tonya's laugh!

Boost your buckaroos' self-esteem with a compliment roundup! Cut a sheet of bulletin board paper equal to the size of your display; then mount the character cutout and title as shown. Nearby, in a cowboy hat, place several watercolor markers. Invite students to write complimentary phrases about their classmates on the bulletin board paper. Also invite other staff members to write positive comments about your students.

Don Reiffenberger—Gr. 3, Laura B. Anderson Elementary, Sioux Falls, SD

Hold your horses, Hollywood! These stars are ready to shine. Invite students to discuss people in their lives that "shine" with goodness; then have each complete and cut out a duplicated copy of the star pattern on page 32. Staple each of these pages between two slightly larger yellow construction paper star cutouts. Attach photographs or draw pictures of the "stars" on the front covers; then decorate with glitter if desired.

Carol Kenney and Lois W. Jones—Gr. 3, Scenic Hills School, Springfield, PA

Dish up an attractive May display with paper plate art. To make a flower, cut a paper plate into six equal sections. Using Q-tips, garnish each "petal" with several colors of paint. When dry, lay the petals one atop the other. Using a hole punch, punch a hole through the narrow end of each petal. Insert a brad through the center of a muffin liner, then through the hole in each petal. Fasten the brad; then reposition the petals to form a flower. Mount flowers atop crepe paper stems and leaves as shown.

 Vivian Campbell—Gr. 2, Martin Luther King School, Piscataway, NJ

At this display, students "bee-dazzle" onlookers with their best work! Using lengths of yarn, visually divide a bulletin board into multiple sections. Mount the title and characters as shown; then have each youngster showcase his best work in one of the remaining areas. Have each student mount his work atop colorful construction paper before attaching it to the bulletin board. Encourage students to keep their displays current. Now that's something to buzz about!

There's nothing fishy about these facts! On white construction paper, duplicate one fish pattern (page 33) per student. Ask each student to choose one skill that he is especially proud to have learned during the course of the school year. Then have him write one sentence about the skill on a fish pattern. Next have him cut out and decorate the pattern. Mount the completed fish cutouts as shown. Everyone's cool in this school!

Kim VanEvery, McLendon Elementary, Decatur, GA

Here's a fun way to thank your little sluggers for a "winning season." Using the pattern on page 34, duplicate, cut out, and label a construction paper baseball for each student. Write a personal thank-you message on the back of each student's cutout; then display as shown. On the last day of school, step up to the mound and call each slugger into the batter's box. Present each student with his cutout; then praise him for the special contributions he has made. Batter up!

Go ahead! Take down that May bulletin board. Just leave the background paper intact, add the title "I'll Remember When…," and your new display is ready. Using colorful markers, have each student write a special memory from the past school year. Invite students to embellish the completed display with construction-paper confetti. On the last day of school, take down the display and have students cut out and take home their special memories.

Sandy Hawkins—Gr. 2, Richmond Elementary, Fleetwood, PA

Use with "Summer Reflections" on page 4.

Pattern

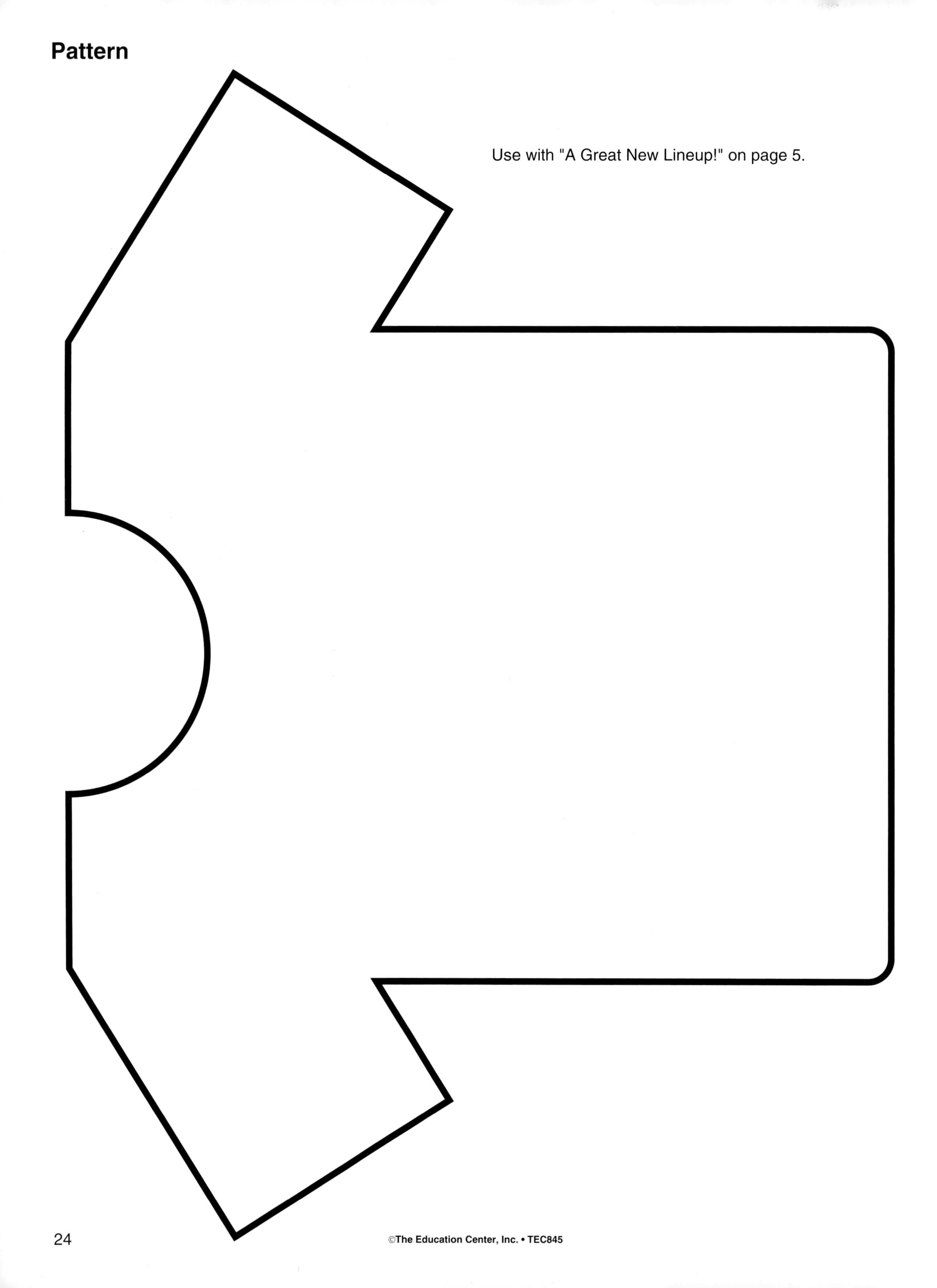

Use with "A Great New Lineup!" on page 5.

Use with "Terrifying And Terrific!" on page 6.

Use with "Welcome To Our Open House!" on page 7.

Duplicate the bat pattern on tagboard to use with "Brew Up Some Great Work!" on page 7.

Use the witch pattern with "Brew Up Some Great Work!" on page 7.

Take A "Batty Break"!

Give this to your teacher
in place of one assignment.

Teacher

Use coupon with "Brew Up Some Great Work!" on page 7.

Use this diagram with "Reading With Petunia" on page 8.

Patterns

Use with "Bright Ideas For A Happy Holiday!" on page 11.

Use with "Dr. Martin Luther King, Jr." on page 13.

Use hat and mitten patterns with "Dressed For Snow And Ready To Go!" on page 13.

Patterns

Use with "Did You Know..." on page 14.

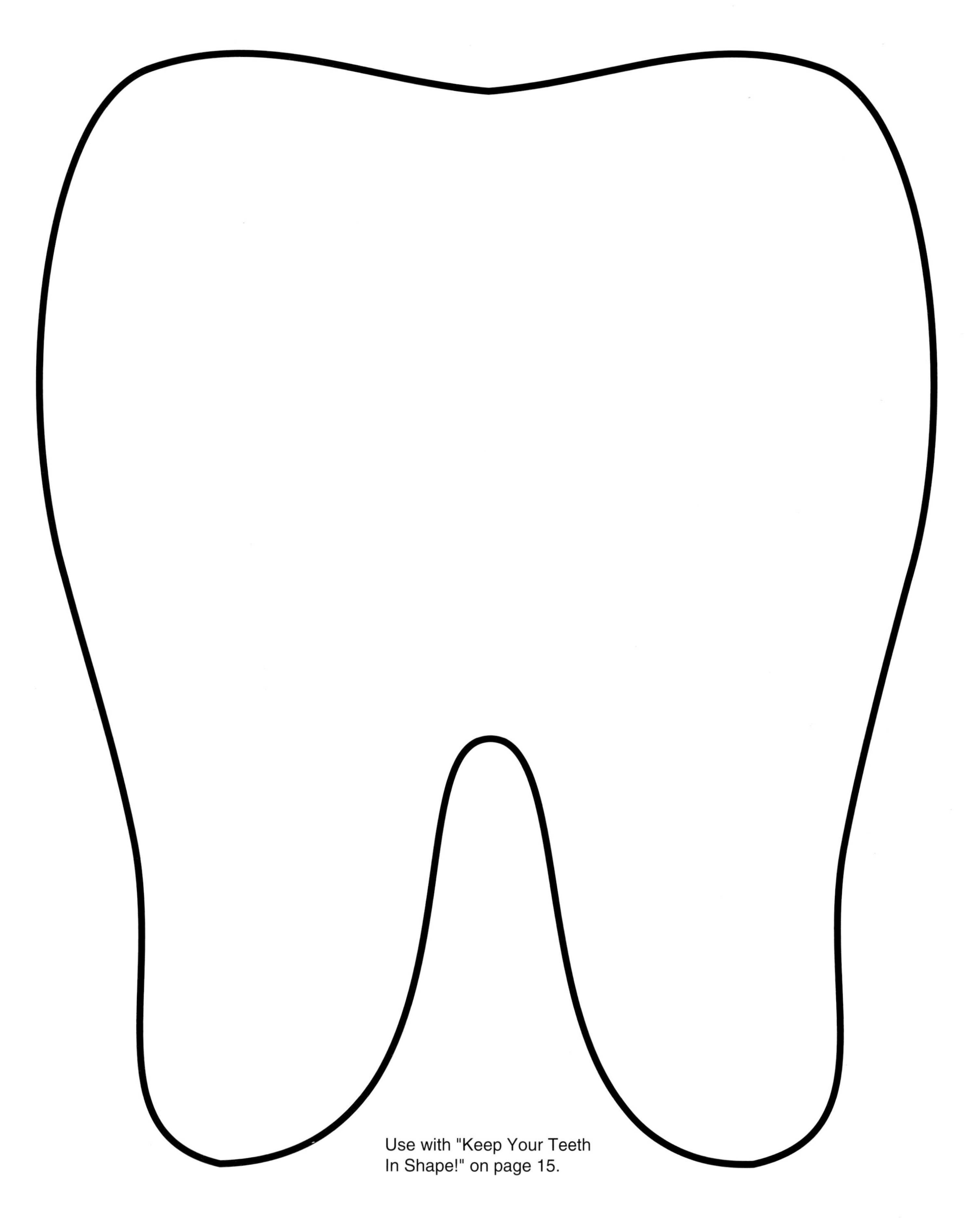

Use with "Keep Your Teeth
In Shape!" on page 15.

Use with "Star Material!" on page 20.

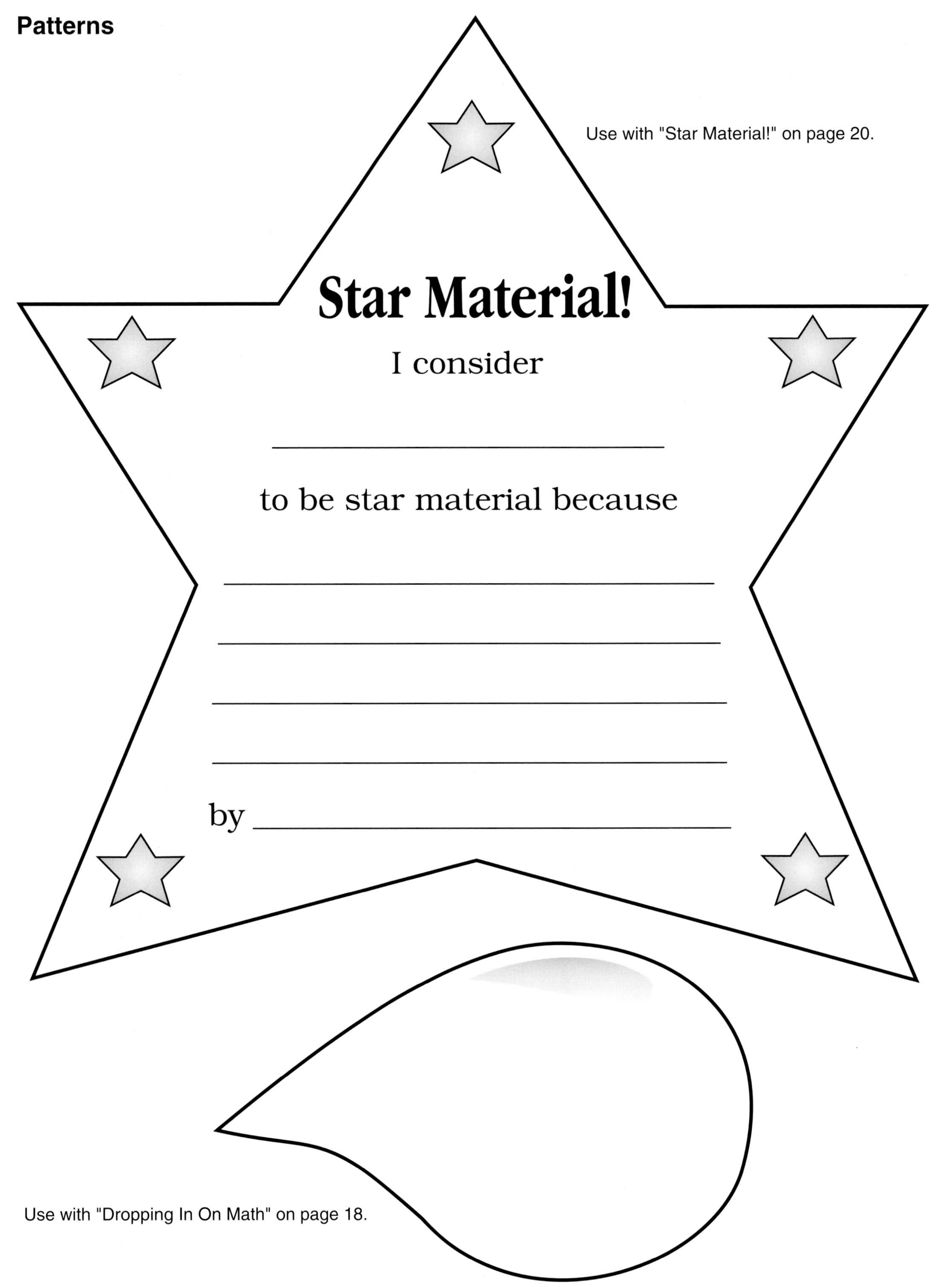

Use with "Dropping In On Math" on page 18.

Patterns

Use with " 'Sea' What We've Learned In Our School!" on page 21.

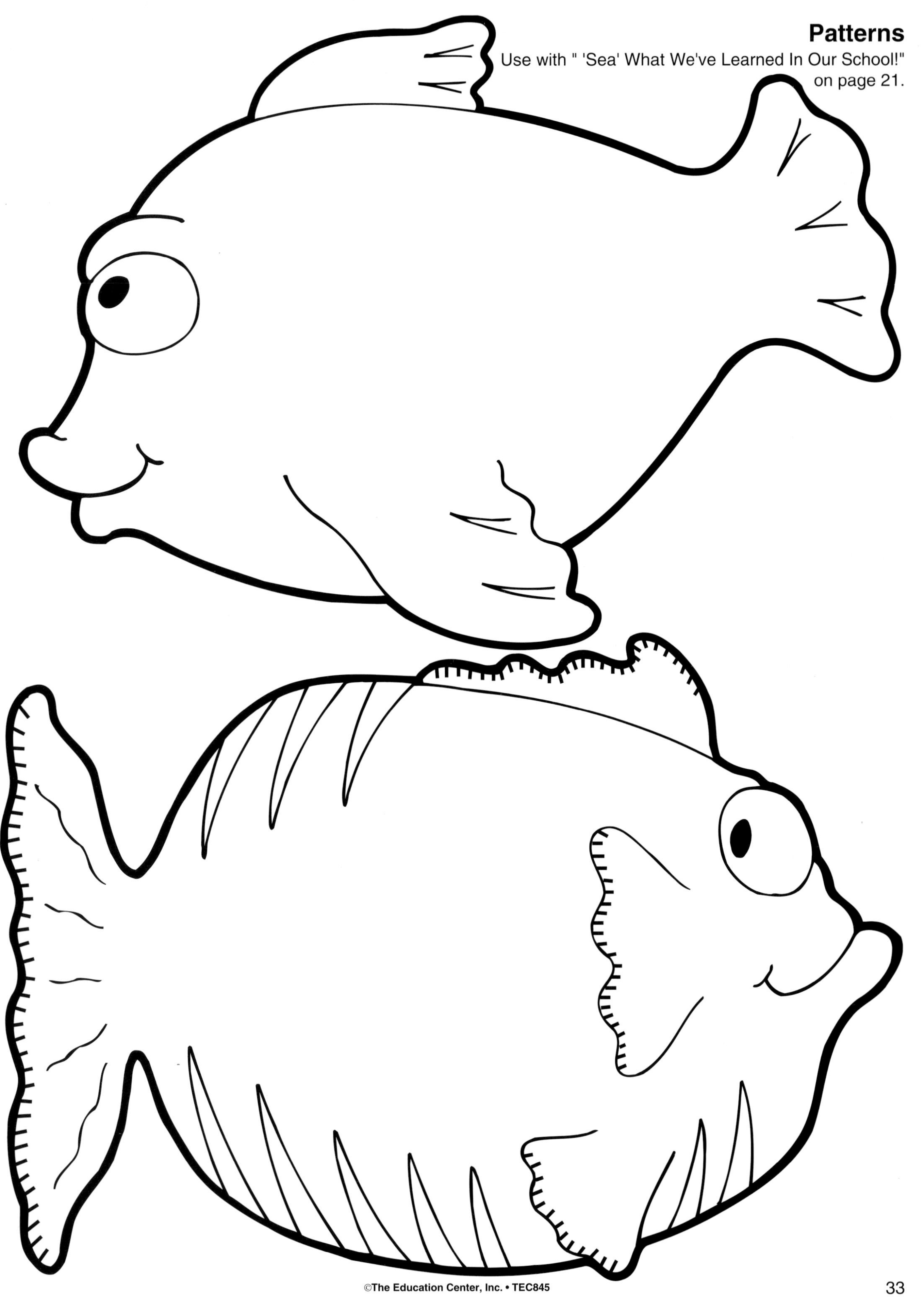

Patterns

Use with "Pitch In And Score!" on page 19 and "Thanks For Pitching In!" on page 22.

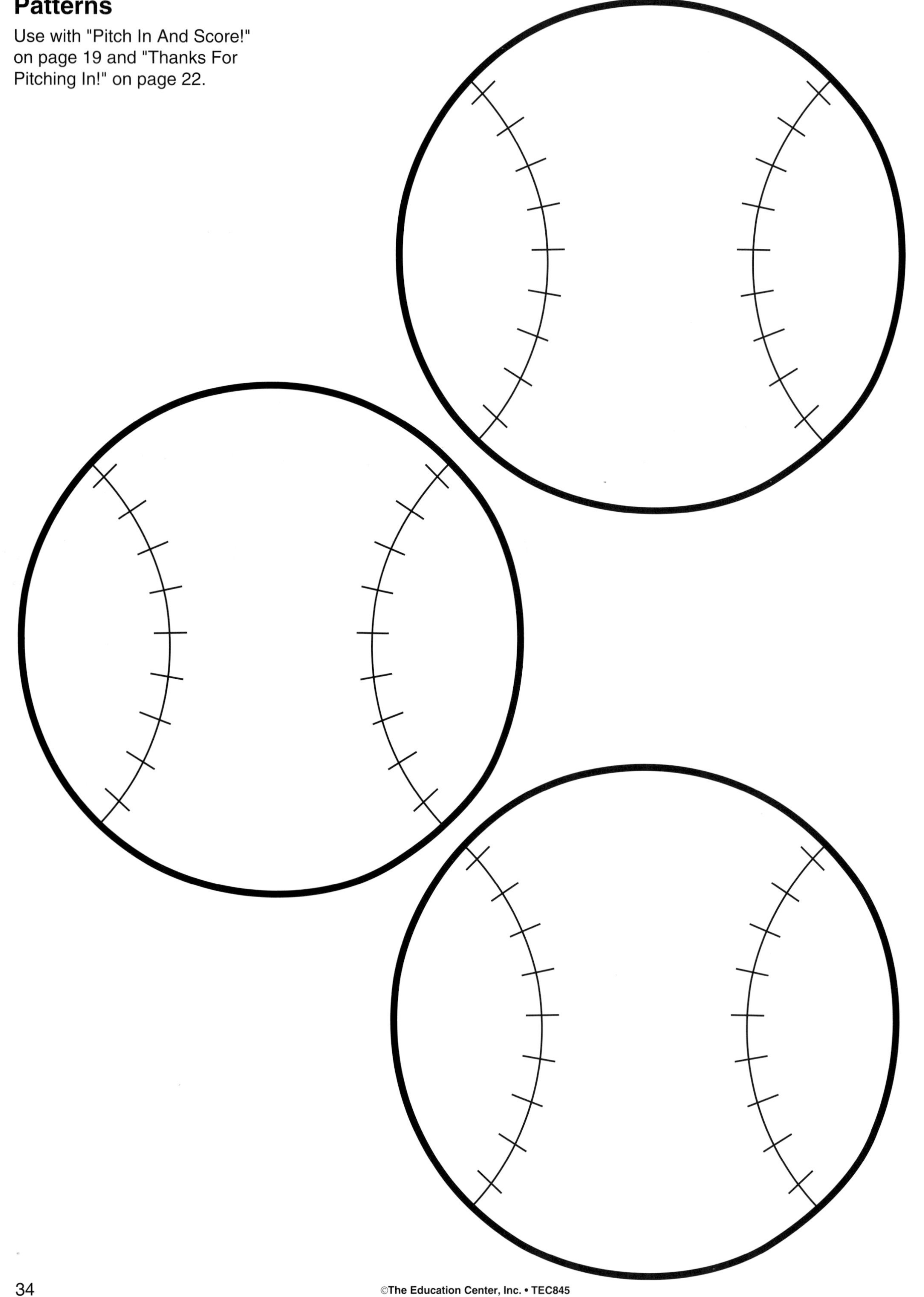

Arts & Crafts

"Apple-tizing" Artwork

Crunchy fall apples are the inspiration behind these bright masterpieces. Begin this project with red, yellow, and green tissue paper squares. Cut several squares into apple shapes. Using liquid starch and a paintbrush, "paint" the tissue paper apple cutouts onto white art paper. Overlap the cutouts as you cover the paper. The following day, brush on tempera paint stems and leaves. Mount the completed projects atop slightly larger pieces of red construction paper. Now that's a feast for the eyes!

Jan Kjelland
Washington Elementary
Valley City, ND

Marker Martians

When you're in the mood for an out-of-this-world art activity, give this one a try. Color one surface of a small, damp, sponge square with your favorite water-based marker. Press the sponge repeatedly onto the bottom of a luncheon-size paper plate. Reload the sponge with marker color whenever necessary. Use assorted sewing notions and arts-and-crafts items to decorate the plate bottom with facial features, hair, and antennae. When you're creating martians, the sky's the limit!

Ping-Pong Paintings

Have a ball! A Ping-Pong ball, that is. To create this abstract artwork, begin by mixing two tablespoons of paint with one tablespoon of water in a cup. Similarly prepare another cup with a contrasting color of paint. Place a Ping-Pong ball in each cup and stir with craft sticks until each ball is coated with paint. In a gift box lid, place a piece of paper and one Ping-Pong ball. Repeatedly tilt the lid back and forth, causing the ball to leave trails of paint on the paper. Replace this ball with the other one to create contrasting trails. When the paint trails are dry, glue the paper to a sheet of construction paper for display.

Michelle Bourlet
Clayton, GA

Creepy Crawlies

Not one youngster will try to wriggle away from this art project. To make a creepy crawly, begin by tearing tissue paper into strips. Using thinned glue and a paintbrush, glue the strips on a 4" x 18" piece of white construction paper. Occasionally overlap the tissue paper strips. Once each strip is attached to the paper, brush a layer of glue atop it. The following day, fold the paper in half and trim to round the ends. Decorate one rounded end with pipe cleaner antennae, a tissue paper topknot, and facial features made from assorted art supplies. Accordion fold the paper. Whether you use your creepy crawlies to brighten up classroom windowsills, bookcases, tabletops, or bulletin boards, they're certain to be lively conversation pieces!

Here's The Rub

This open-ended art idea can be used to complement any unit or holiday. To begin, glue around the outline of a simple coloring book design or an original design. (For best results, use a wide-tipped glue bottle.) Allow the glue to dry thoroughly before placing a sheet of white paper atop the glued design. Use paper clips to hold the pages in place. Rub a crayon or pencil lightly over the top sheet of paper in wide, sweeping strokes to reveal the design below. If desired, use a crayon or pencil to add details to these rubbings. Cut out and mount the completed rubbings on construction paper; then trim this paper to create an eye-catching border. Once your students have tried their hands at this activity, repeat it at a later date, having them replace the thematic designs with their names written in outline letters. Encourage students to make statements about their interests as they embellish these glue rubbings.

Chava Shapiro
Beth Rochel School
Monsey, NY

Look What I've Done!

Students will agree that these easy-to-make refrigerator magnets are perfect for displaying schoolwork. And what better way to receive positive recognition for their hard efforts! Cut out a pencil shape from tagboard and an eraser shape from pink construction paper. Glue the eraser cutout to the pencil cutout; then personalize and add details with markers. Attach a smiley sticker if desired. Laminate; then attach a piece of self-adhesive magnetic tape to the back of the cutout. There you have it—a personalized refrigerator magnet! Encourage students to show off several examples of work each week. To keep students actively interested in their refrigerator displays, make an apple magnet next month!

Kathleen McCann—Gr. 1, Detroit, MI

Merrily, merrily, floating down
Leaves become paint spots on the ground.

Leaf Prints

With this leaf printing suggestion, your youngsters can preserve the fall's finery on fabric. Brush acrylic paint on several leaves. Then place the leaves, paint side up, on a newspaper-protected surface. Place an eight-inch square of white fabric atop the leaves and press without rubbing. Carefully lift the fabric and let it dry. Later add an original thought or verse using a fabric pen.

To frame this artwork, center a seven-inch tagboard square on a nine-inch square of felt. Trace the tagboard; then cut on the lines to create a felt frame. Glue the frame atop the white fabric and display.

Jack-o'-Lantern Delights

Here's a great idea to have in your Halloween bag of tricks. Use pinking shears to cut three inches from the top of an orange, lunch-size, paper bag. (If necessary, substitute a white paper bag which has been painted or colored orange.) On one side of the bag, sketch and cut out jack-o'-lantern facial-feature outlines. To the top, staple a green construction paper stem and curling-ribbon "vines." Line the bag with yellow tissue paper. Scatter student-made jack-o'-lanterns throughout your classroom for a delectable display. On Halloween day, deposit a few treats (candies, stickers, pencils, etc.) into each student's jack-o'-lantern. In little more time than it takes to say, "Bibbity, bobbity, boo!", orange paper bags have become jack-o'-lantern delights.

Pamela Aigner—Gr. 3, Grange Elementary School, Baltimore, MD

Sleepy Hollow Forest

Create an eerie sensation with this artwork reminiscent of the dark and twisted trees in Sleepy Hollow, where poor ol' Ichabod Crane met his tragic fate. On art paper, drip some thinned, black, tempera paint or black watercolor paint. Blow through a drinking straw to transform the paint drips into the shapes of gnarly trees. While this dries, cut out and decorate several orange, construction paper jack-o'-lanterns. Complete the ghastly effect by gluing the jack-o'-lanterns to the tree artwork.

If you're a little more adventurous, heighten the eerie effect by having students create the tree branches atop painted backgrounds. To prepare a spooky-looking background sky, use a wide brush to paint the upper two-thirds of a sheet of art paper purple. Then paint the lower one-third pink, blending it into the purple, and brush a few pink streaks atop the purple. When dry, this uncanny October sky is ready for trees.

Beth Jones, General Va[illegible] School, Niagara Falls, Ontario, Canada

Bewitching Beauties

Dangle these projects from your classroom ceiling to create a bewitchingly whimsical effect. Depending upon the ability levels of your children, you may want to have students make only one part of the witch at a time and assemble the parts on another day.

To make the body:

1. Fold a 12" x 18" sheet of black construction paper in half lengthwise.
2. Beginning at the fold, cut parallel slits approximately 1 1/2" apart.
3. Unfold the paper, overlap the ends to create a tubular shape, and staple in place.

To make the head:

1. Fold a 4 1/2" x 12" sheet of green construction paper in half along its width.
2. Trim to round each corner of the folded piece. (The folded area will be the top of the witch's head.)
3. Glue on marker-embellished construction paper facial features and tissue paper hair.

To make the hat:

1. Fold a 4 1/2" x 12" sheet of black construction paper in half along its width.
2. Draw a hat shape on the paper as shown. Cut on the outline, leaving part of the folded area uncut.
3. Attach Halloween stickers to decorate the hat.

To assemble and display:

1. Glue the hat-shaped halves together, sandwiching the upper part of the witch's head in the hat brim.
2. Glue the witch's head to the body.
3. Embellish the witch, if desired, with hand, broom, and/or magic wand cutouts.
4. Punch a hole near the top of the hat, and suspend the witch from the ceiling.

Beth Jones
General Vanier School
Niagara Falls, Ontario
Canada

Bare Bones

Make no bones about it! Drawing a skeleton isn't nearly as hard as it's cracked up to be. Set the stage for this activity by reading *Funnybones* by Janet and Allan Ahlberg. Then have students complete this project one step at a time, as you demonstrate. To make a skeleton, accordion fold a 6" x 18" strip of black construction paper so that the paper is visually divided into eight (approximately 2 1/4") strips. Unfold a portion of the paper as shown. Using a white crayon, draw the upper skull onto the unfolded section, referring to the sample diagram. Unfold the second section of paper, conceal the third section, and draw the lower half of the skull, referring to the diagram. Continue drawing one section at a time until the entire skeleton is complete. Chances are, you'll be surprised by how well these skeleton drawings turn out.

Phyllis Kidder—Gr. 1, Kadena Elementary School
APO San Francisco, CA

Cornfield Guard

As the corn tassels turn to golden brown, turn your youngsters' harvest thoughts to bushels of creative fun. Have each student make a scarecrow using the directions below. If desired, youngsters may also mount colored crow cutouts (pattern on page 54) atop their scarecrows. Caw! Caw!

To make the scarecrow's overalls:

1. Make an overalls template using the pattern on page 54.
2. Place the template on a folded 9" x 12" sheet of blue construction paper as directed on the pattern.
3. Trace and cut on the resulting outline.

To make the scarecrow's arms:

1. Fold a 12" x 2 1/4" strip of red construction paper in half (to 6" x 2 1/4").
2. Cut two notches near the unfolded end as shown.

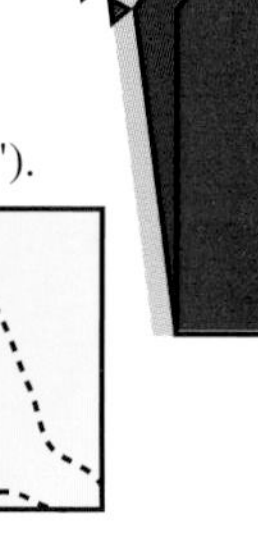

To make the scarecrow's face and hat:

1. Cut out and decorate a tan circle approximately 5 1/2" in diameter.
2. Place the hat template on a folded 7" square of yellow construction paper as directed on the pattern on page 54.
3. Trace and cut on the resulting outline.

To assemble and complete the scarecrow:

1. Glue the scarecrow's red paper arms to the back of the overalls, the face to the top of the overalls, and the hat to the top of the head.
2. Glue 2 1/2" x 1/2" yellow paper strips to the backs of the pant bottoms, sleeves, and face.
3. Glue small paper squares atop the overalls and the shirt. Add stitches with crayon.

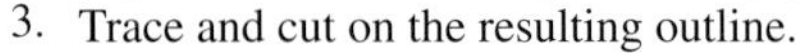

Jill Putnam—Gr. 1
Lanikai Elementary School
Kailua, HI

Hoot Owls

Here's an art project that won't ruffle any feathers! To make an owl, fold and glue three corners of a 9" brown paper square so that they touch in the center of the paper. For tail feathers, use scissors to fringe the unfolded corner. Gently pull some of the fringes forward and some backward for dimension. For the owl's beak, fold a 1 1/2" orange paper square in half diagonally and glue it on. For eyes, cut two 2 1/2" yellow paper circles and two 2 3/4" black paper circles. Glue each yellow circle atop a black one. Use a black marker to make a pea-size dot in the center of each yellow circle before gluing each eye in place. Create a spooky spectacle by displaying your youngsters' owls perched on a bare tree cutout.

Gobble Gobble Gallery

Just in time for Thanksgiving, have your youngsters create an entire flock of grinning gobblers from scratch. To make a scratchboard turkey, begin with a 5" x 7" poster board rectangle. Using red, orange, yellow, green, purple, and blue crayons, heavily color a bull's-eye pattern to cover your poster board. Atop this, apply a thick coat of black crayon. Reapply black crayon, if necessary, to cover the brighter colors. Cut a toothpick in half. Alternately use the resulting "thick" and "thin" toothpick ends to "scratch" a turkey design on the crayon-covered board. Mount the completed turkey scratchboards onto contrasting tagboard for display. Great gobblers! Look what you've scratched up!

Fowls From Filters

Making these gobblers is not only an artistic endeavor—it's also an exercise in listening and following directions. Referring to the materials list, provide the necessary supplies. Read aloud and demonstrate each step of the oral directions. For display, these turkeys may be glued or stapled to sheets of construction paper.

Materials Needed For Each Turkey:

coffee filter
5" brown construction paper square
3" brown construction paper square
2" yellow construction paper square
3" x 1" red construction paper rectangle
watercolor paint set with brush
water
scissors
glue
marker

Oral Instructions:

1. Paint a line from the center of the filter to the outer edge. Change colors and do this over and over. It's okay for the colors to run into each other. Set the filter aside to dry. This will be the turkey's feathers.
2. Trim off the corners of each brown square to make a circle.
3. For the turkey's body, glue the larger brown circle to the bottom of the filter.
4. For the turkey's head, glue the smaller brown circle to the filter. The smaller circle should overlap the larger one just a little.
5. For legs, cut two thin strips from the edge of the yellow square. Set the legs aside.
6. Fold the remaining yellow rectangle in half. Draw a giant capital *v* on the paper as shown. Cut on the *v*. The folded piece is the turkey's beak. Two of the triangles are feet. You will not need the other two.
7. Glue each triangle foot to a leg.
8. Glue the legs to the turkey's body. Then glue the beak to the turkey's head.
9. Cut a wiggly-shaped wattle from the red rectangle. Glue it by the beak.
10. Use a marker to draw the turkey's eyes.

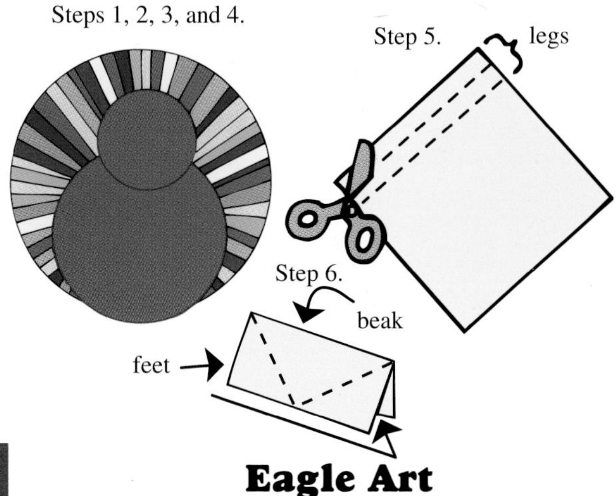

Diane R. Johnson—Gr. 1
Lincoln Elementary
Alpena, MI

Eagle Art

Whether you use this activity to raise your students' consciousness about the endangered status of our national bird or to fascinate your youngsters with a bit of seasonal historical trivia (Ben Franklin wanted the turkey—rather than the eagle—as our national bird), it will be a hit. Cover a 12" x 18" tagboard rectangle with aluminum foil. Duplicate or trace the eagle pattern (page 55) onto brown construction paper. Cut out the eagle; then cover it with balled-up squares of brown, white, and yellow tissue paper which have been dipped in glue. When dry, glue the eagle atop the foil-covered rectangle. To complete the patriotic effect, add foil stars and strips of red-white-and-blue ribbon or bulletin board border.

Sr. Ann Claire Rhoads, Mother Seton School
Emmitsburg, MD

Menorahs and Christmas Trees

With paper loops and glue, youngsters can create bright, three-dimensional holiday artwork. And with their unmatched eye-appeal, you're going to love the festive holiday flair these projects bring to bulletin boards and classroom displays.

Menorah

For each menorah you need:
one 9" x 12" sheet of dark blue construction paper
ten 3/4" x 6" strips of yellow paper
18 3/4" x 6" strips of light blue paper
nine 1 3/4" squares of yellow tissue paper
glue
diluted glue
paintbrush
clear or gold glitter

Directions:

1. For each of the 28 strips, glue one end atop the other end to form a loop.
2. For the menorah, center and glue two yellow loops horizontally at the bottom edge of the dark blue paper.
3. Center and glue another yellow loop above the first two.
4. Glue six yellow loops in a row above the last one.
5. Glue one yellow strip vertically above the center of the row.
6. To make each of the nine candles, glue two light blue loops vertically, one atop the other.
7. "Light" each candle by wrapping a tissue paper square around a pencil eraser, dipping it in glue and pressing it onto the top of the "candle."
8. Brush the yellow loops with diluted glue and sprinkle on glitter.

Christmas Tree

For each tree you will need:
one 9" x 12" sheet of dark blue construction paper
fifteen 1" x 6" strips of green paper
two 1" x 6" strips of brown construction paper
glue
diluted glue
paintbrush
glitter

Directions:

1. For each of the 17 strips, glue one end atop the other end to form a loop.
2. Center and glue one green strip at the upper edge of the construction paper sheet.
3. Working down the page, center and glue a row of two strips beneath the original one. Repeat with rows of three, four, and five loops.
4. Center and glue two brown strips vertically side by side for the tree trunk.
5. Add a cut-out star if desired.
6. Brush the green loops with diluted glue and sprinkle on glitter.

Kathy Mobbs—Gr. 1
Farmington, MI

Hearty Santa Place Mats

Ho! Ho! Ho! You'd better watch out—Santa's on his way! Once these place mats are completed, students can "do lunch" with Santa on a daily basis. Or, if desired, the place mats can be saved for a special holiday party. If your students can't bear the thought of soiling Santa, mount the completed projects on a bulletin board for a jolly display.

Directions:

1. From one pink, one red, and one white sheet of 12" x 18" construction paper, cut large hearts of equal size.
2. To make Santa's face and beard, cut a medium-size heart from the white heart. Then glue the resulting "heart border" atop the pink heart.
3. To make Santa's hat, cut away the pointed section of Santa's face; then mount the face cutout atop the red heart as shown.
4. For the hatband, fold and trim a 3" x 9" strip of white construction paper as shown; then unfold and glue the band to Santa's hat.
5. Glue on marker-embellished construction paper eyes.
6. Cut a mouth, mustache, nose, eyebrows, and hat ball from scraps of red and white construction paper. Attach the features in the order listed.
7. For durability, laminate the completed project.

Barbara Wilson
Port Monmouth Road School
Keansburg, NJ

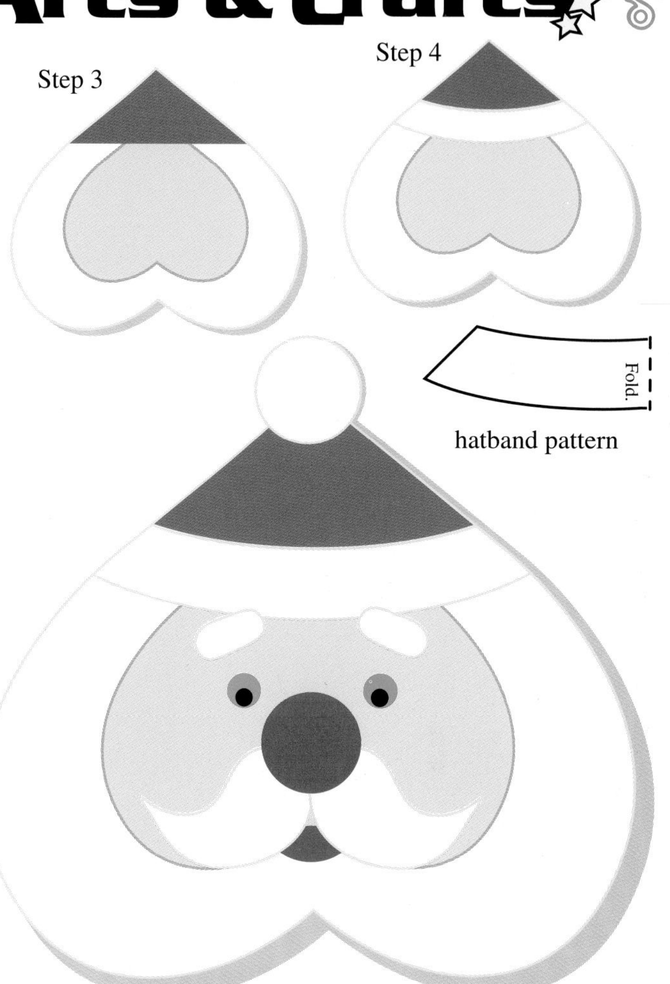

Angelic Art

These adorable angels make a heavenly display! In advance, have each student bring a six-inch square of holiday gift wrap to school. From poster board, cut a six-inch equilateral triangle to use as a template. Then let the creating begin!

For each angel you will need:

a 6" square of holiday gift wrap
a 2" pink construction paper circle
a 3" yellow construction paper circle
(two) 1" yellow construction paper circles
a 9" x 12" sheet of red, green, or blue construction paper
two quarter sections of an 8" gold doily
five pasta wheels
a black marker
foil stars
scissors
glue

Directions:

1. Trace the template onto the square of gift wrap. Cut out the tri (body).
2. Glue the 1" yellow circles (feet) to the base of the triangle.
3. Mount the body and feet on the sheet of construction pape
4. Glue the gold doily sections (wings) and the large yello in place.
5. Using the marker, draw an angelic face on the pink circle on the halo.
6. Attach the pasta wheels (hair) and foil stars.

Virginia L. Kroll
Hamburg, NY

"Berry" Best Ornaments

If you're nuts about inexpensive and attractive student-made ornaments, you're going to love these strawberries. To make a strawberry ornament, paint a walnut red using tempera paint. Allow to dry. To create the strawberry's seeds, first dip a toothpick in white tempera paint. Then repeatedly touch the toothpick to one side of the walnut to create small dots. Place the walnut, dotted side up, in an empty egg carton cup to dry before dotting the other side in the same manner. Use craft glue to attach green felt (leaves) and a green, looped pipe cleaner section (stem) to the top of the walnut. Again the walnut may be placed in an egg carton cup while the glue dries. Then use a needle to pull thread through the felt leaves. Tie the thread off to make a hanger.

Shelly Johnson, Fairfield, MT

Bright, Lighted Christmas Trees

Warn your winter classroom with the bright glow of student-made trees. To make a tree, you will need one small brown rectangle and one green and one white construction paper triangle of identical size. Using a variety of markers or crayons, completely color the white triangle in random fashion. Fold the green triangle (as shown) and cut or tear openings along the fold. Repeat this step several times. To complete your Christmas tree, glue the green triangle atop the white one, wedging a bit of the brown rectangle in between to create the tree's trunk. Display your trees in a window so that sunlight will set them aglow.

Joyce Montag
Slippery Rock, PA

Noteworthy Ornaments

Here's a festive project that students will be proud to give as holiday gifts. For each ornament, use a photocopier to reduce two pages of Christmas music to approximately 5" x 7" each. To "age" the carols, blot each using a damp tea bag. When dry, roll each carol into a tight tube and fasten its loose edge with a dab of glue. Glue the "scrolls" together side by side. Tie a length of red ribbon around the scrolls; then fashion a bow from the ribbon ends. Attach a sprig of holly and an ornament hook to complete the project.

Cheryl S. Johnson—Gr. 3, East Elementary, Monroe, NC

Garland Galore

If you're into recycling, you're going to love these decorative garlands made from grocery bags. To make teddy bear, gingerbread man, or reindeer garland, make a tracer using the selected pattern on page 56. Cut a 15" x 4" strip from a large brown paper grocery bag. (From one bag, you can cut six strips of this size.) Accordion-fold the strip every three inches. Trace the design onto the folded strip. Cut on the lines and unfold. Decorate your teddies with twisted tissue paper bows and facial features drawn with markers. Put the icing on your gingerbread men using paper-punch dots and markers, and put the gleam in your reindeers' eyes and the shine on their noses with paper-punch dots.

Make a garland of snowmen using the patterns on page 56 and large white paper bags. Cut and decorate the snowmen in the same way as the garlands described above. Then top off your snowmen with black hat garland. Look at Frosty go!

Try these garlands as tree trimmers and bulletin board borders.

Sr. Ann Claire Rhoads
Mother Seton School
Emmitsburg, MD

Thumpity thump, thump!

Well, Frosty said he'd be back again some day. And you can help him live up to that promise. To make a snowman suitable for suspending from the classroom ceiling, you will need: two paper plates, two 9" x 12" sheets of black construction paper, two 4" x 7" rectangles and two 1" x 7" bands of fabric or tissue paper, orange construction paper, glue, scissors, stapler, thread, and a hole puncher. Begin by gluing the paper plates rim-to-rim. Cutting through both thicknesses of the black paper, cut a top hat shape. Glue the hat cutouts together, sandwiching some of the paper plates between the cutouts. Using torn black paper scraps, glue "coal" eyes and mouth on both paper plate bottoms. Complete the snowman's faces with torn orange paper noses. Pinch and staple the middle of each 4" x 7" fabric or tissue paper rectangle, and staple them back to back at the lower edge of the paper plates. Glue a fabric or tissue paper band to each side of the hat, and trim to fit. Punch a hole near the top of the hat, and suspend the snowman using thread.

Chris Christensen
Marion B. Earl Elementary
Las Vegas, NV

Through And Through—Red, White, And Blue

With Lincoln's birthday, Washington's birthday, and Presidents' Day just around the corner, it's time to be in an especially patriotic mood. Give students an opportunity to show their true colors with these hanging banners. To make a banner, glue three red and two white 20" crepe-paper streamers to the rim of a blue disposable plate, alternating the colors. Squeeze a trail of glue along the highest ridge of the plate rim. Invert another blue plate atop the first one, and allow the glue to dry. Decorate the exposed surfaces of the plates with star-shaped cutouts or stickers. Use a hole puncher to punch a hole in the plate rim opposite the streamers. Then attach a yarn length for suspending the banner.

Kathleen Yost and Karen Vernak—Gr. 3, Highcliff Elementary, Pittsburgh, PA

Valentines With Va-voom!

These unusual valentine projects will make great surprises for students' loved ones. To begin, cut two identical heart shapes from transparent vinyl. (Upholstery shops sell this fabric.) With one cutout atop the other, use a hole puncher to punch evenly spaced holes around the edges. Using ribbon or yarn, lace through all but a few holes. Through this opening, insert conversation hearts (or other valentine candy), a handmade valentine, and one or two heart-shaped trinkets. Lace through the remaining holes, and tie and trim the loose ribbon or yarn ends.

This idea may be so popular with your youngsters that they'll want to create shamrock-shaped versions for St. Patrick's Day and egg-shaped versions for Easter. For an end-of-the-year surprise, make sandcastle-shaped versions filled with seashells and other treats to present to your youngsters on the last day of school.

Cathryn Cleaveland, Avondale Estates, GA

Wings Of Love

You've heard of the wings of love. Well, now they can flutter into your classroom just in time for Valentine's Day. To make one of these butterflies, begin by stacking two 4 1/2" squares of paper. Fold the squares in half (one inside the other) and draw concentric half-heart outlines as shown. Cut on the lines you've drawn. (If two-toned butterflies are desired, trade both hearts of one size with someone who has cutouts of another color.)

Decorate each of the smaller heart cutouts. Position a larger heart "frame" atop each of the smaller cutouts so that the pointed heart bottoms meet. Glue or tape each pair at the points. Place the heart pairs with decorated sides together, and staple at the points. Spread the pairs apart and pin them to a bulletin board, so that they stand out like wings from the board. Fluttering around a display of student work, these butterflies can be quite eye-catching.

Carlee McGuire—Grs. K–3, Indian Meridian Elementary, Choctaw, OK

Variation On Valentines

Looking for a Valentine's Day activity which will be a unique expression of each youngster's creativity? Then ask each youngster to bring some gift-wrapping paper for this project. To make this heart art, begin by selecting two pieces of construction paper to complement a sheet of gift wrap. Fold one construction paper sheet in half and cut a large heart shape from it. Unfold the resulting heart-shaped paper frame, and glue it to the other piece of construction paper. Cut your piece of gift wrap into several squares. Fold each one and cut several concentric hearts from it. Unfold the resulting heart shapes and outlines. Arrange and glue them to the construction paper. There you have it—original heart art.

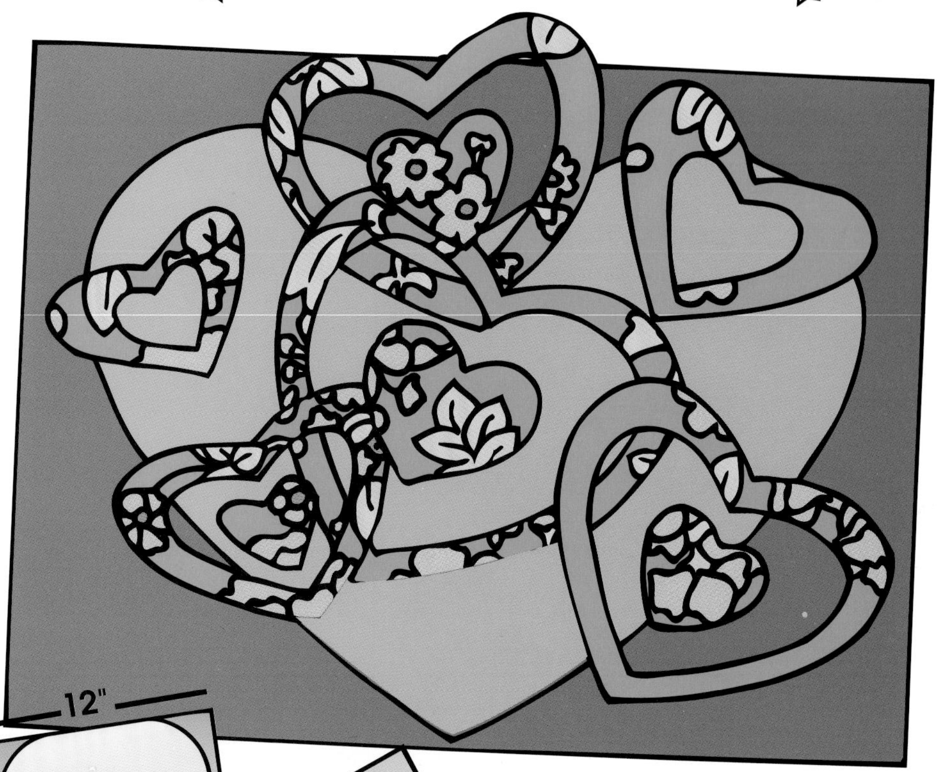

12"

18"

Derrick

Hoppy Holders

If you're hoping for a "toad-ally" new look for Valentine's Day this year, this valentine holder might just get you hoppin'. Begin by creating a tracer like the one shown. Trace this pattern onto a 12" x 18" sheet of green construction paper; then cut on the outline. Cut out, decorate, and attach white, construction-paper eyes. Complete the face by drawing on additional features. Cut another sheet of green construction paper into fourths as shown. Trim one end of each resulting strip for feet. Glue each of the untrimmed strip ends to the back of the body. From a 12" square of red construction paper, cut a heart shape. Attach the heart cutout to the body section of the frog so that it creates a pocket. Without folding the strips, curve them toward the valentine, and staple them in place. If desired, personalize the heart cutout and slip a bag inside it for holding valentines and treats. "Hoppy" Valentine's Day!

This idea can be modified to create other animal characters. For a bear, cut a head-and-body shape, attach ears and eyes, and draw facial features. Attach a heart cutout; then attach decorated paw cutouts.

Sharon Conley—Gr. 1, Port Monmouth Road School, Keansburg

A Good Luck Charm

Just in time for St. Patrick's Day, bedeck your classroom with showers of emerald shamrocks. For this project you will need three 12"-square samples of original artwork featuring the color green. Use a different medium (such as chalk, tempera paint, or watercolor) for each sample, if desired. (Any other green paper such as computer paper or gift wrap can be substituted for the artwork.) Make a half-shamrock pattern similar to the one shown. Cut out and place this pattern on a folded artwork square. (Fold the artwork to the inside.) Trace and cut out the design. Repeat this process with the remaining two pieces of artwork.

To assemble this project, place one folded shamrock cutout on a tabletop. Glue the upper paper surface. Lining up the edges, place another folded shamrock cutout atop the first one. Glue its upper paper surface, and place the remaining folded shamrock atop the second one. Attach several crepe paper streamers or strands of curling ribbon to the exposed shamrock stem. When the glue is dry, pick up the folded shamrock cutouts and bend the top and bottom surfaces toward one another until they meet. Glue in place. Suspend the shamrock from monofilament line, and watch it dance and twirl in the springlike breezes of St. Patrick's Day.

Cynthia Goth—Gr. 1, Glen Elder Grade School, Glen Elder, KS

Shamrock Shenanigans

Think green! It's nearly St. Patrick's Day. To make these shamrock works of art, you'll need a shamrock tracer and two octagonal tracers, one just a little larger than the other. Trace the smaller octagon onto a white sheet of paper and the larger one onto a green sheet of paper. Using the shamrock tracer and a green crayon, trace shamrock shapes onto the white paper, without overlapping the designs. Decorate each shamrock with a different design; then glue the white paper octagon to the green one. Glancing at these fields of green shamrocks may just put a little Irish lilt into your stride.

Clara Turton—Art Instructor
Henry County Public Schools
Martinsville, VA

Whiskers And Fur

Tuck a few treats into these student-made baskets to top off your Easter festivities. Begin with three paper plates per basket. To create the ears, draw two curved lines on a plate as shown. Cut on the curves; then discard the middle section. For the bunny's face, draw a single curve (as shown) on another plate. Cut on the curve; then discard the smaller piece. Invert the face piece and glue or staple it atop an uncut paper plate. Glue or staple one end of each ear beneath the uncut plate. Using a makeup brush and blush, apply color to the cheeks and the insides of the ears. Cut out and attach construction paper features; then draw on whiskers. To complete the project, tuck some cellophane grass into the opening. To create a carrying handle, punch two holes in the uncut plate and thread with yarn. Before long your classroom will be brimming with bunnies!

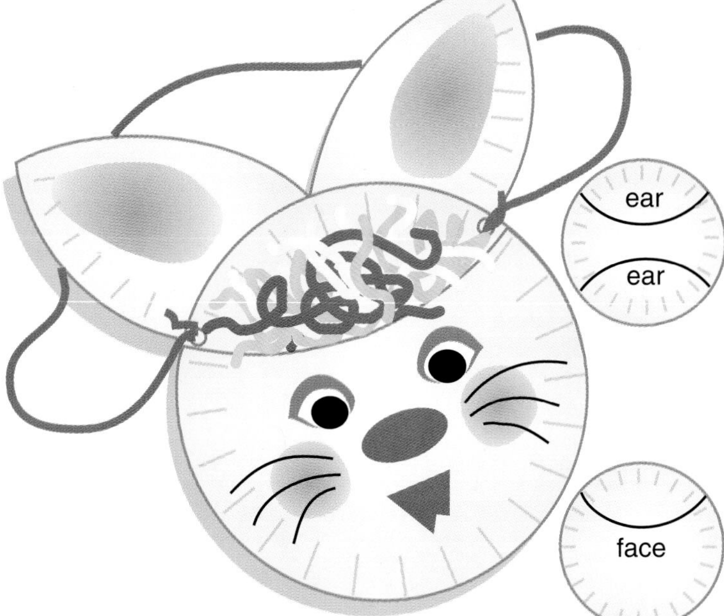

Springtime Vases

Since imitation is the sincerest form of flattery, Mother Nature should be rather proud of these pussy willow and forsythia impostors. Begin by cutting a vase shape from construction paper, wallpaper, or fabric. Glue the vase cutout near the bottom of a large piece of construction paper. Use brown crayon to draw stems extending upward from the vase. For pussy willows, decorate some stems by gluing on puffed rice cereal. For forsythia, decorate the remaining stems with small pieces of yellow tissue paper. Is that the faint, sweet fragrance of forsythia that I smell, or is it just my imagination?

Sharon Haley
Jacksonville, NC

Boppin' Bunnies

Like Weebles, these bunnies wobble but they don't fall down! Mix plaster of paris according to box directions, and fill the bottom section of a L'eggs egg 2/3 full of the mixture. Place the egg on an upside-down egg carton, so that the plaster of paris will dry level. (You may want to do this the day before you intend to decorate your egg.) Glue the top section of the egg to the bottom section. To transform your egg into a bunny, use craft glue to attach felt or construction paper ears and facial features, as well as a cotton ball tail. Add finishing touches with a permanent marker. Not only are these bunnies beauteous, but they can also bop with the best of them!

Laurie Vent
Upper Sandusky, OH

Leap Into Spring

Get the hop on springtime art with these paper plate amphibians. For this project, you will need a thin white paper plate, a pencil, a paintbrush, green tempera paint, a red crayon, scissors, glue, a 3 1/2" x 2" red construction paper rectangle, two 2" white construction paper squares, two 1" black construction paper squares, and four 6 1/2" x 3 1/2" green construction paper rectangles.

To make a frog, fold a paper plate in half and color one inner half red. Then paint the outer surfaces of the plate green. Allow for drying time. From the red paper rectangle, cut a tongue. From the white and black paper, create eyes. From the green paper cut "arms" and "legs." Glue the eyes, tongue, arms, and legs in place as shown. Look out, Kermit; more great "hoppers" are on the way!

Donna Turner—Gr. 1, Stevenson Elementary, Burbank, CA

Shy Violets

Set the mood for this activity by displaying several colors of blooming violets. To make a flowerpot, cut a 4 1/2" x 6" sheet of yellow construction paper into a rounded shape. Then cut ovals from 1 1/2" wide blue, pink, or lavender crepe-paper strips. Also cut several heart-shaped leaves from green construction paper. Glue the yellow pot cutout near the bottom of a sheet of black construction paper. Glue leaf shapes near—but not above—the top of the pot. Then glue the crepe-paper ovals in clusters of five above the pot to resemble violet petals. Glue only near the center of each cluster. Glue a yellow circle cutout (cut from the remaining yellow scraps) in the center of each cluster of ovals. Voilà, a floral masterpiece!

Beth Jones, Niagara Falls, Ontario, Canada

Perky Posies

If your youngsters gather the flowers for this project in April, the flowers will be ready to become part of a masterpiece in May. To make a pressed flower bouquet, choose and locate several delicate flowers. Flowers like primrose, bluebonnet, and black-eyed Susan are especially good choices for this project. Press the flowers between the pages of weighted catalogs. Several weeks later, glue a few of the dried, pressed flowers to a mat board or a piece of construction paper or tagboard. When the glue is dry, laminate the project. Display each project on a tagboard easel for easy viewing. (See the diagrams for an easy-to-make easel.)

Peggy Coe—Gr. 2
Wells Branch Elementary
Austin, TX

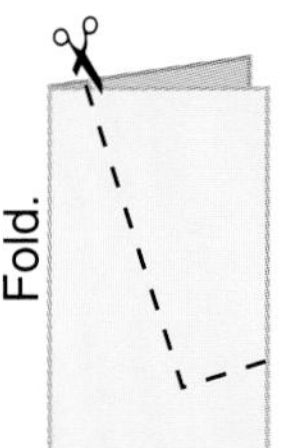

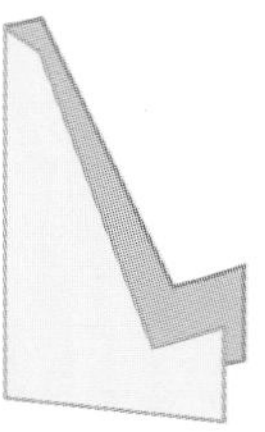

Tulips For Mom

Have your youngsters make colorful floral greetings to surprise and delight their moms on Mother's Day. To make a greeting, trace a symmetrical tulip shape onto 9" x 12" (or larger) wallpaper samples two times and onto colorful, lined paper once. Cut out each tulip shape. After writing and correcting a first draft of your message, use a colorful felt-tip marker to copy it onto the lined paper cutout. Place the message between the tulip-shaped wallpaper covers, punch holes in the left margin, and fasten the sheets together with brads. Attach a 1 1/2" x 12" strip of green construction paper at the lower edge of the inside back cover. Using a contrasting marker, write "Happy Mother's Day!" on the front cover and "Love, [your signature]" on the strip. Fold the strip so that it is concealed between the covers if desired. Happy day, Mom!

Kathy Quinlan—Gr. 1
Lithia Springs Elementary
Lithia Springs, GA

Sweets For The Sweet

What a sweet way to treat Mom on Mother's Day! To make this Mother's Day greeting card, fold a sheet of 12" x 18" art paper twice to create a 3/4" spine. Decorate the front of the card with flowery art. Write "A big bunch of kisses just for you! Love, [your name]" on the inside left side of the card. Around this writing, draw additional flowers. Next decorate the inside right side of the card with four candy-kiss flowers.

To make a candy-kiss flower, begin with two 3 1/2" squares of construction paper. Cut each square as shown to create flower petals. Then cut a 3 1/2" x 1 1/2" green piece of construction paper to make a leaf. Glue the leaf, then the two petal pieces, to the card. Glue on a foil-wrapped candy kiss for the flower center. Repeat this process to create three additional flowers.

Giovanna Anzelone—Gr. 3, Frank A. Sedita #38 School, Buffalo, NY

Take Note

Your youngsters can fashion these note holders to give to their mothers on Mother's Day. To make the back of the note holder, position one craft stick horizontally on a sheet of waxed paper. Above the stick, place ten more. Press all 11 sticks together. Along each side, run a trail of glue. While the glue is drying, create and glue a similar configuration of seven sticks (front of the note holder) and another of two sticks (bottom of the note holder). For each of the two sides of the note holder, glue eight sticks one atop the other. When all of these sections have dried, glue them together. (Use rubber bands to hold the pieces in place until the glue dries.) For a hanger, glue two sticks to the back of the note holder and to each other in an inverted *v* shape. When the glue is dry, decorate the note holder with a photograph, fabric notions, flowers, or other miscellaneous craft supplies. Complete the project by slipping a stack of 3 1/4" x 4" notes in the holder.

Karen Frandsen, McLendon Elementary School, Decatur, GA

Quilled Butterflies

A display of these fancy fliers attracts lots of attention! To make a butterfly, cut out a tagboard tracer using an enlarged version of the butterfly pattern on page 57. Also cut a supply of 6" x 1/2" strips of black construction paper. Using the tracer, cut a butterfly shape from colorful construction paper. One at a time, wrap each of several black strips around a pencil; then slide the strip off and glue it—standing on edge—to the cutout. Hold each "quilled" strip in place until the glue has dried enough to hold it. Continue in this manner until the cutout is filled in. When the project has dried, mount it atop another sheet of construction paper; then trim this paper to create an eye-catching border. Repeat this step a second time. Attach bent pipe-cleaner antennae and your project is complete. Now that's a fancy flier!

Sr. Ann Claire Rhoads
St. Pius X
Greensboro, NC

Folded Fliers

Your recycling enthusiasts are going to love making these eye-catching butterflies! To make a butterfly, tear two brightly colored pages from a discarded magazine. Fold one page in half; then trace the half-pattern on page 57 onto the page. Cut on the resulting outline—not on the fold. Next unfold the paper and refold it so that the rounded ends meet. Starting at the fold and working toward one rounded end, accordion fold one-half of the pattern. Fold the remaining half of the pattern in the same manner; then set the piece aside. Next cut a 6 1/2-inch square from the second magazine page. Fold the square in half, making a triangle. Starting at the fold and working outward, accordion fold one-half of the pattern. Fold the remaining half of the pattern in the same manner. Join the two folded pattern pieces with a length of black pipe cleaner as shown; then gently spread the wings of the butterfly. There you have it! A one-of-a-kind folded flier!

Donna Dayer—Gr. 2, Anne Watson Elementary, Conway, AR

All Aflutter!

These eye-catching butterflies can be created in just a flit and a flutter! Place each of several colors of tempera paint in individual containers. Cut three 18-inch lengths of string. Dip each length into a different paint container. Arrange the strings inside a folded sheet of 9" x 12" construction paper in a twisted fashion. Make certain a portion of each string touches the fold line, and the unpainted ends of the strings extend off the paper. Place one hand on top of the folded paper and pull out the strings. Unfold. When dry, center a tagboard butterfly cutout (pattern on page 58) atop the painted project and trace using a marker or crayon. Cut out the butterfly. There you have it! A spectacular and symmetrical butterfly cutout!

Joan Steele—Gr. 1
Queen Of All Saints School
St. Louis, MO

What A Catch!

Here's an art project youngsters will fall for hook, line, and sinker. To make a fish for your stringer, trace a fish shape onto a large sheet of art paper, and cut it out. Use a ruler to draw an assortment of lines; then color each resulting space a bright, cheery color. Glue on foil fins and a button eye for a fishy finish. To display your classroom catch, connect the fish cutouts to a crepe paper "stringer." Ah-h-h, the fish are biting today!

Sue Hancock
Seaford, DE

I'm so glad there are family "ties" between us! Happy Father's Day!
Love, Nicki

Just For Dad!

Strengthen family ties with these colorful cards! To make this unique Father's Day greeting, fold a 4" x 18" strip of construction paper in half; then trace the tie pattern (page 57) onto the folded paper. Cut on the resulting outlines—not on the fold. Next trace the tie pattern onto colorful lined paper. (Do not fold the lined paper.) Cut approximately 1/8 inch inside the resulting outline. After writing and correcting a first draft of a personalized Father's Day message, use a colorful felt-tip marker to copy it onto the lined paper cutout. Glue this message inside the folded tie cutout. Using crayons or markers, decorate the front cover of the resulting card. Happy Father's Day!

Sr. Carolee Vanness, Holy Family School, Lindsay, NE

A Fishy Footprint

Get right to the point with this fishy art project! Place several colors of tempera paint in individual containers. Trace the outline of your shoe onto white construction paper. Dip one end of a Q-tip into one color of paint. Blot the Q-tip on a paper towel to remove excess paint; then paint dots inside your shoe outline. Paint the dots close together so just a small amount of white shows between each dot. Use a different Q-tip for each color of paint. When dry, cut out and mount the shoe shape on a 12" x 18" sheet of light blue construction paper. Add construction paper fins and tail. Use markers, crayons, or construction paper scraps to add details and create a habitat for your fish.

Pamela L. Fulton—Gr. 1, Lewisville, NC

Patterns Use with "Cornfield Guard" on page 40.

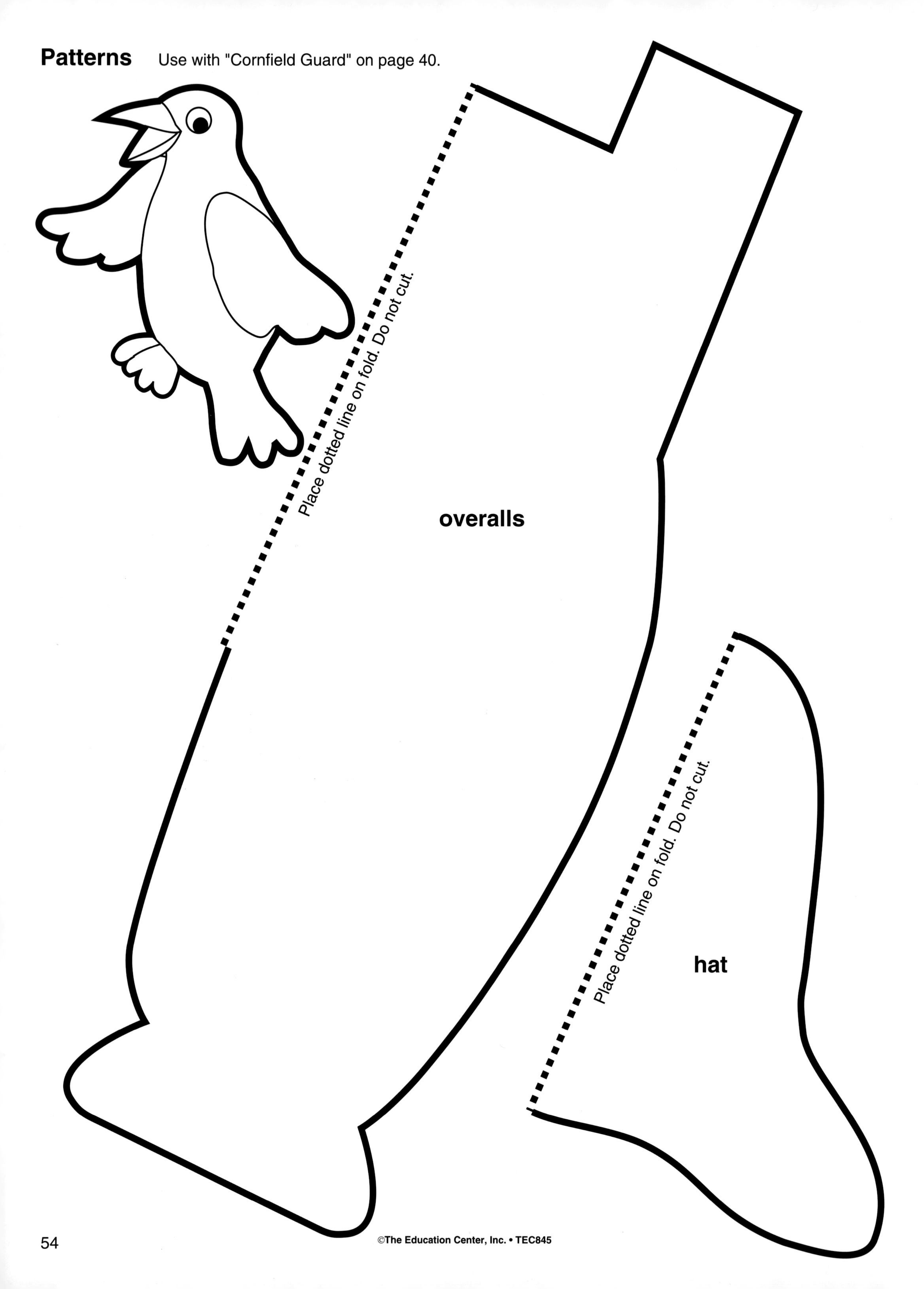

Pattern

Use with "Eagle Art" on page 41.

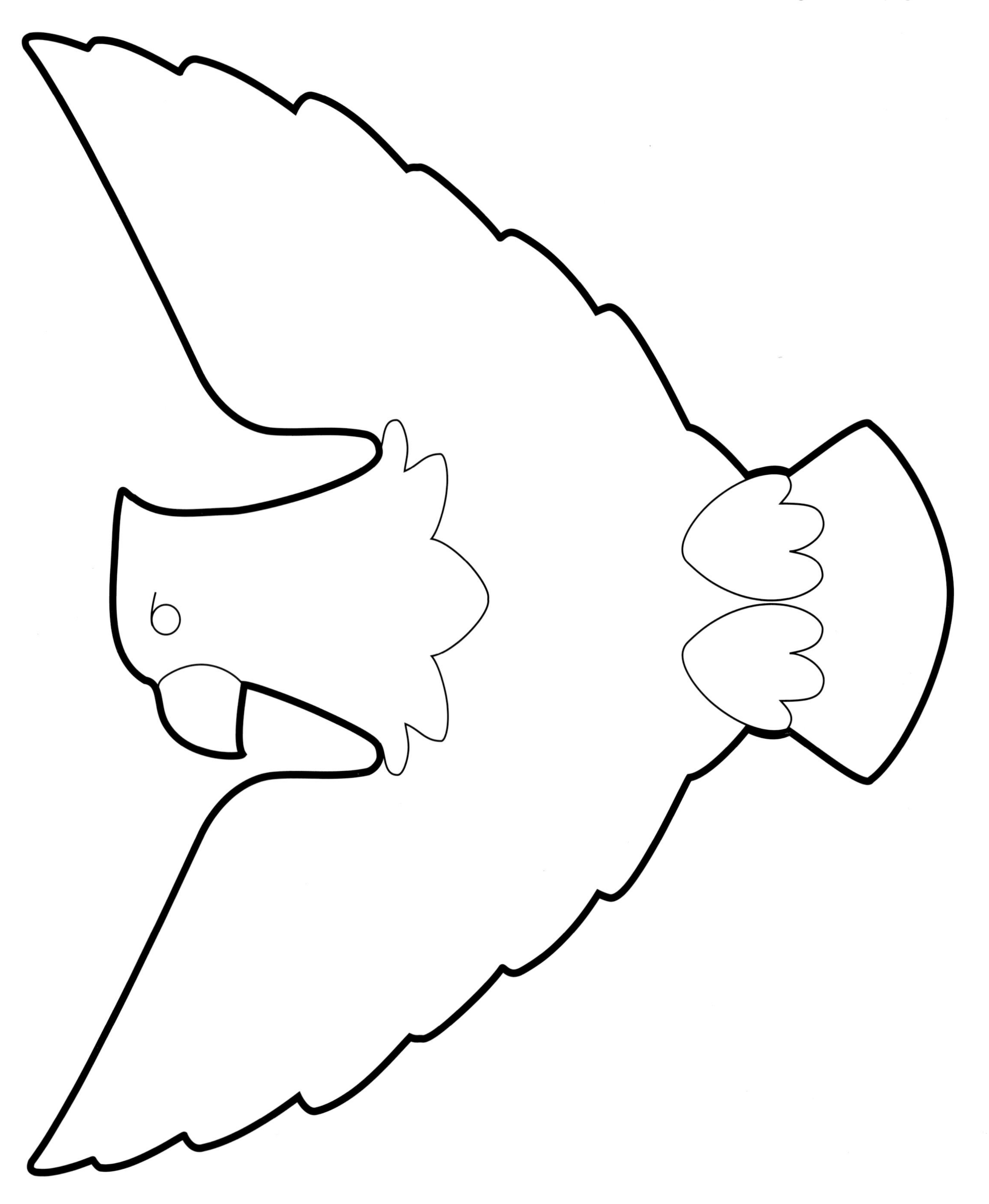

Patterns

Use with "Garland Galore" on page 45.

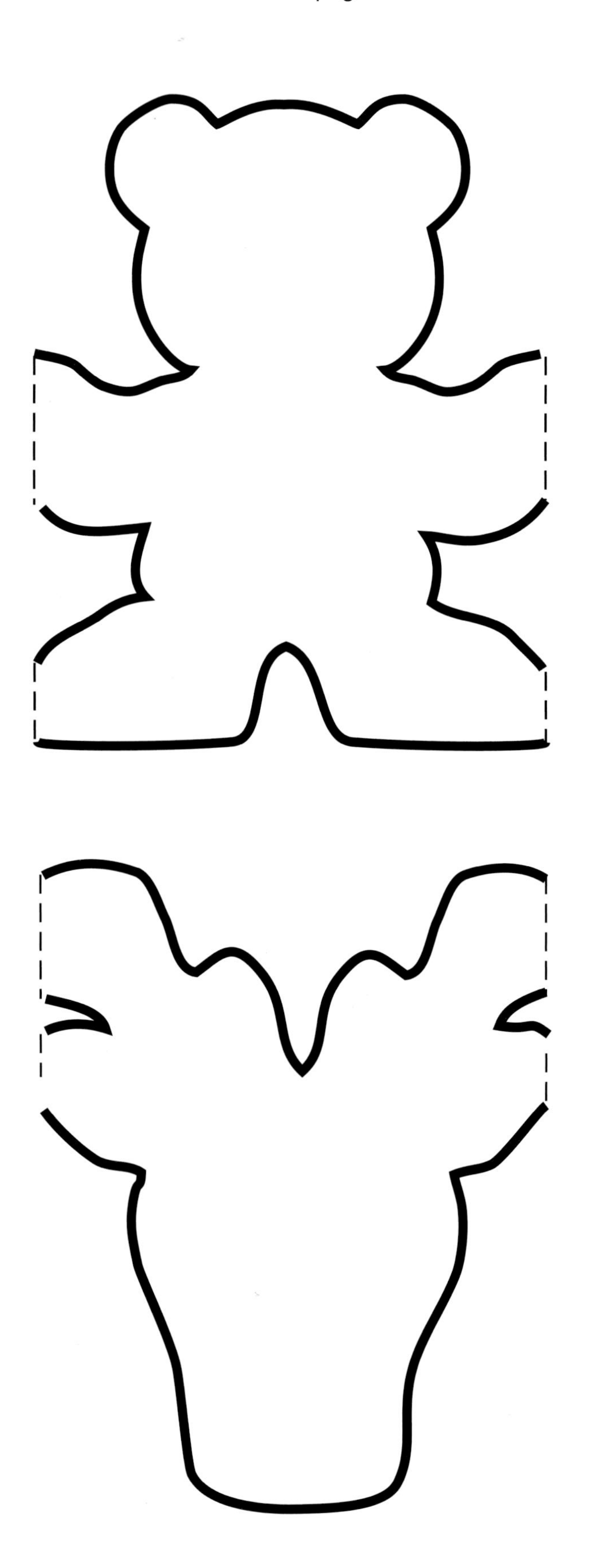

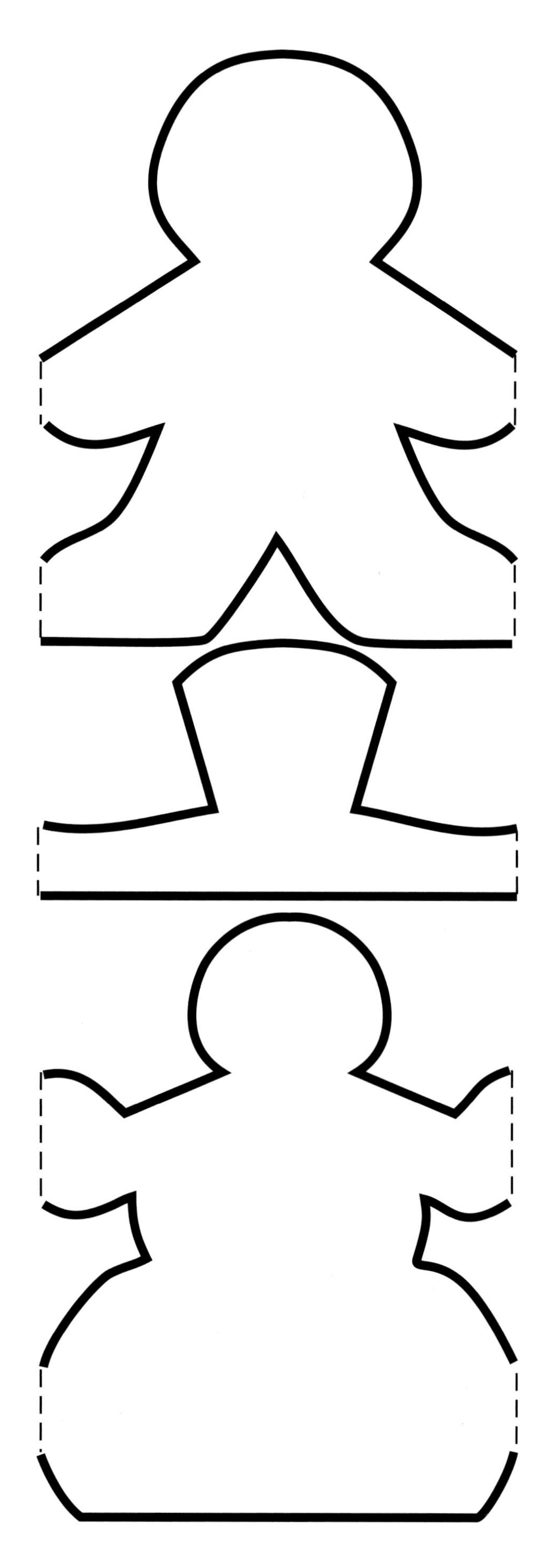

Place on fold.
Use with "Quilled Butterflies" on page 52.
Use with "Just For Dad!" on page 53.
Place on fold.
Use with "Folded Fliers" on page 52.

Pattern

Use with "All Aflutter!" on page 52.

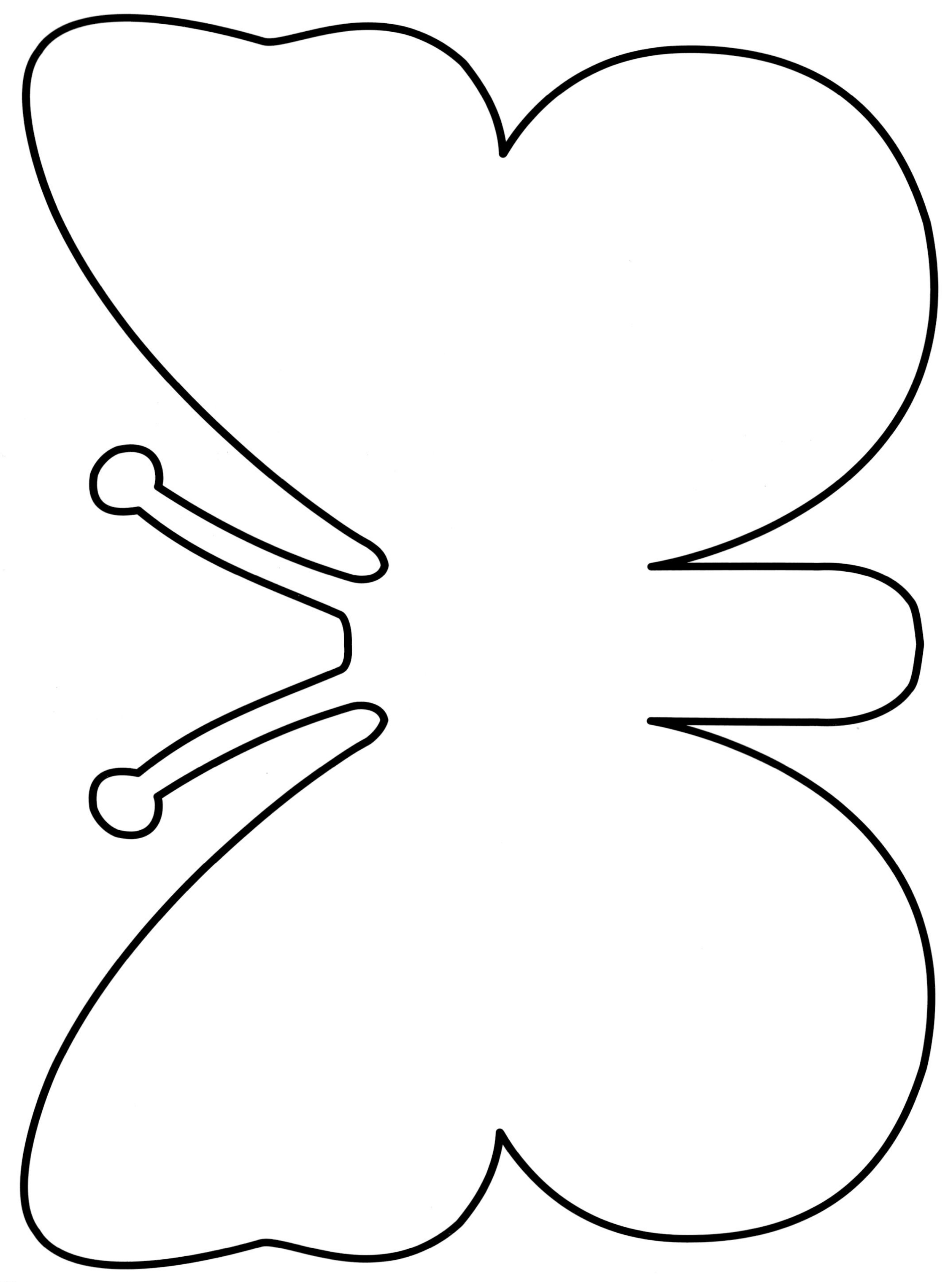

Lifesavers
Management Tips For Teachers

Helping Hat

Avoid interruptions when providing individualized instruction by donning a colorful "helping hat." Place this colorful hat on your head whenever you need several uninterrupted minutes to work with a student. Students will know to keep their questions under their hats until you remove yours!

Sally Thomson
Brown School
Schenectady, NY

Sharing The Bucket

Students will delight in this unusual sharing procedure. Each afternoon select one student to "share" the following day. Present the student with an empty, plastic bucket as you verbally recognize him for an outstanding deed or behavior he displayed. The bucket serves as a reminder for the student. It also prevents an overabundance of sharing items since all items must fit inside the bucket!

Sarah Fergus—Gr. 2
Christian Life Academy
Baton Rouge, LA

Classical Classroom Management

I have found that playing classical music after high-energy activities, such as P.E. and recess, helps to calm my students. In addition, I also prepare a brief, transitional activity such as a handwriting assignment for the students to complete as soon as they return. The students' energies are quickly soothed and redirected with a minimal amount of effort.

Wiley W. Blevins
Frederick, MD

Poems To Pass By

If your students become restless waiting for their papers, consider this poetic approach! On a weekly basis, as papers are being distributed, have students recite a chosen poem. When several poems have been learned, volunteers can lead their classmates in reciting the poems of their choice.

Judy Covington—Gr. 3
Alba Elementary, Coden, AL

At The Drop Of A Circle

Organize your small groups quickly and quietly using this management tip. Assign each group a number; then number a large circle cutout for each group. Laminate the cutouts for durability if desired. When it's time for youngsters to work in their assigned groups, place the circles where you'd like the groups to meet. You'll have a smooth transition into group work and the flexibility to choose the work location that you feel is most appropriate for each group.

Marilyn Haynos
Scranton, PA

Open House Drawing

Encourage parent involvement and gather classroom supplies with this idea. Place index cards labeled with needed supplies (such as paper plates, lunch bags, and waxed paper) in a large, decorated container. Invite each parent who expresses an interest to draw a card from the container, then provide the item on the card for classroom use. You'll have a bounty of supplies and numerous parents who are pleased to have been able to help.

Debbie Neumann
Pecan Park Elementary
Ocean Springs, MS

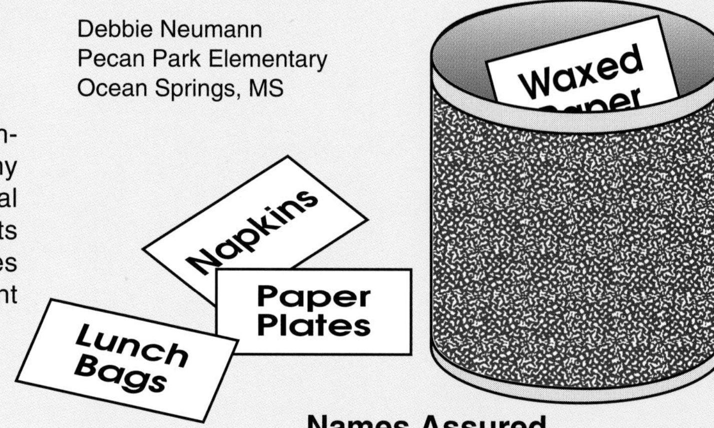

Names Assured

You'll never have another USP (unidentified student paper) again with this idea. Prior to collecting students' assignments say, "If your name is on your paper, draw a valentine heart [or other simple object] beside it." Since students like to draw, you can rest assured their names will be on their papers!

Sherry Gurka
Montgomery Elementary
Montgomery, TX

Restroom Reminder

Know at a glance which student is taking a restroom break by providing a restroom block for your students. Paint and decorate a small block of wood, and glue felt to the bottom. When a child leaves to visit the restroom, he quietly places the block on his desk, then replaces the block when he returns. A decorated chalkboard eraser works well also.

Kenneth T. Helms—Gr. 3
Irving Park Elementary
Greensboro, NC

Fair Chance

To keep students from monopolizing favorite centers, folder games, or skillboards, I tape a class list to each activity. Students cross their names off the lists as they complete the activities. When all names are crossed off a list, a new activity is introduced, or the list is replaced and children may complete the activity again.

Kathy Quinlan—Gr. 1
Annette Winn Elementary
Lithia Springs, GA

Luck Of The Draw

Here's a fun and fair way of choosing students to respond, line up, or be helpers. Write each student's name on a Popsicle stick. Store sticks in a small decorated container. Instead of choosing individual students, simply take the appropriate number of sticks from the can and read the student names. It's also a great way to form teams!

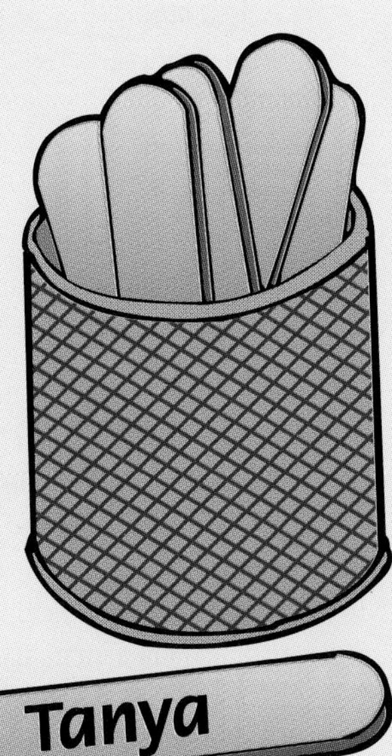

Diane Richwine—Gr. 3
York Springs Elementary School
York Springs, PA

A Calm Way To End The Day?

How do you keep 25 excited first graders quiet as they wait for their buses to be called at the end of the day? We have a sharing time. After the room has been straightened and the children are quiet, one child is allowed to sit in the teacher's chair and share his topic with the class. Because first graders *always* have something to share, this activity really helps us end the day on a calm note.

Susan Valenti—Gr. 1
Emmitsburg, MD

The End-of-the-Day Box

If your students' small toys seem to appear at inappropriate times, try this safekeeping system. Cover a shoe box with Con-Tact paper; then label it as shown. Program the clockface cutout with your dismissal time. If a student is playing with a toy during an inappropriate time, ask him to put it in the End-of-the-Day Box. The box will safely hold your students' treasures until the end of the day.

Bernadette Carnevale—Gr. 1
Buffalo, NY

Checking Manipulative Boards

Finding time to check our manipulative bulletin board seemed impossible during my busy day. And by the end of the day I was often uncertain which student had completed the work. I solved this problem by leaving an extra pushpin and a container of small laminated name tags at the bulletin board. After a student completes the activity, he attaches his name tag to the board. Now I can check and record each student's work as time permits.

Amelia K. Wallace—Gr. 1
Hopkins Elementary
Mentor, OH

Have I Or Haven't I?

How often do you wonder if you've already used a particular page from a ditto book? I eliminated this problem by placing a form on the inside cover of each ditto book. When I use a page, I write the page number, date, and group of students who used it. Replace the forms at the end of the school year and you'll be ready for fall!

Patsy Flynt
Monor Elementary
Lilburn, GA

Page #	Date	Group
15	9-26-93	everyone
5	11-4-93	Stars
20	1-18-93	Dudes

Hats Off To Cleanup!

Painters' hats will give the members of your weekly cleanup committee added prestige. Each afternoon, have the members don painters' hats. Students will enthusiastically complete their cleanup responsibilities at the drop of a hat!

Debbie Schneck
Schnecksville, PA

Math Tool Bag

I organized my math manipulatives into individual math tool bags and saved precious time. Inside each bag (a handy bag available from The Education Center) I placed a small clock, a 35 mm film can filled with buttons, a ruler, a small piece of cardboard, clothespins, a Ziploc bag of money, and a Ziploc bag with fraction pieces. Then I attached a teddy bear shape labeled with "Math Tool Bag" to the bag front. At math time we quickly pass out the bags and begin. My students eagerly await a chance to use their "tools" and look forward to math each day.

Dorothy P. Schenk—Gr. 1
Huntingtown Elementary
Sunderland, MD

Classroom Closeout

On the first school day in June, I begin taking down classroom posters, charts, displays, and learning centers, one at a time. Each day after the students leave I put away one item. The following morning the students guess what item is missing. The student with the correct guess receives a reward, often an old poster or leftover award. This method is fun for the students and a timesaver for me.

Julie Renkes
Hutchinson, MN

Secret Word

Are you tired of having to repeat classroom rules several times a day? Then a secret word is just what you need! Choose a secret word, such as "excel." Explain to your students that every time they hear the secret word, they should think about the classroom rules. When entering gym, music, or art class have each student whisper the secret word to you. If a student misbehaves, whisper the secret word to him. This quiet reminder will help to insure good conduct.

Joan M. Sewell—Gr. 2
Brookwood Elementary School
Snellville, GA

Memory Jogger

Post a wipe-off board near your desk to cut down on interruptions. When you're busy, a child who needs assistance may write his name on the board with one word to describe the nature of the question. As soon as you're available, you can glance at the board to see who needs your attention.

Sr. Mary Catherine Warehime
Mother Seton School
Emmitsburg, MD

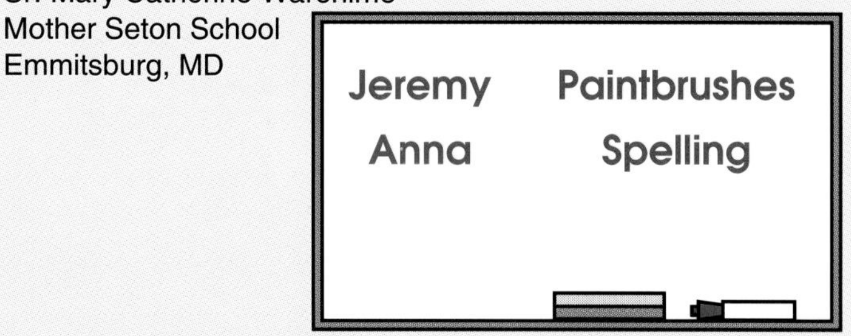

Quick Transitions

Before students leave for lunch, recess, or special classes, ask them to place the books and materials needed for their next lesson atop their desks. Students are motivated to get ready quickly, and the succeeding lesson can begin immediately upon their return.

Geraldine Fulton—Gr. 3
Meadow Heights Elementary
Sedgewickville, MO

Cleaning Out Desks

When cleaning out desks, instruct students in the "four pile system." Have children remove all items from their desks and sort them into piles to go in the trash, home, into the desk, and elsewhere in the classroom. With a little guidance every student can learn to eliminate a mess!

Ruth Wolery—Gr. 1
Glendover School
Lexington, KY

Spotlight On
Centers

Spotlight On Centers

A Truckload Of Short Vowels

Students fill dump trucks with picture cards for loads of short-vowel practice. Purchase five, inexpensive, plastic dump trucks. Label each truck with a different short-vowel sound. Make picture cards to represent these vowel sounds. Program the backs of the cards for self-checking and laminate if desired. A student loads the trucks by sorting each card into its matching dump truck.

Kathleen Darby—Gr. 1
Cumberland, RI

Sentence Building Blocks

Copying sentences from the board can be a tedious chore for beginning writers. To encourage students to create long sentences without labored handwriting, substitute sentence building blocks for pencil and paper. Write six sentences having an equal number of words on strips of masking tape. Use a different-colored marker to write each sentence. Cut the masking tape to separate the words in each sentence. Attach one word from every sentence to each block. A student chooses a color, then moves the blocks around until the sentence is in the correct word order. Students will love manipulating the blocks to find the mystery sentences.

Elizabeth Harris—ESL
Kimball Elementary
Mesquite, TX

"Packed" With Punctuation

This center is "packed" with punctuation practice. Using a permanent marker, program one resealable plastic sandwich bag to show each of the following ending punctuation marks: period, exclamation mark, question mark. On each of several bread slice cutouts, write a sentence, omitting its ending punctuation. Program the backs of the cutouts for self-checking, and laminate if desired. Store cutouts and bags in a lunch box. A student "packs" each cutout in a bag by identifying its missing punctuation mark.

Ready, Set, Begin!

Here's a fun way for students to improve rapid and accurate recall of math facts without creating competition between classmates. Place an assortment of math fact drill sheets, corresponding answer keys, and a three-minute hourglass egg timer in a center. A student turns over the timer when he begins his drill sheet, then stops working when the timer runs out. He then checks and evaluates his work. The student can focus on his own gains (rather than those of his classmates) and strive to improve at his own pace.

Susie Petges—Gr. 2
St. Dennis School
Lockport, IL

Student-made Flash Cards

Reinforce ABC order and enhance vocabulary development with student-made flash cards. Students cut out and glue magazine pictures of familiar home products onto construction-paper flash cards. Completed cards are displayed at a center for students to alphabetize.

Christina R. Seanor
Oakland Elementary
Suffolk, VA

Surprise Box Writing Center

Who wouldn't want to sneak a peek inside a surprise box? Decorate a large box and lid with a theme or wrap them with seasonal paper. Inside the box, place several interesting items such as a plastic dinosaur, a silver dollar, a skeleton key, and a used ticket stub. Place the closed box at your writing center to create lots of curiosity. A student who visits the center peeks inside the box, then includes each item in his story or poem. Maintain that exciting element of surprise by changing the items frequently. Watch out as eager students rush to the surprise box to see what's inside!

Sr. Ann Claire Rhoads
Mother Seton School
Emmitsburg, MD

Spotlight On Centers

A Poetic Hangout

Your young poets can put the finishing touches on original poetry at this unique center. Each student mounts an original poem on the bottom half of a sheet of 12" x 18" construction paper. Using markers, crayons, or paints, he then illustrates his poem on the top half of his paper. To display his completed project, the student folds back and staples the top corners of his construction paper around a hanger as shown. The poem can be hung from a chart rack or suspended from a clothesline for fellow poets to read and admire. Encourage students to create additional poems to add to the display.

A Chain Of Thanks

Here's a seasonal center that's certain to stir up thoughts of thankfulness. Each student needs 14 construction paper strips. Label one strip for each of the following letters: *T, H, A, N, K, S.* Label each of six more strips with a thankful thought. Glue the ends of a blank strip together to form the first loop of the chain. Attach the strip labeled *T* to the beginning loop; then attach a strip labeled with a thankful thought to the second loop. Continue in this manner—alternating between the two types of labeled strips—so the word "THANKS" is displayed down one side of the chain. Color and personalize a seasonal cutout; then loop the remaining construction paper strip through the chain, and glue the completed cutout between its ends. Suspend the completed chains from lengths of yarn or monofilament line for an attractive display.

Sr. Ann Claire Rhoads
Mother Seton School
Emmitsburg, MD

Feeding The Birds

This following-directions center is sure to be favored by your students and their feathered friends. Place pinecones attached to lengths of string, spoons, a jar of peanut butter, a large container of birdseed, and Ziploc bags at the center. Display written directions similar to the ones shown. Each student reads and follows the directions to make a bird feeder. The center is a fun way to reinforce the importance of carefully reading and following directions. And students are learning something they can do to help care for our wildlife. Encourage students to replenish their bird feeders throughout the winter months.

Sue Hancock—Gr. 1
Seaford Christian Academy
Seaford, DE

Spotlight On Centers

A New Look

Handwriting practice takes on a new look at this center. Cut out large shapes representing letters introduced for handwriting. Use a ghost for *g,* a corncob for *c*, a feather for *f,* and so on. During center time, students practice writing upper- and lowercase letters on the cutouts. As a variation, cut shapes from tagboard, laminate, and provide wipe-off markers. Or duplicate smaller shapes for individual student copies.

Sara McCormick Davis—Gr. 1
Wiley-Post-Putnam City Schools
Oklahoma City, OK

Spill And Sort

Recycle juice or soup cans with this fun sorting center. Cover several empty cans with construction paper. Glue a category picture on each can; then label with a category and number as shown. Label tongue depressors with words to be categorized. Code the backs of the word sticks with numbers for easy self-checking. Place the word sticks in the appropriate cans.

To play, two students select three cans, remove the sticks, and mix them up. They place the word sticks faceup and take turns reading and sorting them. When all the sticks have been placed in the cans, the students check the number codes on the backs of the sticks. Try these categories for lots of sorting challenges: Vegetables, Pets, Planets, Months, Continents, Transportation, States.

Guess And Prove It

Name______

Item	Guess	Proof
sneaker	7 in.	8 in.
	in.	in.
	in.	in.
	in.	in.

Guess And Prove It!

Here's an activity that sharpens students' measurement and estimation skills. Arrange six items at a center, each atop a sheet of paper labeled with the item's name. Place a duplicated worksheet (similar to the one shown) and a ruler at the center. A student writes the item names on his paper, records an estimated length for each item, then records a measurement for each item. He then compares his estimations to his measurements. If desired, provide a key of actual measurements. Change the center items weekly. Students will soon notice improvements in their powers of estimation and measurement!

Susan Voss—Gr. 1
Central Elementary
Michigan City, IN

Flapjack Facts

Cook up a "stack" of math fact practice! Label several pancake cutouts with math facts. Program the back of each cutout for self-checking; then laminate the cutouts for durability. Store the pancakes in an empty container that once held pancake mix or frozen pancakes. Place the container, a spatula, and a paper plate at a center. A student places the pancakes "on the grill" so each fact is displayed. After solving a fact, he uses the spatula to flip the pancake. If his answer is correct, he transfers the pancake to the paper plate. If his answer is incorrect, he flips the pancake to its original side. The student continues until all the pancakes are on the plate. Order up!

Tonya Byrd
Shaw AFB, SC

"En-deer-ing" Homophones

'Tis the season for homophone fun! To make each reindeer folder, diagonally fold a nine-inch, brown, construction-paper square. Program a pair of construction paper antlers with a homophone word pair; then attach the antlers to the folder as shown. Inside the reindeer folder, write four corresponding "fill-in-the-homophone" sentences. Number the sentences; then use the numerals to program the back of each antler for self-checking. Also use each numeral to program both sides of a clothespin. To complete each folder, attach wiggle eyes and a red, pom-pom nose; then place the folders and the four clothespins at a center. A student selects a folder; then, after reading each sentence, he clips the corresponding clothespin to the appropriate antler. He then flips the folder to check his work.

Alice L. Bennett—Gr. 1
Richmond Hill Elementary School
Richmond Hill, GA

The Stockings Were Hung

Fill these stockings with number-sequencing activities. Cut stocking shapes from red or green poster board. Beginning at the top, program each stocking cutout with a number sequence. Laminate the cutouts for durability; then cut the stockings apart so each piece features a number. Place the pieces of each stocking in a Ziploc bag. Store the bags in a Christmas stocking; then suspend the stocking at a center. A student sequences the pieces in each bag to make a stocking.

Kathleen Darby
Cumberland, RI

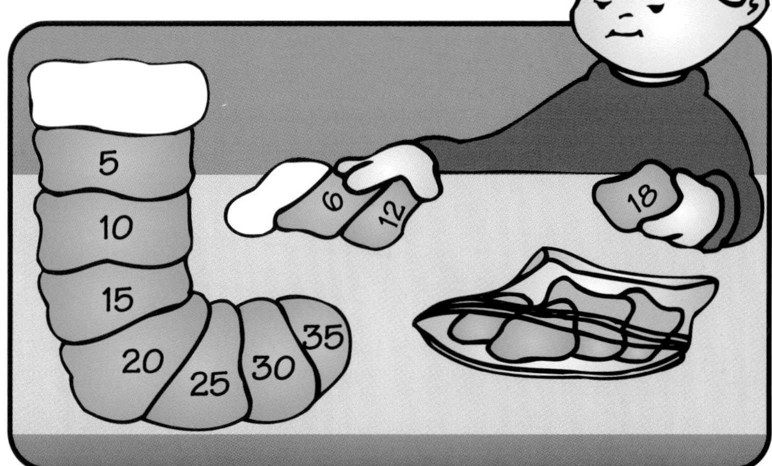

Spotlight On Centers

'Tis The Cooking Season

This independent cooking activity will be a holiday favorite. Display the recipe and needed ingredients at a center. Each student reads the recipe and follows the directions to create an edible Rudolph.

Judy Goodman—Gr. 2
Perryville Elementary
Perryville, MO

Undercover Noun Work

Noun classification skills are a must at this undercover center. Label three file folders "Top Secret! Missing People," "Top Secret! Missing Places," and "Top Secret! Missing Things." Students sort labeled cards into the correct top secret folders. Program the backs of the folders with corresponding answer keys if desired. For added fun, provide a trench coat and spy cap to wear while working undercover!

Mary Anne Haffner and Sue Ireland
St. Andrew School
Waynesboro, PA

Book Order Forms

Here's a resource that's free, comes in classroom quantities, promotes interest in books, and is extremely versatile! That's right—student book orders! Place copies of outdated order forms at a center along with a variety of task cards. Students attach order forms to completed tasks. Enlist the help of fourth- and fifth-grade student volunteers to check the completed tasks. Try it! They'll like it!

Deb Walter
Roscoe, IL

Spotlight On Centers

Valentine Mail

All you need to sweeten money skills is a package of commercial valentines. Using money stamps, stamp a coin amount on the back of each valentine. "Address" the envelopes with matching amounts. The student inserts each valentine inside its matching envelope. For self-checking, "hide" the correct amount somewhere on the front of each valentine. Store the valentines and envelopes in a valentine candy box or canister.

Tally The Tapes

Cash in on easy-to-make math center activities by using cash register receipts. Number several receipts of assorted lengths. Next program task cards with math activities related to the receipts. Activities might include measuring the receipts to the nearest inch or centimeter, finding the sum of designated receipts, or counting out the amount of play money needed to make the purchase indicated on each receipt. Program the back of each card for self-checking and laminate the receipts and cards for durability, if desired. Store the receipts in a gift bag and the cards in a decorated box. Place the bag, box, and other needed materials at the center.

Diane Vogel—Grs. 2–3
W.B. Redding School
Macon, GA

Candy Box Contractions

Here's a sweet way for your students to practice forming contractions. Cut a large heart shape from red poster board. Laminate the cutout and attach muffin tin liners labeled with contractions as shown. This will serve as your candy box. From construction paper, cut circular candy shapes to fit inside the liners. Program the cutouts to correspond with the candy box. Label the back of each candy cutout for self-checking. If desired, laminate the cutouts for durability. Students place the cutouts in the candy box, then flip the cutouts to check their work.

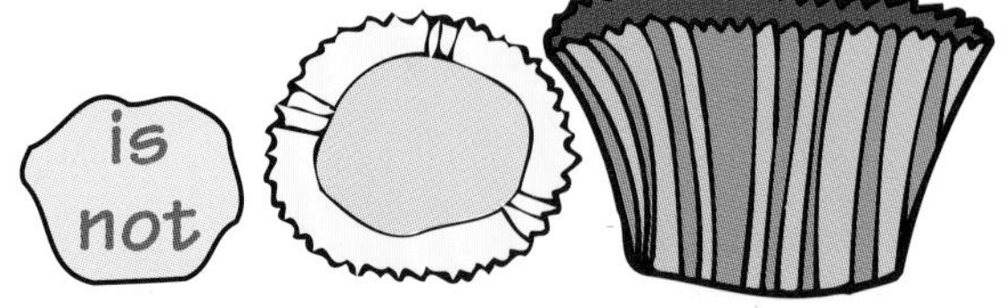

Spotlight On Centers

Fact Finders, Inc.

Here's a seasonal center idea that's easy to make no matter what the time of year. Cut out several large seasonal shapes from colorful poster board. Write a number in the center of each shape; then laminate the shapes. Place the cutouts and a supply of wipe-off markers at a center. A student chooses a cutout and uses a marker to write corresponding math facts around the number. Challenge students to write as many different facts as possible.

Isobel Livingstone
Rahway, NJ

Silly Tails

Snickers and giggles will be plentiful at this creative writing center. Fill a box with an assortment of yarn, ribbon, fabric, and gift wrap scraps and other arts-and-crafts materials. Place the box at a center along with a supply of drawing paper, glue, scissors, and a copy of *The Silly Tail Book* by Marc Brown (Parents Magazine Press, 1983). After reading the book, a student creates a unique tail atop a sheet of drawing paper. He then writes a story about the imaginary owner of this silly tail! Tickle your young authors' funny bones by rewarding them with Snickers candy bars!

Jolene Vereecke—Gr. 1
Lafayette Co. C-I School
Higginsville, MO

"Egg-ceptional" Families

Crack open some fascinating facts about animal names at this center. From wallpaper, cut a supply of matching egg shapes. Program the top half of each cutout with the name of a female animal. Program the bottom half of the cutout with the name of the animal's offspring. Using a different jigsaw-style cut for each egg shape, separate the programming on each egg. Place the cutouts in a basket filled with cellophane grass. A student removes the cutouts from the basket, then matches the egg halves. What an "egg-ceptional" way to hatch new vocabulary!

Tonya Byrd—Gr. 2
Shaw Air Force Base, SC

Spotlight On Centers

What's The Attraction?

This hands-on center attracts lots of interest in magnetism. Cut pictures of magnetic and nonmagnetic items from workbooks and magazines. Glue the pictures to the inside of a file folder and number each picture. Put a sample of each pictured item in the center along with a variety of magnets. A student numbers his paper to match the folder, then determines the magnetic property of each item. He writes *yes* for a magnetic item and *no* for a nonmagnetic item. Provide an answer key on the back of the folder for self-checking.

Gloria Wisniewski—Gr. 1
Buffalo, NY

Sentence Shenanigans

Reviewing subjects and predicates can lead to some pretty silly sentence shenanigans. Working from a list of descriptive sentences, program one set of sentence strips with the sentence subjects and a second set with the sentence predicates. (Use one color of sentence strips for subjects and another for predicates so that the strips are easily identifiable.) Tuck the strips in a Ziploc bag; then place the bag and a supply of paper, pencils, and crayons at a center. A student removes the strips from the bag and randomly pairs each subject strip with a predicate strip. After reading each of the sentences he has created, the student chooses the sentence he thinks is the silliest. He then copies and illustrates that sentence on a sheet of paper.

Marilyn Borden—Gr. 3
Castleton Elementary School
Bomoseen, VT

Recycling Center

Students will enjoy this center activity over and over again. Leaving the handle intact, trim the top half from a clean, empty, gallon-size milk jug. Using a permanent marker, label each of three Press-on Pockets (available from The Education Center, Inc.) "glass," "paper," and "plastic." Attach each pocket to a different side of the milk jug. Glue pictures of recyclable glass, paper, and plastic items to index cards; then code the backs of the cards for self-checking. Laminate the cards for durability; then place them in the milk jug. A student removes the cards from the milk jug and places each one in its corresponding pocket. After sorting the cards, he checks his work by referring to the programming on the backs of the cards.

Diane Vogel—Gr. 3
W. B. Redding School
Lizella, GA

Spotlight On Centers

Two dogs ate two biscuits each. How many did they eat in all?

Give A Dog A Bone

Real dog biscuits encourage students to "paws" at this center! Duplicate several dog patterns (page 74) on construction paper for each child. Cut out and store the patterns in a large Ziploc bag. Provide a box of small dog biscuits. On index cards, write math word problems such as the one shown. Program the backs of the cards for self-checking if desired. A student reads a problem, then solves it by "feeding" the dog(s) the appropriate number of dog biscuits. It's more fun to practice math with a canine companion!

Patsy Higdon
Arden, NC

Duty Calls!

There's plenty of work to be done at this center, and every bit of it will be done with enthusiasm! Create an office setting suitable for two working students. Include two desks or a table, two chairs, a manual typewriter, two real (disconnected) phones, two phone books, "in" and "out" baskets, blank order forms (gathered from magazines, catalogs, or book orders), a trash can, an assortment of pencils and markers, a stapler, and paper clips. Allow student pairs to role-play various office occupations (secretary, boss, client, janitorial service) while quietly performing office tasks such as talking on the phones, locating numbers in the phone books, filling out forms, or cleaning the office area. Besides feeling very grown-up, students can better understand what adults do when they "go to the office."

Kim Bohl—Gr. 1
Blissfield, MI

Place Value Toss

This action-packed center inflates place value skills! Program each indentation of an inflated air mattress with a numeral from one to nine. Place the air mattress in a center along with a red and a blue beanbag. To determine a two-digit number, a student tosses the red beanbag to discover the tens digit and the blue beanbag to discover the ones digit. A beanbag that does not fall into an indentation counts as a zero. He then tosses the beanbags again to determine a second number. Next he compares, adds, or subtracts the two numbers that he created. For an added challenge, place a green beanbag (hundreds digit) in the center. Both individuals and partners will enjoy this hot math activity!

Amy Barsanti—Gr. 1
St. Hilda's and St. Hugh's School
New York, NY

Pattern

Use with "Give A Dog A Bone" on page 73.

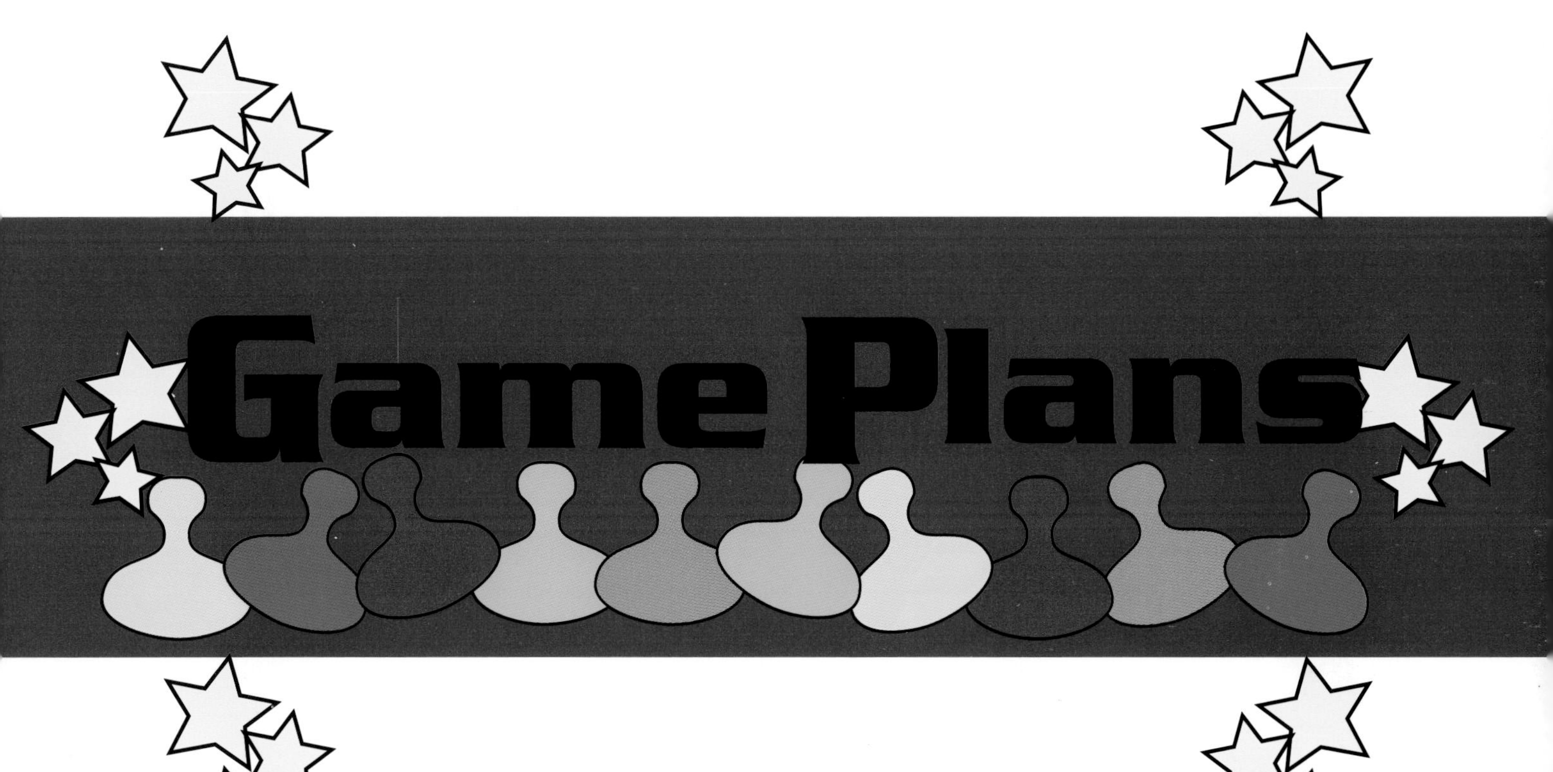
Game Plans

Getting Acquainted

This game takes the jitters out of first-day introductions. Clip ten clothespins onto a hanger. A student, holding the hanger in one hand, says his name, then uses his free hand to remove and hold a clothespin from the hanger. The student continues to remove and hold an additional clothespin for each personal detail he shares. When he drops a clothespin, he counts the clothespins in his hand, then passes the game to another student. Continue until all students have introduced themselves. The student who held the most clothespins in one hand wins.

Deanna Groke
Medical Lake, WA

Vocabulary Checkers

Check out this new twist on an old-time favorite game! Program a set of construction paper cards with vocabulary words. Store the cards in a Ziploc bag; then place the cards and a checker set at a center. To play, students follow the rules for playing checkers with one exception. Before making a move, a player must draw a card, read the programmed word and use the word correctly in a sentence. If a player is unsuccessful, he loses his turn. Your students are sure to be "jumping" with their new vocabulary words!

Cindy Callahan
Stewart's Creek Elementary
The Colony, TX

Spin To Win

The element of chance adds excitement to flash card drill! For this large group game you will need a large spinner labeled as shown and a stack of flash cards. Divide students into two teams. Have one member from each team draw a flash card from the stack, then copy and solve the fact on the chalkboard. If both players answer their facts correctly and their answers are the same, award each team one point. If the correct answers differ, spin the spinner to determine which team scores one point. If only one player has a correct answer, that player automatically scores one point for his team. Continue in this manner until all team members have taken one or more turns. The team with the larger score wins!

Deb Walter
Roscoe, IL

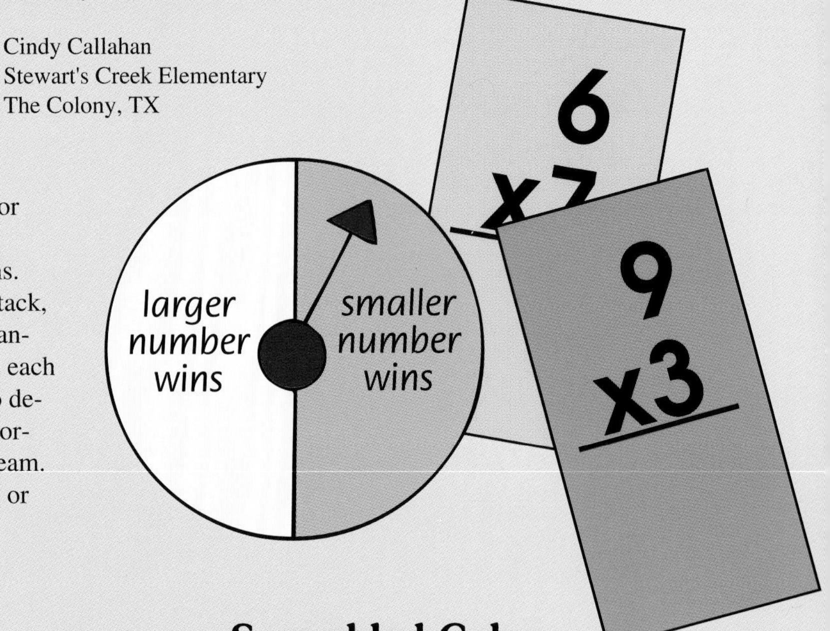

Scrambled Colors

Here's a great, large or small group game for reviewing color words. Write the letters of each color word to be reviewed on individual cards. Code the cards with small colored dots as shown. Distribute the cards so that each student has cards which bear different-colored dots. Call out a color word. Students with cards bearing dots of the called color come to the front of the room. Holding their cards, these students arrange themselves in order to correctly spell the color word. Continue in this manner until all color words have been spelled.

Vivian N. Campbell—Gr. 1
Grandview School
Piscataway, NJ

Mental Math

Here's an instant math game that's perfect for math warm-up or filling extra minutes. Orally, give students a sequence of calculations to complete mentally such as: begin with six, add two, subtract four, double your answer. Have students record their answers on pieces of scrap paper. Complete four or five sequences; then check the answers together. Kids love it!

Kathy Mobbs—Gr. 2
MacArthur Elementary
Southfield, MI

Spell Ball!

Careful spelling and good aim earn points in this game. On the floor, position a length of tape perpendicular to one end of a chalkboard. Place a trash can on the tape. Label the chalkboard with point values as shown, with the largest number being the farthest from the tape. Divide students into two teams. In turn, a player from each team positions the trash can beneath a point value, then stands behind the tape, faces the trash can, and awaits his spelling word. A player earns half the points by correctly spelling the called word. To earn the remaining points, he must toss a yarn ball (or similar device) into the trash can from his position. Continue play until all students have participated. The team with the most points wins.

Kimberle S. Byrd
Wyoming, MI

Under Your Thumbs

This fast-paced math fact game will be favored by your students. Visually divide a rubber ball into sections using a permanent marker. In each section, write a numeral. A student tosses the ball to a classmate. He catches the ball, locates the sections in which his thumbs have landed; and either adds, subtracts, or multiplies the two numbers. The ball is then tossed to the next student.

Patti Jones—Gr. 2
East Elementary School
Monroe, NC

Brainstorming Bonanza

Challenge your students with this category mind game! Prepare a deck of category cards. Have students arrange their chairs in a large circle. Select two students (seated beside each other) to stand; then display a card to begin play. Taking turns, the two players name items that fit in the displayed category. If a player gives an inappropriate word or is unable to brainstorm a suitable word, he must sit down. The remaining player advances clockwise to the next student in the circle. Play continues in this manner, until one student has advanced all the way around the circle or time runs out.

Sister Ann Claire Rhoads
Mother Seton School
Emmitsburg, MD

Cooperation Relay

This team relay promotes cooperation and generates giggles! Divide students into two teams. Have each team pair off into partners. (If necessary, one team member may have two partners so the team can be evenly paired.) Instruct each team to line up (in pairs) behind a designated line. On a given signal, the first pair on each team together carries a rubber ball (without using their hands!) to a predetermined spot, then back to the next pair in line. The first team to complete this task wins.

Suggest that partners hold the balls between their knees, their heads, their stomachs, or their elbows, or devise their own methods of movement! A dropped ball must be retrieved. Resume play where the ball was dropped. Because travel speed is minimized by these unusual positions, accident potential is reduced. Whether the game is played indoors or outdoors, one thing is certain—everyone will have a good giggle!

Marilyn Borden—Gr. 3
Castleton Elementary
Bomoseen, VT

Erase-A-Word

Pep up vocabulary practice with this game. Write eight words on the chalkboard in a scattered arrangement. Call out a task for each word. (For example: Circle a word that rhymes with *bees*. Circle a word that is the opposite of *noisy*.) When all the words have been circled, have the students "hide" their eyes while you erase a word. The students uncover their eyes and identify the missing word. Continue in this manner until each word has been erased.

Gertrude Faulkner
Elk Valley Elementary
Lake City, PA

Unlikely Pairs

For a quick five-minute game, have students list the similarities and differences in a pair of given objects, places, or animals. Then have students share their lists aloud. Students will be strengthening their thinking and vocabulary skills each time they play. The list of possible pairs is endless! Try these for starters: starfish—crab, Mississippi River—Atlantic Ocean, scissors—pencil.

Mary Anne Haffner—Gr. 2
St. Andrew School
Waynesboro, PA

scissors—pencil

similarities	differences
sharp	one is for writing and one is for cutting
held in the hand	
different sizes and styles	different shape
used at school	made out of different materials

Directional Moves

Play this small group, partner game to reinforce directional words. Using masking tape, create a six-foot-square grid on your classroom floor and "star" one square as shown. Label the north, south, east, and west sides of the grid. Provide a large spinner (labeled north, south, east, west) and a die. Pair students; then have one student from each pair stand on the grid square of his choice. In turn, the remaining students spin the spinner and roll the die to indicate how many steps and in which direction their partners may move. If a spin/roll takes a student beyond the perimeter of the grid he remains in his original position. The first student to conclude his move on the starred square wins the game.

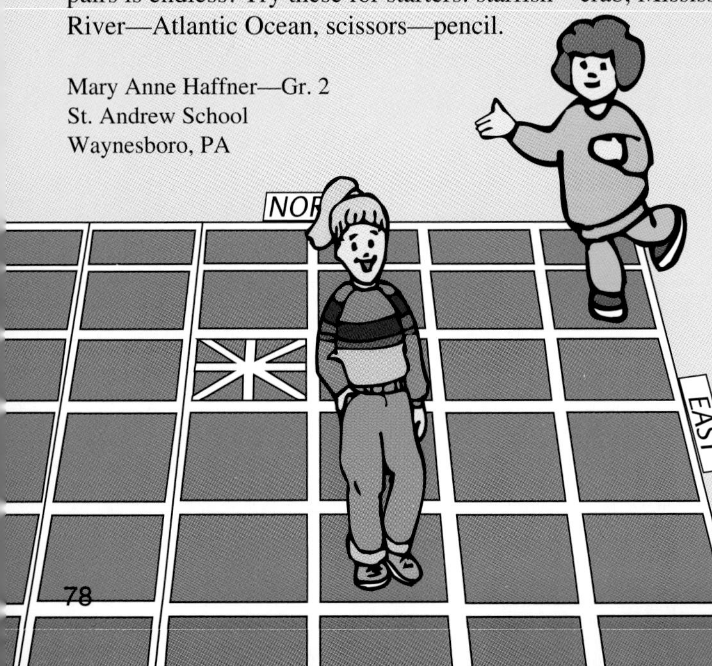

Sue Fowler—Special Education
Green Elementary School
Portsmouth, OH

Write
About It

Who-ooo's Who?

Here's a fun way to showcase your students' writing skills during Open House. On brown construction paper, duplicate or trace owl shapes. Have each student cut out a shape, then add facial and body features to his cutout using construction paper scraps or markers. On a piece of writing paper cut to fit the owl's breast, have each student write an anonymous description of himself. Mount the descriptions atop the owls; then display the completed projects with the caption "Who-ooo Are We?" Students will be delighted as their parents try to guess "who-ooo is who!"

Kenneth T. Helms—Gr. 3, Irving Park School, Greensboro, NC

Author Vests

Showcase students' literary talents with these author vests. Cut vests from bulletin board paper or brown paper bags. Have each student write a story or poem and then illustrate it on his vest. Then have each author don his vest, sit atop a special stool, and share his story or poem with his classmates.

Lisa Heintz, St. Mary School, Cincinnati, OH

Seasonal Shape-ups

Shape up your students' writing skills with the help of Bill Martin, Jr.'s *Brown Bear, Brown Bear, What Do You See?* For each child, program and duplicate several copies of a seasonal-shaped booklet page onto white paper. After sharing Bill Martin, Jr.'s book, show students an unprogrammed booklet page. Enlist their help in brainstorming seasonally appropriate adjectives and nouns for its completion. Next have each student refer to the list to complete a series of booklet pages. Staple each student's pages between two slightly larger construction-paper covers of the same shape. Have students personalize and decorate their booklet covers as desired.

For a cooperative learning activity, divide students into small groups. Have each group create a large-size booklet. Place the completed booklets in your classroom or school library.

Ellen Bruno and Esta Fowler, Rio Rancho Elementary, Rio Rancho, NM

Now That's A Tall Tale!

Familiarize your students with a few legendary tall-tale heroes, and they'll be ready to embark on this writing experience. Have each student compose a tall tale about an "unknown" hero; then have each student create a life-size cutout of his character creation. Mount the character cutouts around the room. As a finale, have each student read aloud his tale while standing alongside the cutout he created. If desired, invite students from a neighboring classroom to witness this storytelling affair.

Diane Afferton—Gr. 3, Morrisville, PA

Silent Films

Students re-create familiar classics with this writing activity. Show the filmstrip version of a well-known story such as *Cinderella.* There should be no sound accompaniment or words shown on the screen. Instruct students to write the story as it unfolds before their eyes. The visual clues are great writing motivators. And the activity is a fun way to reinforce story sequence.

Carol Cave—Gr. 3
Lexington, KY

Videorama
Cinderella
Rating G

The Weekly News

This writing activity is enjoyed by students and parents! Each Monday give students 3" x 5" pieces of paper. Instruct students to label the papers with their names; then have them write about or draw something they have recently done at school or at home. Collect and attach the papers to 8 1/2" x 11" sheets of paper. Make student copies of these papers, and staple into student packets to form "The Weekly News." Students enjoy reading their own writing and the writing of other students in their classroom newspaper. Parents enjoy the newspapers as well.

Pamela Myhowich—Grs. 1 & 2
Auburn, WA

Decorating With Details

Students trim these trees with well-organized paragraphs. Have students brainstorm a list of Christmas-related topics. Then have each student copy one topic and write a related topic sentence on his paper. Have him write several detail sentences to support his topic sentence, then revise and proofread his work for publication. To publish his paragraph, have each student use a green marker to draw a large outline of a Christmas tree on a sheet of chart paper. Have him copy his topic on a star cutout and glue it to the top of the outline. For the effect of colored lights, have each student copy his paragraph inside the tree outline, using a different-colored marker for each line. Have students cut out and share their trees with their classmates. Display the completed projects as desired.

Jacqueline D. Radford—Gr. 3, Suwanee Elementary School, Suwanee, GA

Tree Trimming

It is fun to trim a tree. Put the tree in a stand. String lights on the branches. Hang ornaments with little hooks. Drape garland around the tree. Then put a gold star on the top. What a beautiful tree!
Kelly

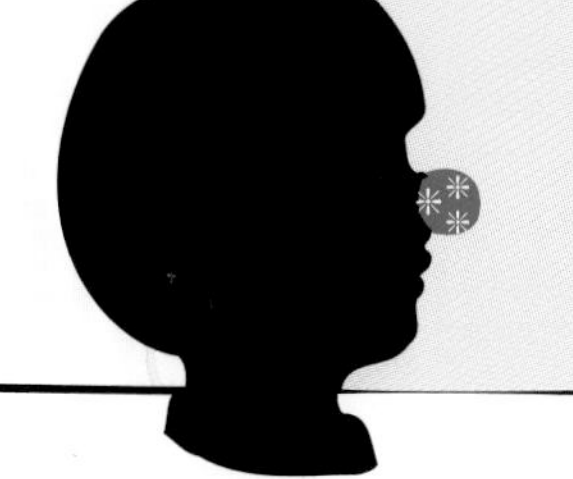

If I had been born with a shiny, red nose, I could help people. I could flash my nose to warn people of danger. I could help people find things in the dark. I might even be a hero!
Scott

Red-nosed Revelations

The story of Rudolph, the Red-nosed Reindeer, provides the perfect springboard for a discussion of individual differences. Follow up the discussion by having each student write how he would feel if he had been born with a shiny, red nose. To create story toppers, project and trace each student's silhouette on black construction paper. After cutting out his silhouette, have each student embellish a red, construction-paper circle with red glitter and glue it atop the nose of his cutout. Attach each child's story to his topper; then display the completed projects in the hall for passersby to admire. From this activity, you can glean much about each child's self-concept.

Bonnie Preston—Gr. 2, Ideal Elementary School, La Grange Park, IL

Signed, Sealed, Delivered

These personalized special deliveries recapture memories of the school year. Have each child write a letter to his parent(s), recounting his most memorable experiences from the year. Then have him seal his letter inside an envelope which he has addressed to his parent(s) and marked *special delivery*. For an official touch, add a sticker in place of a postage stamp. This is a first-class delivery parents are sure to appreciate.

Mary Dinneen—Gr. 2, Mountain View School, Bristol, CT

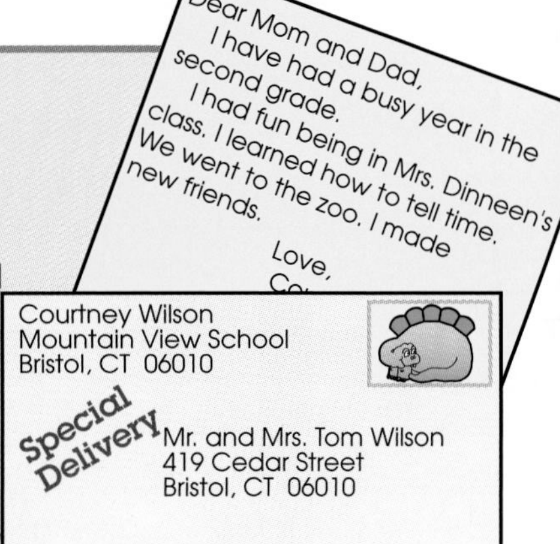
Dear Mom and Dad,
I have had a busy year in the second grade.
I had fun being in Mrs. Dinneen's class. I learned how to tell time. We went to the zoo. I made new friends.
Love,

Courtney Wilson
Mountain View School
Bristol, CT 06010

Special Delivery

Mr. and Mrs. Tom Wilson
419 Cedar Street
Bristol, CT 06010

Surprise Packages

Pique students' natural curiosity as you develop writing skills. Heighten suspense by displaying three different-sized, colorfully wrapped, empty surprise packages labeled *A, B,* and *C.* On the chalkboard, write *who, what, where, when, why,* and *how* questions pertaining to the packages. Students choose lettered packages, then they use their imaginations to write answers to the questions. After illustrating their packages' contents, invite students to share their "surprises" with their classmates.

Mary Rubino Kibbey—Gr. 1, Earlton, NY

Sticker Stories

Having a problem finding a quick and easy, end-of-the-year writing activity? Then you'll love this instant solution! Gather the unused stickers you've accumulated during the school year and place them in a shoe box. Have each child select a sticker, attach it to a sheet of paper, and write a story about the illustration featured on his sticker. Students will be stuck on these fun-to-write sticker stories.

Eleanor Beson—Resource Room, Ballard School, South Glens Falls, NY

My Dirt Bike

This is me on my dirt bike. I am in first place. All of a sudden a deer jumped in front of me. I ran over the deer. I fell off my dirt bike and one wheel fell off. The dirt bike was totaled. I broke my leg, but I hope to ride again in a couple of months.

by Carl Donaldson
June 5, 1991

News Flashes

Periodically add a little spice to your normal routine with news flashes. During class or for homework, have each child prepare a news flash by selecting a short newspaper article, writing a brief summary of the information given, and drawing an illustration of the event. The next day, interrupt your regularly scheduled "programming" at regular intervals. During these pauses, youngsters take turns presenting their news flashes to classmate "viewers". For added fun, have each student newscaster sit inside a cardboard box which has been decorated to resemble a TV.

Velma Maclin, Memphis, TN

Getting Kids
Into Books

Getting Kids Into Books

Sprout new interest in reading with this reading corner. Create a "couch potato corner" by placing a used love seat in a cozy nook of your classroom. Or create your own makeshift version by tossing two plump pillows on the floor and attaching a matching poster-board couch back on the wall behind them. Each day select two students to "plant" themselves amid the comfortable surroundings to read the books of their choice.

Cathy Cavasos—Gr. 2, Hickok School, Ulysses, KS

A classroom mascot makes a great read-aloud buddy! Place a stuffed animal and a spiral notebook in a canvas bag. Each day, select a different student to take the bag home. Have the selected student read at least one story to the furry friend, then record his name and the title of each book he read in the notebook. The next day, ask the student to give a brief report about each book he shared with the mascot. When the titles of 50 books have been recorded in the notebook, reward the class with a special treat.

Mary Anne Haffner—Gr. 2, Andrew School, Waynesboro, PA

Nurture your budding illustrators' creativity with Caldecott books. Each month feature a Caldecott award-winning book. After reading the book aloud, examine the illustrations and discuss the illustrator's medium (such as collage, watercolor, or pen and ink). Place the book at a center along with the art supplies necessary for students to create personal renderings of their favorite illustrations from the book. Display the completed works of art on a bulletin board captioned "Caldecott Corner." At the end of the month, select and present one outstanding student illustrator with a paperback copy of the featured book. Students' interest in reading additional Caldecott books is sure to blossom!

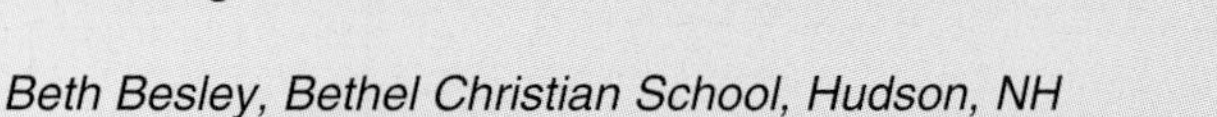

Beth Besley, Bethel Christian School, Hudson, NH

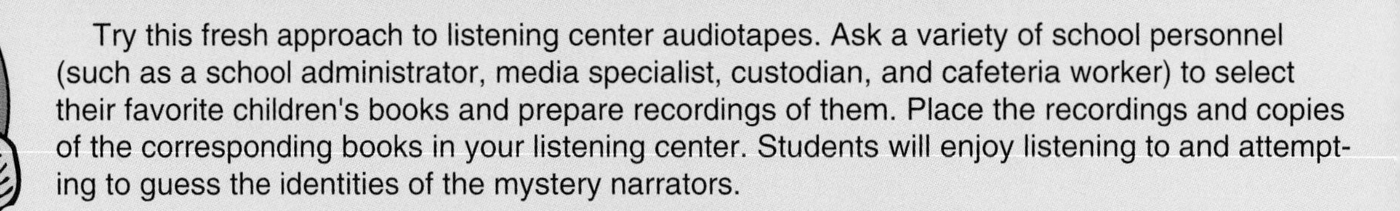

Try this fresh approach to listening center audiotapes. Ask a variety of school personnel (such as a school administrator, media specialist, custodian, and cafeteria worker) to select their favorite children's books and prepare recordings of them. Place the recordings and copies of the corresponding books in your listening center. Students will enjoy listening to and attempting to guess the identities of the mystery narrators.

Sue Zimmerman—Gr. 1, Spruce Street School, Sauk City, WI

Students will be delighted to play this literary version of the well-liked game Pictionary time after time! Write book titles familiar to your students on individual cards; then place the cards in a small container. To play, divide students into two groups. In turn, one student from each team chooses a card and draws pictures to indicate the title of the book he has chosen. If his team correctly guesses the title in the allotted time, his team earns a point. If his team is unsuccessful, the opposing team may make a guess. A correct guess earns one point. Continue play in this manner. At the end of the game time, tally the points to determine the winning team. Or record the existing scores, and continue play the next time you find yourself with a few extra minutes to spare.

Chris Christensen, Marion B. Earl Elementary School, Las Vegas, NV

Getting Kids Into Books

Encourage students to share read-aloud books with these headband headliners. Duplicate strips containing the message, "Today we read __________ by __________________. Ask me about it!" After sharing a read-aloud book, distribute duplicated strips to students. Have students fill in the title of the book and the author's name; then glue the duplicated strips to sentence strip headbands. Have students decorate their headbands with drawings of favorite characters or story events, staple them to the correct size, and don their creations. Students are sure to feel head and shoulders above the crowd as they proudly share their read-aloud experiences with others.

Mary Ann Smith—Gr. 1, Muskegon, MI

Using lunch boxes, you can pack reading activities to go! Pack each lunch box with a book and cassette set, a corresponding activity worksheet, and a special edible treat for students to enjoy while completing the activities. Send the lunch boxes home with different students each night. When the lunch boxes are returned, remove and evaluate the completed worksheets; then replace the worksheets and treats for the next students. Continue until each student has had a chance to take a lunch box home; then select new materials and start again. Students will enjoy sinking their teeth into these great activities.

Georgia Darrah—Gr. 2, Longcay Elementary, Kent, OH

Invite students to share the gift of reading with their classmates. Separately wrap and decorate the lid and box portions of a hatbox. Place a read-aloud book inside the box, replace the lid, and display the wrapped "gift." Discuss intangible gifts such as smiles, hugs, and kind words with students. While opening the gift, tell students you have a similar gift to share with them; then reveal the book! Read the book aloud; then invite students to place "gifts" in the box. Set aside time each day for students to read aloud their "gifts."

Amelia K. Wallace—Gr. 1, Hopkins Elementary School, Mentor, OH

The whole family can put their hearts into this fun reading activity! Glue white construction paper heart cutouts atop larger red heart cutouts. Send home a heart and a note of explanation with each student. In the note, request that each family identify its favorite book and then decorate the heart accordingly. When the completed hearts are returned, display them on a bulletin board entitled "Our Family Favorites."

Mary Vondrak—Gr. 1, Seth Paine School, Lake Zurich, IL

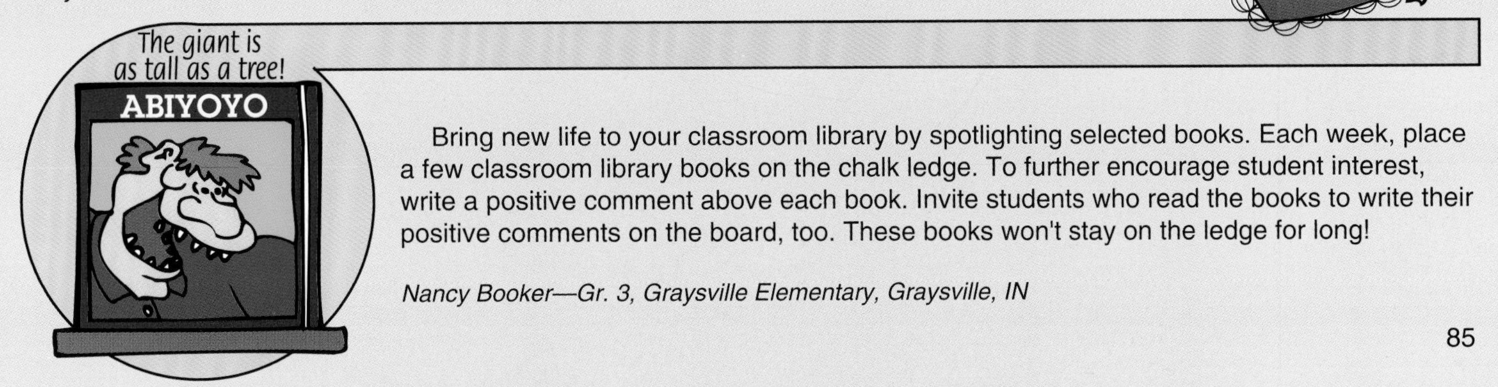

Bring new life to your classroom library by spotlighting selected books. Each week, place a few classroom library books on the chalk ledge. To further encourage student interest, write a positive comment above each book. Invite students who read the books to write their positive comments on the board, too. These books won't stay on the ledge for long!

Nancy Booker—Gr. 3, Graysville Elementary, Graysville, IN

Here's a way students can enjoy drawing during storytime, and you can rest assured they are listening. As you begin a novel, supply each student with a construction paper folder containing sheets of drawing paper equal to the number of novel chapters. As you read (one chapter daily), students draw illustrations. Students label their drawings with captions, then place them in their folders. When the novel is completed, students design cover art for their folders, punch holes, and tie their pages and covers together with yarn lengths. They now have their own picture book versions of the completed novel!

Pamela Myhowich—Grs. 1–2, Auburn, WA

Weekly Mystery Book Contests will surely get your students interested in reading! Display 25 to 30 books for a two- to three-week period. During this period, challenge students to read as many of the selected books as possible. Each Friday read a brief description of one of the books. Have students cast ballots to guess the title of the summarized book. Reward two correct entries with bookmarks or fancy pencils and the additional correct entries with stickers.

Barbara Dixon, Loveland, OH

Encourage students to read at home by giving their parents a reading homework assignment! In a note home, request that each parent read a book with his child. Also ask that the parent and child locate one or two household items that in some way represent the book they have shared. Have students share these items and books during a weeklong celebration. In addition, ask parents to illustrate book covers for their favorite childhood books. Invite the parents to share their covers and related book memories with the students during another fun and motivational book week celebration.

Susan Holtkamp—Gr. 3, Terra Linda Elementary, West Jordan, UT

Watch youngsters join in the fun of reading when you introduce author fan clubs! Display sets of books by each of several different authors. When a student has read a predetermined number of books from a set, present him with a tagboard membership card. Have the student complete a card and decorate it with art which relates to his favorite book in the set. Sign; then laminate the completed cards for durability. For additional reading motivation, hold monthly membership drives for selected fan clubs. Students will be proud to be card-carrying members of numerous author fan clubs.

Mim Dilmore—Gr. 1 and Pam Tinker—Librarian, Thorntons Ferry Elementary, Merrimack, NH

How can you get the word out about good books to read during the summer? Let your kids do it for you! A week or two before summer vacation begins, set aside five to ten minutes each day for informal "book talks." Ask students to discuss and recommend books they've read during the year. Your children will be eager to check out books that they've discovered through a friend's book talk. To make summer library trips even easier, keep a list of the books your students recommend during these talks; then duplicate the list and send a copy home with each child on the last day of school!

Susan Grimm, Lukeville Elementary, Brusly, LA

Our Readers Write

A Loop-A-Day Diary

Keep a paper chain diary of the daily events that happen throughout the school year. Each afternoon review the happenings of that day. Using a marker, record the most important event or events on a strip of construction paper. After forming the first loop of the chain, attach each strip around the previous day's loop. Near the end of the school year, begin to disassemble the chain (beginning with the first loop) and share the recorded events. Your paper chain diary will bring back many happy memories of the past school year.

Marilyn Borden—Gr. 3
Castleton Elementary School
Bomoseen, VT

We learned about Johnny Appleseed while we ate apples. Yummy!

"Magic" Red Shoes

Add a little pizzazz to ordinary lessons with "magic" red shoes. Coat an old pair of shoes with glue; then sprinkle the shoes with red glitter and sequins. When a lesson needs a little extra zip, don your shoes and watch your students "magically" transform into terrific listeners and sensational workers. "Click! Click! Click! There's no place like...*school!"*

Sara G. McGee—Gr. 1, Bel Air Elementary, Evans, GA

A Warm Welcome

Create a nonintimidating environment in the school office by displaying student work throughout the year. Feature student work from individual classrooms and special groups on a weekly, biweekly, or monthly basis. What a sense of pride students will have when they view their work in such a prominent location!

Melba S. Vokosky—Gr. 2
Newcomb Elementary School
Newcomb, NM

Classroom Cleanup

Classroom cleanup is a snap when your students work together as a lean, mean, cleaning machine! Choose two or three students to role-play machine nozzles; then have the remaining students hum like the machine's motor. Signal the student machine to begin operation with a "click" of an on switch. Periodically "click" the machine off and have the student nozzles exchange places with other classmates. Your room will be in tip-top condition in no time at all!

Suzanne Edmunds—Gr. 1
Forest Elementary School
Forest, VA

Student Art Gallery

Personalize a display of student artwork by attaching each student's photograph to his completed art project. Attach the photographs (I use a roll of student photos that accompanies our school pictures) to the corners of the artwork with masking tape. When the display is taken down, the photos can be easily removed and saved for the next showing!

Sr. Ann Claire Rhoads
Mother Seton School
Emmitsburg, MD

Open House Bookmarks

Student-made bookmarks are sure to attract the attention of Open House visitors. Have each child decorate a construction paper strip as desired, then use his resulting bookmark to indicate a favorite story, an interesting chapter, or an especially challenging page in one of his textbooks. Parents are sure to notice the specially marked pages and will enjoy discussing them with their children when they return home.

Joan D. Light—Gr. 2, Seattle, WA

LOOK!
This is my favorite story.
Blake

Getting Acquainted

Try this fun, getting-acquainted activity. Ask each child to bring his favorite board game with him on the first day of school. (Have some extra games on hand for those students who are unable to bring them.) Randomly divide students into groups. Have each child teach the members of his group how to play his game. As students play and get acquainted, you can observe how they relate to one another.

Marge Westrich—Gr. 2
Colby Elementary School
Colby, WI

Too Much Paste

Put an end to extra blotches of paste on student projects or desks. Cut a regular-sized sponge into two-inch pieces. (One sponge will yield about 12 pieces.) Lightly dampen the sponge pieces and distribute to students at the beginning of any pasting project. Students can use the sponge pieces to wipe away extra paste. The result will be neater projects and cleaner desks.

Pamela McKedy
Durham, NC

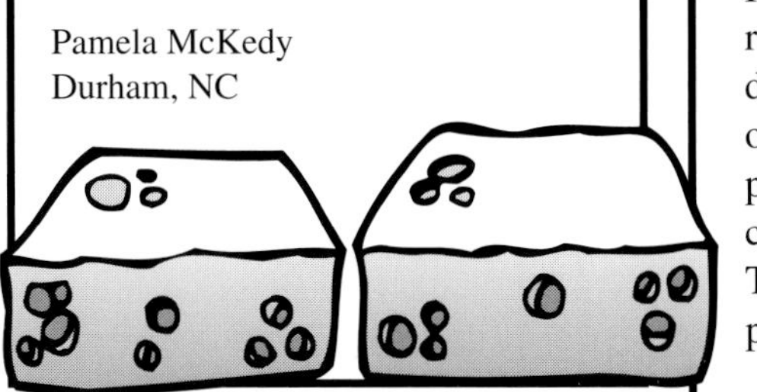

Spooky had a tiny boo!
Tiny boo! Tiny boo!
Spooky had a tiny boo!
But it was scary, too!

Haunted Lyrics

Challenge students to write spooky lyrics to familiar tunes such as "Twinkle, Twinkle, Little Star" or "Mary Had A Little Lamb." This makes a great seasonal creative writing assignment, and students can share their masterpieces at a Halloween sing-along. This idea works well with other holidays and themes, too!

N. Jean Ellis—Gr. 3, Lorenzo Elementary, Lorenzo, TX

Our Pen Pals

I keep a display of pen-pal photographs on exhibit year-round. As new pictures arrive, they are added to the display. In this way, each student can enjoy a photograph of his own pen pal and photographs of his classmates' pen pals, too. My students enjoy visiting the display and chatting about their faraway friends during free time. They also like to refer to the photographs as they compose their pen-pal letters.

Debbie Wiggins
North Myrtle Beach Primary, North Myrtle Beach, SC

Instant Number Line

Use chalk to create an instant number line on a classroom carpet or rug. Students can walk, hop, or stand along the number line to reinforce a variety of math concepts. When the lesson is over, the number line can be quickly wiped away!

Marci Haber—Transitional First
Nashville, TN

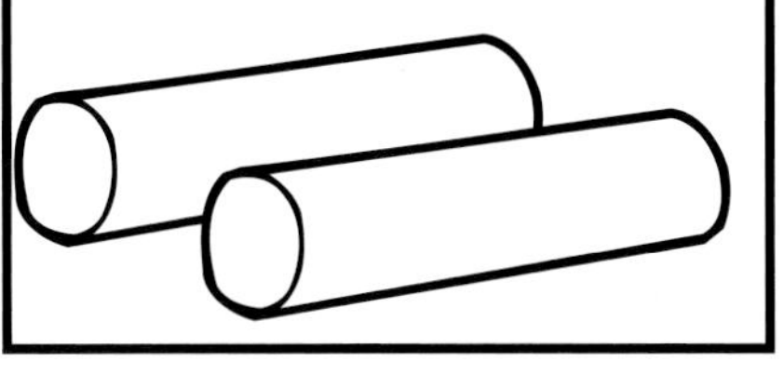

Autographs, Please

Motivate your youngsters to complete their assignments with this suggestion. Each morning, sketch an open seasonal shape on the board. For extra appeal, use colored chalk. Students who finish all their assignments to your specifications sign their names inside the shape.

Pat Smith—Gr. 1
Linda Sandlin—Gr. 2
Jackson R-2 Schools
Jackson, MO

Writing Without Lines

Here's a tip that enables young authors to successfully write on unlined paper. Using a dark marker, trace the lines on a sheet of lined writing paper. Laminate the paper for durability. When a young author wishes to write a story on unlined paper, tape the lined and laminated sheet to his desktop. Then have the student place a piece of lightweight, unlined paper atop the laminated sheet. The lines from the laminated sheet will show through the unlined paper and serve as writing guidelines!

Sara Kennedy
Bedford, VA

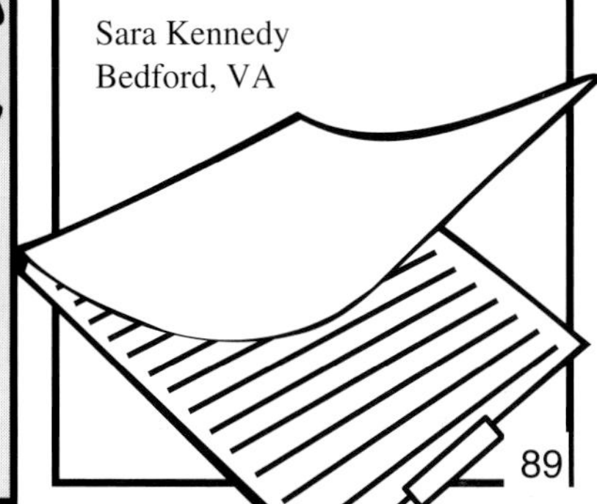

Principal's Pals

This idea promotes positive interaction between students and their principal. Display a large, laminated envelope labeled "Principal's Pals." Place an assortment of colorful stickers inside the envelope. When appropriate, use a wipe-off marker to write on the outside of the envelope the names of students who deserve special recognition for positive behaviors, outstanding work, or good deeds. Arrange for your school principal to make daily or weekly visits to present stickers to the listed students. After each visit, wipe the envelope clean and begin a new collection of student names.

Jill K. Dean—Gr. 3
Our Lady Of Guadalupe, Topeka, KS

Thankful Boxes

This Thanksgiving emphasize thankfulness with these special boxes. Label and cut a slit in the top of a shoe box for each student. Introduce the activity by brainstorming a class list of thankful thoughts. Each student then copies one thankful thought on a slip of paper and places it in his shoe box. Have students write one or more thankful thoughts each day to place in their boxes. When Thanksgiving arrives, students will have generous collections of thankful thoughts to share with their families.

Cindy Villavaso—Teacher's Assistant, Gr. 1
Overstreet Elementary
Starkville, MS

Teacher's Report Card

I turn the tables on my students at the end of each report card period. How? By letting them grade me! In his journal, each child writes comments about how he thinks I'm doing, what he likes and dislikes about being in my class, and suggestions for the future. This exercise lets me know how my students perceive me and life in our classroom. The children also enjoy knowing that they aren't the only ones being graded!

Don Reiffenberger—Gr. 3
Laura B. Anderson Elementary
Sioux Falls, SD

"I Feel Good About..."

On the day that my students are to receive their first report cards, I give each child an "I Feel Good About..." badge. Each student completes his construction paper badge, colors it, and proudly wears it all day. These little motivators really give my students positive feelings about themselves as they take home their report cards.

Cathy E. Caudill—Gr. 1
North Drive Elementary
Goldsboro, NC

A Sneak Preview

A laminated message center posted outside your classroom can provide a sneak preview of each day. Use a wipe-off marker to write daily messages. Messages can remind students of special events or build excitement about a lesson. Sneak previews are a fun way to build students' enthusiasm before the day begins!

Joan Light—Grs. 2 & 3
Seattle, WA

The Worry Box

A class worry box can help students solve problems. Separately cover a shoe box and its lid with Con-Tact paper. Cut a slit in the lid and label the box "Worry Box"; then set the box (with its lid) on your desk. A student can discreetly slip a note stating a problem or concern into the box; then, when appropriate, you can talk over the problem privately with the student. Sometimes just getting a problem off his chest can help a student feel much better.

Barbara Doughty—Gr. 3
Esther Jackson Elementary
Roswell, GA

Class Outing

Promote class spirit and unity by planning a special outing for students and their parents. Check with local theaters, skating rinks, or miniature golf courses about special group rates; then invite your students and parents to join you for an evening of fun. The casual atmosphere provides the opportunity for everyone to get to know one another a little better.

Rebecca Abney—Gr. 3
Kingston Elementary
Richmond, KY

Travel Log

When family vacations are taken during the school year, present the traveling student with his own travel log before he leaves. To make a travel log, staple alternating sheets of writing and drawing paper between construction paper covers. Ask the traveler to decorate the cover, then write a short entry for each day, illustrating it on the adjacent page. A small memento of the day may also be glued atop the illustrated page. Each traveler will delight in sharing the memories of his travels upon his return.

Vivian Campbell—Gr. 2
Martin Luther King School
Piscataway, NJ

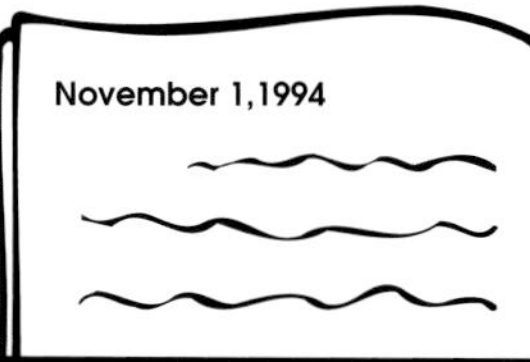

Sticker Books

These sticker books are not only a breeze to make; they're inexpensive as well. Fold a half sheet of construction paper in half for a sticker book cover. Then place folded microwave, waxed-paper sheets between the halves of the cover and staple. Stickers can be attached to the waxed-paper sheets in this booklet and easily removed for trading.

Sheilah Champion
Brethren Navajo Mission
Counselor, NM

Holiday Greetings

Here's a great way to inspire creativity and promote recycling. Place artwork cut from previously used cards in a seasonally decorated gift box. Display the box, a supply of construction paper cards, markers, glitter, glue, and other desired supplies at a holiday art center. Have students design and personalize holiday greeting cards for their friends and family members. Happy holidays!

Diane McAdams—Gr. 2
Paul Pewitt Elementary
Omaha, TX

Reindeer Gift Bags

Students can make these eye-catching gift bags as quick as a wink! Open a brown lunch bag and attach a red pom-pom nose near its base. Glue in place eyes made from black and white construction-paper scraps. Trace both hands on brown construction paper and cut out the resulting "antler" shapes. Approximately two inches from the top, attach one antler to the pleat at each side of the bag. Fill the bag as desired; then fold down and staple the top in place. Or, for a festive finish, fold down the bag top and punch two holes near the center of the folded portion. Thread the ends of a curling ribbon length through the holes and through a jingle bell; then tie and curl the ribbon ends.

Alice L. Bennett—Gr. 1
Richmond Hill Elementary School
Richmond Hill, GA

Sideways Math

Help your students achieve straight columns while calculating math problems with this little math twist. Instruct students to turn their papers sideways and use the lines as column dividers. A new angle can make all the difference in the world!

Cindy Newell
Washington Irving Elementary
Durant, OK

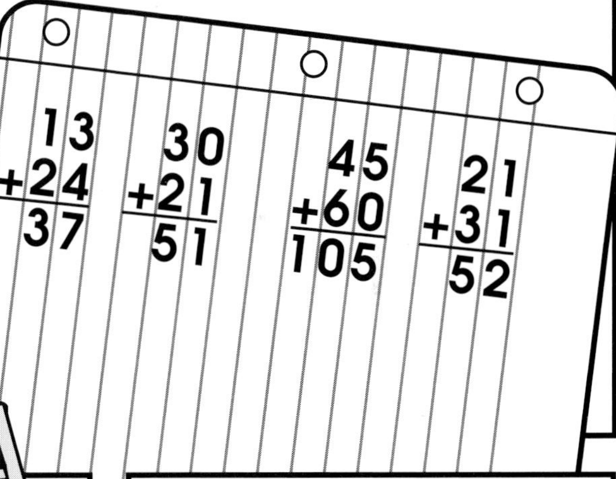

Indoor Recess Options

When winter weather prohibits outdoor recess, my students play indoor games or visit our pattern table. Scissors, a variety of seasonal tracing patterns, and construction paper are placed at the table. Students trace and cut out patterns as they chat. It's a fun diversion for students and I benefit by having an ample supply of ready-to-use patterns on hand.

Paula K. Holdren
Prospect, KY

Big Book Storage

Hung up on how to store your collection of big books? Try using a clothes-drying rack. Open; then drape each big book over a bar on the rack. Books can be identified, removed, and replaced with ease.

Cindy Cribbs—Gr. 1
Northwoods Elementary School
Jacksonville, NC

Sealing Tip

Take the air out of resealable plastic bags with this handy tip. Using a hole punch, punch a hole directly beneath the seal of each bag. Later, when the bags are being sealed, any air trapped within them can escape through the holes. The "airless" bags will also be flatter and easier to store.

Tara Kayrouz—Gr. 2
St. Raphael School
Louisville, KY

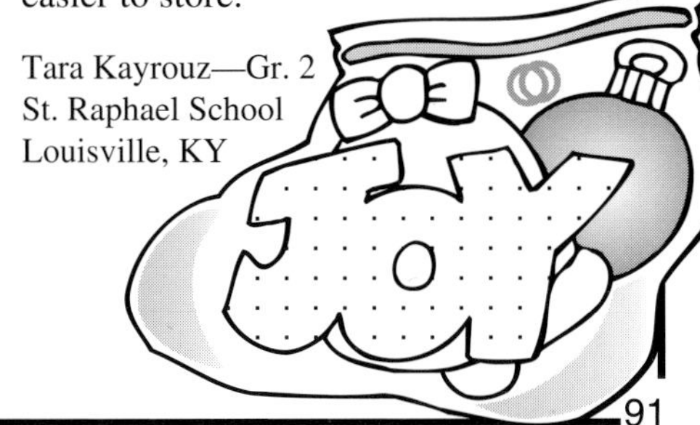

Grading By Another Teacher

We taught cursive handwriting this year in second grade. The children loved it, but soon the newness wore off and they wanted to print again. To keep interest high, I occasionally asked a friend who taught third grade to grade my students' papers. This seemed to keep them motivated for several weeks. Use this idea in other subjects to keep interest high!

Betty Ann Morris—Gr. 2
Liestman Elementary
Houston, TX

The Special Sack

When introducing a new concept, heighten students' interest with a Special Sack. In advance, fill a brightly colored sack with items that correspond to the concept you plan to introduce. For example, to introduce homophones, place a pear and a pair of shoes in the sack. Give students oral clues about what is in the sack. After students have guessed its contents, reveal the items and introduce the concept. With the Special Sack, students are motivated and eager to learn new things.

Michele Cantwell-Copher—Gr. 2
Jefferson School
Clovis, CA

Multiplication Manipulatives

Six-pack rings clearly define sets for multiplication manipulatives. Provide each student with one or two six-pack rings and a supply of counters. To illustrate the concept of multiplication, have students place counters in the rings. For example, to illustrate 3 x 4, a student would place four counters in each of three rings. The rings can also be used to illustrate division facts or introduce division with remainders.

Janis Dorsey—Gr. 3, Colwyck Elementary, New Castle, DE

Plush Puppets

Give new life to discarded stuffed animals by creating these delightful hand puppets. To make a puppet, carefully slit the seam at the bottom of a stuffed animal. Remove the stuffing; then finish the raw edges. Insert your hand into the opening and move your fingers to manipulate the puppet's arms and head. These plush pals are sure to get rave reviews from your students!

Louise Philpot
Brushy School
Sallisaw, OK

Sweetheart Lunch

Surprise your students by inviting them to join you for lunch during the week of Valentine's Day. Cover a large table with a red-and-white tablecloth and provide chairs for one-fifth of your class. Each day invite a new group of sweethearts to eat their lunches around the table with you. Add to the festivities by providing holiday napkins and dinner music.

Wendy Brunker—Gr. 1
Spruce Street School
Sauk City, WI

Start The Day With A Smile

Start each school day with a smile, and maybe even a giggle, by allowing students to read selected jokes from a joke box. Choose a different student each morning to read a joke to the class. Not only will children become more accustomed to reading in front of the class, but they'll also have a chance to exercise their senses of humor. You'll find that laughing with your students is a great way to start the day!

Jennifer Gardner—Gr. 2
Galax Elementary
Galax, VA

A Gift For George

Say "Happy Birthday, George!" with a unique homework assignment. Tell students that the class will hold a celebration on George Washington's birthday. Each child is to look through catalogs and magazines and cut out a picture of something he'd like to give George as a gift. The student must be ready to tell about his gift, give his reasons for choosing it, and describe how George Washington would have used it. During the celebration, children are also encouraged to share any information they know about our first president. What a fun way to wish George a happy birthday!

Kathy Shanko—Gr. 1
Erie View School, Avon Lake, OH

Super! Fantastic! Terrific!

Do you sometimes find yourself in a verbal praise rut? Then here's a way to put a little zip into your repertoire. With your students, brainstorm a list of positive reinforcement words. Write each word on a separate card and showcase the cards on a wall. Each day, have one student choose a word from the display to be used throughout the day to reinforce positive behaviors. Outstanding!

Sue Zimmerman—Gr. 1
Spruce Street School
Prairie du Sac, WI

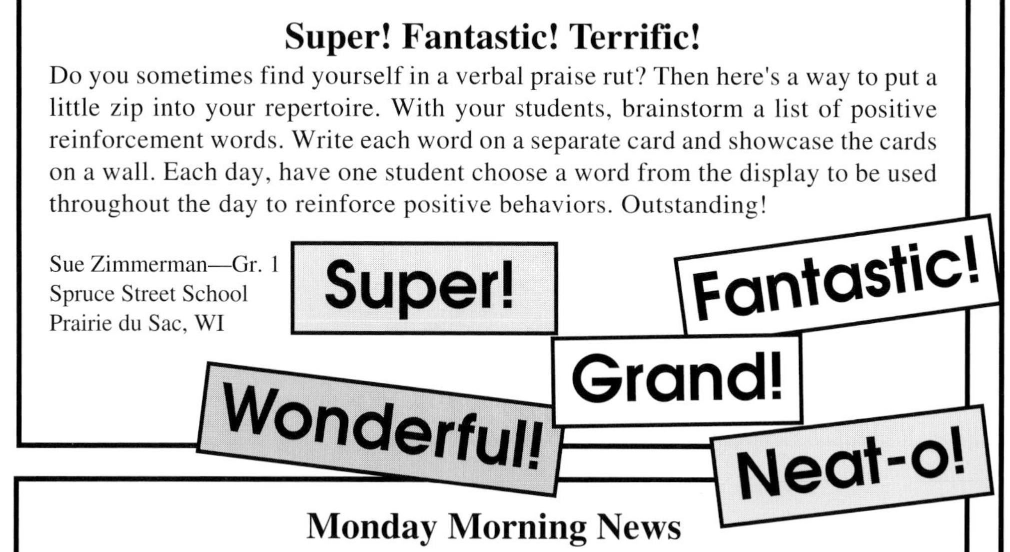

Monday Morning News

This great Monday morning icebreaker gives students an opportunity to share the excitement of their weekend experiences. Have each student tell a partner about his weekend. After a few minutes, invite students to share something about their partners' weekends with their classmates. Students' listening and speaking skills will improve using this simple activity.

Betsy Jackson—Gr. 1, Ottawa School, Buchanan, MI

Easy Squeezin'

Quickly refill paint containers at your easel with this easy squeezin' method. Mix individual colors of paint in large, squeezable plastic containers. Each day, use the containers of premixed paint to refill the paint containers at your easel. All it takes is just a squeeze!

Louisa Cahan—Gr. 1
Lynchburg, VA

Reading With Feeling

To encourage students to read with feeling, I provide time for willing students to share favorite passages (from books, poems, and cartoons) with their classmates. Students quickly learn to identify and express feelings of sadness, joy, anger, and fear. As classmates listen and enjoy the readings, they are also inspired to express feelings in their everyday readings.

Rebecca Gibson Calton
Auburn, AL

Roll A Reward

A roll of the die adds suspense to reward time! On poster board, number and list six rewards. Also duplicate a supply of coupons for each reward listed. When a student earns a reward, have him roll a die. Then present him with a personalized coupon that matches the number he rolled. Students will love this exciting twist!

Eleanor Sardo—Gr. 3
Thornton Elementary, San Antonio, TX

Edible Birds' Nests

Edible birds' nests are a "tweet" addition to a spring or bird unit. To make 20 nests, melt a stick of butter or margarine in a saucepan. Stirring constantly, add a ten-ounce package of large marshmallows one at a time. When the marshmallows have melted, remove the pan from the heat and stir in 12 crumbled, shredded-wheat biscuits. Let the mixture cool until it's slightly warm to the touch. Then have each student roll one tablespoon of the warm mixture into a ball and shape it into a bird's nest. When the nests are cool, have students add a few candy robin eggs or jelly beans to complete their springtime treats.

Melanie Taylor—Gr. 1
Sandston Elementary
Sandston, VA

Bulletin Board Tip

After taking down a bulletin board, give students magnets to clean up the staples or tacks that have fallen to the floor. They'll have firsthand experience in applying the principles of magnetism.

Lisa Etchason
Shelbyville, IN

Recess Tickets

Sharpen problem-solving skills with recess tickets. Each day, a few minutes before recess, give each student a construction paper "ticket." Read aloud a word problem; then have each student solve the problem on his ticket. When a student completes the problem, she turns in her ticket. If her answer is correct, she lines up. If her answer is incorrect, she solves the problem again. Problem-solving skills will improve in no time!

Tonya Byrd—Gr. 2
F.J. DeLaine Elementary
Shaw Air Force Base, SC

Gifts For Book Characters

Students will delight in choosing "gifts" for favorite book characters. For each student, write the name of a book character on a slip of paper; then drop the slips into a container. Have each student draw one name from the container, then decide upon an appropriate gift idea for her character. Have students illustrate their gifts or bring items from home that represent their gifts; then have them share their selections with their classmates. What a lovely new hat for Amelia Bedelia!

Kathleen Darby—Gr. 1
Community School, Cumberland, RI

Class Booklet Giveaway

Chances are, by the end of the year, your students have created many class booklets. To distribute these treasured booklets fairly among your students, hold a booklet giveaway. In advance, have each student write his name on a slip of paper and drop it into a container. Periodically select a class booklet and read it aloud. Then draw a name from the container and present the winning student with the booklet. Students will enjoy hearing their stories again and winning the booklets.

Jane Cuba—Grs. 1 & 2, Redford, MI

Previewing Audiotapes

Make good use of daily travel time. As you drive to and from school, listen to tapes that accompany books and filmstrips. It's a convenient way to select tapes that are appropriate for your students.

Bonnie C. Dennis
Chapter I Reading
Bailey's
Elementary
Vienna, VA

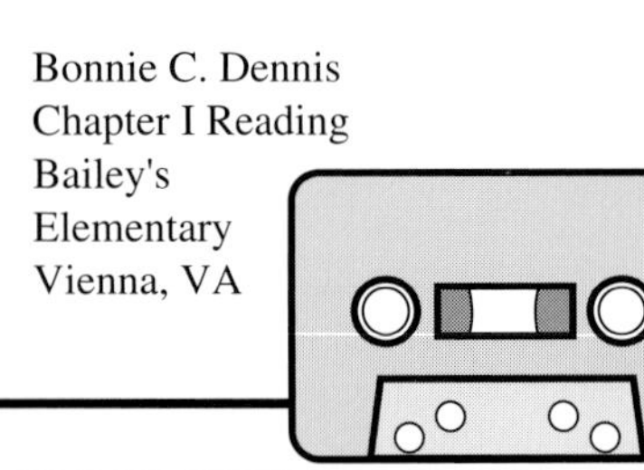

Handy Teaching Coat

Here's a great way to keep pens, paper clips, stickers, and other teaching essentials close at hand. Dye and/or decorate a lab coat as desired. Fill the pockets of the coat with teaching supplies; then slip the coat on over your clothes. You'll have your essentials with you as you move around the classroom, and your clothes will be protected from messy mishaps.

Anne Spets—Grs. 1 & 2
Good Steps School
Scottsdale, AZ

Quick Covers

Instantly cover classroom furniture for the summer with plastic drop cloths. Drape the cloths over bookcases, shelves, or cubbies; then tack or tape the cloths in place. In the fall, remove the drop cloths to find your furniture clean and dust-free. Plastic drop cloths are durable, waterproof, and reusable!

Dana Peck
Clinton, TN

Keeping In Touch

Here's a quick and easy way to provide students with the names and phone numbers of their classmates. Type a brief note to parents in the center of a ditto; then have students write their names and phone numbers around the note. (This gives my students a chance to show off their newly acquired cursive writing talents!) Duplicate the completed ditto, and distribute on the last day of school.

Roberta Fields—Gr. 2
Bridgeville, DE

Literature-Related Units

Three Cheers For Arthur!

Arthur, the lovable aardvark, is sure to win the hearts of your youngsters. The star of his own adventure series, Arthur brings a sense of humor and comfort to a variety of childhood tribulations. And, whether you read one or all of Arthur's adventures, the following teacher-tested ideas are certain to add to the fun! Hip! Hip! Hooray!

Meet The Author And Illustrator

As a child, Marc Brown's creative instincts were inspired primarily by his grandmother, who supplied him with lots and lots of paper, pens, and pencils. During his high school years, he became impressed with Maurice Sendak's *Where The Wild Things Are* and the potential for a career in children's books. Although his parents would have preferred a more "respectable" course of study, he went to art school, launching what has become a distinguished career as a writer and illustrator of children's books. Many of the elements in Marc Brown's books are based on events and people from his own life. And, come to think of it, there's probably a Francine, a D.W., or even an Arthur in your classroom!

Use these suggestions with specific book titles.

Arthur's Birthday

Birthday parties are supposed to be lots of fun, but poor Arthur has a problem! Before reading aloud *Arthur's Birthday*, share a letter like the one shown with your students. Have students tell how they would respond to Arthur's letter. Or have each student write a response and share it with his classmates. Then read the story to find out how Arthur handles the problem. Compare your students' predictions to the actual outcome of the story.

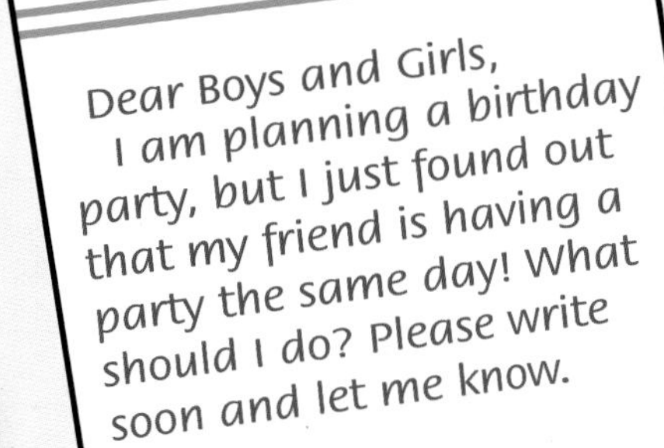
Dear Boys and Girls,
I am planning a birthday party, but I just found out that my friend is having a party the same day! What should I do? Please write soon and let me know.

Love,
Arthur

Arthur's Eyes

Arthur feels proud of his new eyeglasses—that is, until he wears them to school! Arthur's trying experience is a fun learning experience for all. As a follow-up activity, have students create personalized eyeglasses. Using a variety of arts-and-crafts materials, have students decorate tagboard eyeglass cutouts to their liking. Invite students to don their creations for activities requiring "extra concentration." Or have your bespectacled students "peer" through their eyeglass creations to write predictions about upcoming events.

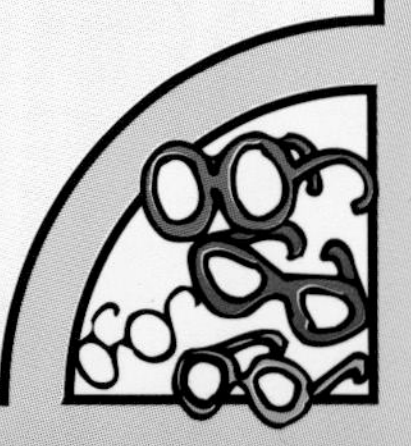

Spelling

ball, cream, disk, pot, may, pizza, ape

hat, monkey, paper, mouse, house, lamp, desk, tape

Arthur's Tooth Troubles

Each of Arthur's classmates has lost at least one baby tooth, but Arthur hasn't lost any. If only his loose tooth would fall out! After reading the story aloud, have each student write a tale about the time he lost a tooth. If desired, have the student trace and cut out a large tooth shape, then write his story on the resulting cutout. Displaying the completed tooth tales along with the caption "Sink Your Teeth Into These Tales" will produce lots of toothy grins.

Arthur's Teacher Trouble

With Mr. Ratburn as his teacher, Arthur is sure that third grade means nothing but trouble. But when Arthur is picked to represent his class in the all-school spellathon, he discovers that hard work can pay off! As a follow-up to the story, divide students into "study" groups. Have the groups meet daily for predetermined amounts of time to study spelling words or math facts, or to play small group games. The extra study time is sure to build academic confidence and boost self-esteem.

Arthur's Baby

Arthur is full of questions when he learns his family is expecting a new baby. What will life be like with a new baby in the house? Will it be as bad as his friends say? After reading the story, have students discuss the types of changes that occurred in Arthur's home as a result of his new baby sister. Then have students share other changes that might occur. Discuss which changes they think would be the most fun and which would be the most difficult. Then take a vocal poll—those students wanting younger siblings say, "Waaa!" All those opposed, say, "Naaa!"

Arthur's Pet Business

Arthur wants a puppy! But first he must prove to his parents that he can be a responsible pet owner. As a follow-up activity, have each child illustrate one thing he wishes his parent(s) would let him have or let him do. Beneath the illustration, have the student list the ways he could demonstrate his responsibility.

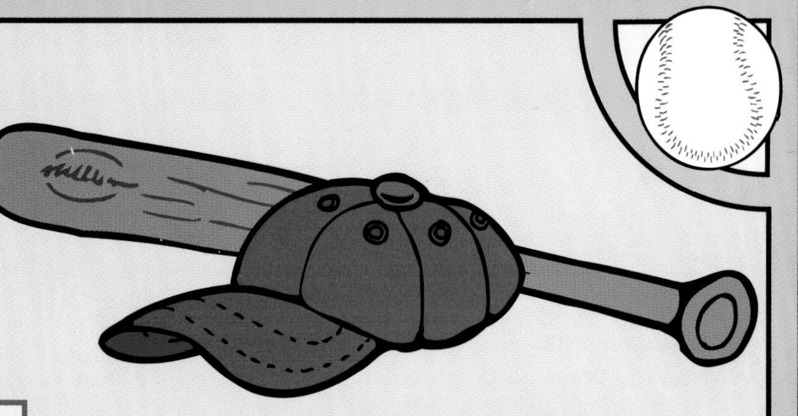

The True Francine

In this book, Francine and Muffy learn valuable lessons about honesty and friendship. After reading the story, discuss some consequences of Muffy's lie: Francine was blamed for something she didn't do, her friends were disappointed in her, and she missed ball practice. Muffy felt guilty because she had lied, and she lost Francine as a friend. Then discuss how Mr. Ratburn handled the situation. Next divide students into groups of three. Have each group role-play the interaction between Mr. Ratburn, Francine, and Muffy as it happened in the story; then have them role-play other possible outcomes of this situation.

Arthur's Halloween

Arthur finds everything about Halloween scary! Set the scene for this holiday read-aloud with an Arthur look-alike. Fill a one-gallon plastic bucket with sand. Place a blue sweatshirt over the bucket. Using crumpled newspaper, stuff the sweatshirt and a matching pair of sweatpants. Attach the pants to the shirt. Refer to the book illustrations to add shoes, gloves, a cape, and other desired decorations. Then, using construction paper cutouts and permanent markers, decorate an oval-shaped pumpkin to resemble Arthur's head. Attach a black mask; then place the decorated pumpkin atop the sand-filled container.

At the completion of the story, serve "bat-wing brownies" (bat-shaped brownies) and "vampire blood" (cherry-flavored Kool-Aid). Then have each student write a sequel to Arthur's spine-tingling Halloween adventure. Compile the stories into booklet form; then place the booklet in the "hands" of your Arthur look-alike.

Arthur's Thanksgiving

Arthur has been selected to direct the class Thanksgiving play. And he has a problem. No one wants to play the turkey! Stop reading when you reach the part of the story when the cast threatens to quit. Ask students to predict what Arthur will do. Then continue reading to find out how Arthur casts the unpopular role. The show must go on!

Arthur's Christmas

Choosing the perfect Christmas gift can be difficult—especially when it's a gift for Santa Claus! Have each student illustrate what his perfect gift for Santa would be; then have him explain his choice as he shares his illustration. Next read aloud the story to find out what Arthur chose as his perfect gift.

For some holiday hilarity, have each student illustrate and name an outrageous snack for Santa. Then videotape each student holding his illustration and repeating, "Papa Piper's pickled peppers may be pleasant, but my sensational snack will surely make Santa smile!" As a finale, arrange for "Santa" and your students to view the unedited video. Ho! Ho! Ho!

Arthur's Valentine
by
Marc
Brown

When the story began, Arthur had a secret admirer.

Then Arthur pretended to be sick.

When the story ended Arthur gave Francine kisses.

Arthur?

Arthur's Valentine

Arthur has a secret admirer! Who can it be? Have each student summarize the events of this heart-warming story on a "heartstring" mobile. To make, cut five heart shapes from pink construction paper. Punch a hole in the top and bottom of each cutout; then tie the cutouts together using red or white yarn lengths. Write *Arthur's Valentine* by Marc Brown on the first heart cutout. Then copy and complete the following sentence starters in order on the next three cutouts: *When the story began...*, *Then...*, *When the story ended...*. On the final cutout draw and color a favorite scene from the story.

POPCORN

BE MINE

Use these suggestions with any books in the Arthur Adventure series.

Chocolate Chip Arthurs

These special cookies are definitely chips off the old aardvark! Give each child a 2" slice of refrigerated, chocolate-chip cookie dough. From his slice, have the student form two 1" balls and one 4" log. Arrange the pieces on an ungreased cookie sheet as shown; then bake according to the directions on the cookie dough packaging. While the cookies are still warm, press chocolate-chip eyes and chocolate-chip nostrils in place. When cool, draw Arthur's eyeglasses using chocolate icing. Form a mouth using red licorice laces or decorating gel.

Aardvark Antics

In no time at all, Arthur is sure to be your youngsters' favorite aardvark. Divide a large sheet of bulletin board paper into two columns. Entitle one column "Arthur" and the other column "Real Aardvarks." In the Arthur column, list information about Arthur as provided by your youngsters. Next challenge students to find information about real aardvarks; then write their findings in the remaining column. When the research is completed, help students compare Arthur to real aardvarks. And the winner of the aardvark popularity contest is...!

Character Quilt

Piece together your students' favorite episodes from the Arthur Adventure series with this character quilt. Have each child draw his favorite event on an eight-inch construction paper or tagboard square. Punch holes at even intervals along all four sides of each completed square (making certain the holes are in the same location on each square). Loosely lace the quilt squares together using yarn. Display the completed quilt on a paper-covered bulletin board. Invite students to explain the details of their squares to their classmates.

Vote for Me!

Favorite Character Graph

Which characters from the Arthur Adventure series are favored by your youngsters? To find out, create a character graph similar to the one shown. Have each student indicate his two favorite characters by coloring the appropriate spaces on the graph. Display the completed graph and discuss the results. Have students refer to the graph to identify the most popular and the least popular characters. Then ask students what factors could have contributed to whether specific characters were liked or disliked. Use this discussion to inspire a second discussion about friendships and the importance of getting along with others.

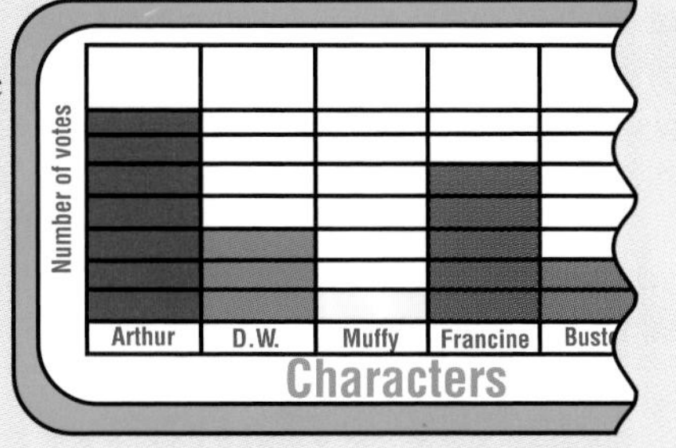

Bright Ideas

Invite your youngsters to share their ideas or new Arthur adventures with his creator, Marc Brown. Have each child write his suggestion on a duplicated idea card (similar to the one shown). Send the completed suggestions to:

Marc Brown
c/o Little, Brown and Company
34 Beacon Street
Boston, MA 02108

A Bright Idea for an Arthur Adventure
Grade
By

Our thanks to the following contributors to this literature feature: Kay Adams—Gr. 1, New Bern, NC; Kimberly Agosta, Raleigh, NC; Lori Bruce, Collinsville, VA; Denise Capozzi, Seneca Falls, NY; Kathleen Darby—Gr. 1, Cumberland, RI; Angela R. Falter—Grs. 1–2, Republic, OH; Delly Ingersoll—Gr. 2, Morrison, CO; Rhonda King—Librarian, Hollidaysburg, PA; Linda Leach—Gr. 1, Chatham, IL; Phyllis McConnell—Art Teacher, Hollidaysburg, PA; Susan Mielnik—Librarian, Duncansville, PA; Rachelle Schneider—Gr. 2, Houston, TX; Donna Young—Gr. 2, Cairo, NE

The Boxcar Children

by Gertrude Chandler Warner

Captivate students with the adventures of Henry, Jessie, Violet, and Benny Alden. Orphaned by the death of their parents, the children are determined to evade the custody of their grandfather and survive on their own. But will the refuge of an abandoned boxcar shield the children from discovery? This first, in a series of 19 enchanting books, will have your students begging for more boxcar adventures.

ideas by Kimberly Spring

Dear Diary

Keeping diaries for the Alden children will be loads of fun! And it's a great way to reinforce your students' comprehension and writing skills. After the first read-aloud session, have each student choose which child's diary he would like to keep. Then, writing from his character's point of view, challenge each student to explain what happened that day, how he feels about it, and what he thinks will happen next. Invite students to illustrate their writings. Repeat the activity after each read-aloud session. When the final entries have been written, have students compile and staple their diary pages in chronological order between construction paper covers. Allow eager students to share their favorite entries with their classmates.

A Family Graph

Number of Families: 8, 7, 6, 5, 4, 3, 2, 1

two members | three members | four members | five members | six members | seven members

Number of Family Members

Family Matters

The makeup of the Alden family is a motive for discussing other non-traditional households. On a sheet of drawing paper, have each youngster illustrate and label himself with the members of his family. Then invite students to tell about their families. Next attach the pictures to a "family graph." (See illustration.) Help students understand that the love and bonding of a family is not dependent upon its structure. Conclude the activity by having each student copy, complete, and illustrate the phrase "A family is...." Compile student papers into a classroom booklet entitled "Family Matters."

On The Run!

The Alden children left their home with a laundry bag, clothes, cake of soap, towels, a knife, a workbag of sewing notions, and a small amount of money. Challenge students to determine the importance of each of these items by recalling how each affected the outcome of the story. List this information on the chalkboard. After each item has been critiqued, have students determine which items were most and least important.

Next have each student determine five items he would take (excluding money) if he had to leave home unexpectedly. Have students draw and color each of their choices, then cut out and mount the drawings on colorful knapsack cutouts. Provide time for students to justify the contents of their knapsacks.

Thinking Beyond The Boxcar

Challenge your students' thinking skills with these critical-thinking questions.

- Why do you think the Alden children never argued or fought? Do you think this could really happen? Why or why not?
- How can you tell this story was written a long time ago?
- What did you learn from the Aldens' adventure about judging people you haven't met?
- Do you think this story could really happen? Defend your answer.

Re-creating The Scene

Students will tackle this project with endless enthusiasm. Challenge youngsters, working in pairs, to re-create the Aldens' boxcar home. Ask students to first recall clues about the home; then, with their help, categorize and list this information under the headings "Inside The Boxcar" and "Outside The Boxcar." To begin the project, every two students will need one shoe box, four thread spools, and a half sheet of poster board. Provide other art media such as colored construction paper, tissue paper, wallpaper scraps, yarn, pipe cleaners, and toothpicks. Request that students resourcefully use their environment, much the same as the boxcar children did, in gathering additional supplies. Display the completed projects in your school or public library to promote interest in the Boxcar Children series.

Kids Helping Kids

The number of homeless children in our country is staggering—and it's on the rise. Invite a community member to speak with students about the plight of the homeless. Ask the speaker to suggest ways children can help improve this devastating situation. Follow up the presentation by selecting and undertaking a related class project. Projects might include organizing a clothing, food, or toy drive; writing and illustrating books for homeless children; producing a video that publicizes and presents possible solutions for the problem; or volunteering to clean up, serve food, or entertain at a homeless shelter. The learning experience for your students will be lifelong, as will the realization that little ones like themselves can successfully contribute to the solution of a big problem.

Would You Or Wouldn't You?

Have students compare their modern-day environment with the environment the Alden children experienced. Introduce the activity by having students complete sentences such as "One thing Henry did that I would do is...." and "One thing Henry did that I would not do is...." Have students explain their responses. Enhance the discussion with issues of present-day personal safety. Ask students to provide answers and explanations for questions such as: *Would it be safe to live alone in the woods? Should children walk alone at night? Is it smart to accept food from strangers?* Next discuss the advantages and disadvantages of each environment. Conclude the activity by having each student cast a vote for the environment he thinks he would most enjoy.

Gertrude Chandler Warner

As a teacher, Miss Warner discovered that young readers had a difficult time finding books that were exciting and easy to read. Inspired by this need and a childhood fascination with trains, Miss Warner authored her first book, *The Boxcar Children.* The success of this book and an onslaught of reader requests impelled her to continue the Aldens' adventures. Though the element of mystery is present in each of her stories, Miss Warner took special pride in the independence and resourcefulness of the Alden children. Miss Warner lived in Putnam, Connecticut, until her death in 1979.

Miss Warner chose a special setting for each story of the Boxcar Children series. Invite each student to illustrate a modern-day story setting in which he would like a personal adventure to take place. Settings might include a 100-story building, a space shuttle, or a subway car!

Name ______________________

Boxcar Buddies

Read each phrase.
Color the circle to show which person it best describes.
Use the code.

- ◯ an older sister ☐
- ◯ very friendly ☐
- ◯ likes to cook ☐
- ◯ likes to talk ☐
- ◯ works very hard ☐
- ◯ likes dogs ☐
- ◯ a good housekeeper ☐
- ◯ an older brother ☐

Color code

Henry	=	blue
Benny	=	green
Violet	=	purple
Jessie	=	yellow

- ◯ likes to sew ☐
- ◯ likes to play games ☐
- ◯ a younger sister ☐
- ◯ learning to read ☐
- ◯ good with money ☐
- ◯ has good ideas ☐
- ◯ runs very fast ☐
- ◯ a younger brother ☐

Bonus Box:
Read each phrase again.
If it describes you,
color the square red.

Once Upon A Classic Tale

Set a magical mood with this fresh approach to folklore. You'll find creative activities to enhance the traditional tales of *Cinderella*, *Jack And The Beanstalk*, *Little Red Riding Hood*, and *The Three Little Pigs*. You'll also find imaginative ideas to accompany selected contemporary versions of these tales. Pick and choose to your youngsters' delight!

From Rags To Riches

With a wave of a magic wand, gather your youngsters together and read aloud the classic tale of Cinderella. Amy Ehrlich's adaptation, which is beautifully illustrated by Susan Jeffers, will have your youngsters oohing and aahing to their hearts' delight. Students will also enjoy Peter Elwell's thoughtful and lovely illustrated interpretation. Or, if you prefer a fresh and funny look at Cinderella, Barbara Karlin's retelling (illustrated by James Marshall) is a terrific choice.

The Golden Rule

Even though Cinderella had reason enough to despise her stepsisters, she responded to their demands with kindness. Ask your youngsters to describe situations in which they have felt cheated or unfairly treated; then have them tell how they reacted. Next ask students to describe how Cinderella might have reacted in similar situations. Ask students to decide and explain whether they would choose to act in a manner similar to Cinderella's.

Modern Cindy

As a lead-in, have youngsters imagine Cinderella riding to the ball in a bright red sports car! Then challenge students to retell Cinderella's tale in a modern setting. Divide students into small groups and have each create a sequence of illustrations to accompany its retelling of the story. Then have the groups present their stories to their classmates.

For added fun, challenge interested students to create prehistoric versions of the Cinderella story.

A Contemporary Companion

This companion to *Cinderella* has all the ingredients to make a fairy tale a timeless favorite.

Princess Furball retold by Charlotte Huck

In this variant to the Cinderella theme, a spunky princess overcomes obstacles through her own ingenuity, rather than relying on the wave of a magic wand by a fairy godmother.

- Students will have fun comparing and contrasting Princess Furball and Cinderella. As students brainstorm, list characteristics of Princess Furball on a large soup bowl cutout and characteristics of Cinderella on a large pumpkin cutout. Then compare and contrast the two lists. Find out which princess each youngster would most like to be and why.
- Cinderella and Furball were both nicknames. Cinderella was given her name because she often sat among cinders. Furball earned her name because of a coat she wore. Invite students to share nicknames they have been given and suggest possible reasons for these names. Find out how your students feel about nicknames. Then find out why your students think Cinderella and Furball liked or disliked their nicknames.

Venturing Up The Beanstalk

Fe! Fi! Fo! Fum! Set the stage for this collection of ideas by reading aloud a traditional version of *Jack And The Beanstalk.* Susan Pearson's lively interpretation of this timeless tale is certain to amuse your youngsters, and John Howe's beautifully illustrated version is certain to leave a lasting impression.

Jack Versus The Giant

Did Jack deserve the treasures he took from the giant? Or should the treasures have remained with the giant? To find out how your youngsters feel, have each child design an eight-inch, square, construction-paper poster. If a student believes Jack was entitled to the giant's treasures, have him draw and color Jack on his poster, then write a sentence to explain his reasoning. If a student feels the giant was entitled to the treasures, have him feature the giant on his poster in a similar manner. Have each student tape his poster to one end of his ruler before presenting this poster and viewpoint to his classmates.

Spilling The Beans

Sow a bit of scientific learning into your literary adventure. Toss a handful of dried beans (such as limas) through a classroom window or door to the out-of-doors. Ask students why these beans might or might not grow. After students have identified the basic needs of plants, allow each to plant a similar bean in a recycled milk carton filled with soil. If desired, have each student graph his plant's growth. For added fun, have students predict the growth of their bean plants and comment on the amazing growth of Jack's plants. Students will have discovered an important fairy-tale element when they recognize the magical qualities of Jack's beans.

Mix 'n' Match Giants

Create a gigantic surge of creative energy with this hands-on activity. Divide students into eight groups and give each group a length of bulletin board paper. Ask two of the groups to each draw, color, and cut out the head of a giant. Ask two other groups to each draw, color, and cut out the upper torso of a giant. In the same manner assign the lower torso and the feet of a giant to the four remaining groups. Then challenge the groups to mix and match their resulting cutouts to create a myriad of giants!

Contemporary Companions

Students will enjoy these variations to the traditional tale of *Jack And The Beanstalk.*

Jim And The Beanstalk by Raymond Briggs

This humorous sequel to *Jack And The Beanstalk* shouldn't be missed. Jack's successor, Jim, finds a problem-plagued giant at the end of his beanstalk. Jim helps the giant by fixing him up with super-size glasses, dentures, and a flaming red wig. No doubt about it: Jim earns his gold in this story.

- Students must use their head to complete this activity! First have each student cut a length of string to predict the circumference of his head. After students have evaluated their estimations by holding the strings to their head, ask them to group themselves into three categories: Guessed Too Long, Guessed Too Short, Guessed Just Right.

The Giant's Toe by Brock Cole

In this updated version, a grandfatherly giant is outwitted by his own toe! The toe cunningly disposes of a chicken that lays golden eggs, a golden harp that plays and sings all by herself, and an annoying boy named Jack!

- Keep students on their toes with this role-playing activity. First have students dramatize the giant's reactions to each of the following events: when he cut off his toe, when he discovered he had baked a chicken pie instead of a toe pie, when he found out he had thrown his golden harp down to China. Next have students dramatize the "toe" escaping from the pie and then from the velvet bag. For more toe-tapping fun, have student pairs role-play additional ways the giant could have tried to do away with the toe.

Giants One And All

How do the giants from each of these stories measure up? To find out, ask students to examine the characteristics of each giant. List their findings on a chart. Ask students to use this information to tell how the giants were alike and how they were different. Conclude the activity by having each student write a letter to the giant he would most like to encounter. Suggest that the student tell the giant why and where he would like to meet him.

Advice From Parents	If the advice is followed...	If the advice is not followed...
Eat your vegetables.	we will be healthier.	we might get sick.
Brush your teeth.	we will have healthier teeth.	we might get cavities.
Walk on the sidewalk.	we should be safe.	we might get hurt.

Off To Grandmother's!

Don a hooded red cloak; then set your sights on Grandmother's cottage! To begin, read aloud a traditional version of *Little Red Riding Hood.* A charming edition of this familiar classic is retold by Armand Eisen and illustrated by Lynn Bywaters Ferris. Another fine version is retold and illustrated by Trina Schart Hyman. Paul Galdone has also adapted and illustrated this favorite tale about a little girl and her encounter with a wolf.

Mother Knows Best

If only Little Red Riding Hood had listened to her mother! Let your students come to grips with this dilemma as they decide how and why this little girl got herself into so much trouble. As a follow-up, have students brainstorm a list of often-heard parental advice. Next have students determine possible outcomes if they follow the advice and possible consequences if they do not. Record this information on a chart similar to the one shown below.

Is A Wolf A Wolf?

Students will enjoy comparing and contrasting the wolf characters in *Little Red Riding Hood* and *The Three Little Pigs.* Sketch the outline of a nightcap and a top hat on the chalkboard. As students tell about the wolves, write their descriptions in the appropriate outlines. Next have students draw lines to connect the similar attributes and draw circles around the contrasting attributes.

Big, Bad, And Ugly?

Why are wolves such convincing bad guys? Ask students why they think a storyteller would choose a wolf to symbolize an evil character. After some discussion, challenge interested students to discover and share real facts about wolves with their classmates.

For a fun storytelling activity, divide students into small groups. Have each student in the group choose an animal to replace the wolf in *Little Red Riding Hood.* Then have the youngsters tell their story versions to the other members of their group.

A Contemporary Companion

Your youngsters are certain to enjoy this award-winning version of *Little Red Riding Hood.*

Lon Po Po: A Red-Riding Hood Story From China translated and illustrated by Ed Young.

Winner of the 1990 Caldecott Medal for the best illustrated children's book of the year, this Chinese version of *Little Red Riding Hood* tells the story of three children who trick the wolf and save themselves.

- Before reading the story aloud, tap into your youngsters' curiosity by presenting the following items: a large basket, a candle, an unshelled nut, a door latch or similar object, a bedspread. Have students use their knowledge of the traditional *Little Red Riding Hood* tale to predict the roles these story elements could have in the Chinese version. Evaluate these predictions after the story has been read. As a follow-up, have students brainstorm a collection of items related to the traditional *Little Red Riding Hood* tale. Write these items on the chalkboard. Use this list to initiate a discussion of the similarities and differences between the two tales.

With A Huff And A Puff!

A dab of straw, a handful of sticks, and a brick will set the tone for *The Three Little Pigs.* Reacquaint students with this classic tale before presenting the following activities. For a retelling faithful to the traditional version try *The Three Little Pigs: An Old Story* by Margot Zemach or *The Three Little Pigs* by Erik Blegvad. The simple text and humorous illustrations of Jean Claverie's retelling will also be well received, as will James Marshall's contemporary retelling.

"Who's Afraid Of The Big Bad Wolf?"

Your little ones will delight in humming "Who's Afraid Of The Big Bad Wolf?" as they work and work all day on these little pig houses. In advance, locate three appliance boxes and trim the top of each to resemble a slanted roof. Also cut doors and windows from the boxes.

Divide students into three groups and give each group an assignment. Using paintbrushes and yellow and orange paint, have one group paint irregular slashes on its box to transform it into a straw house. Have another group decorate its box as a stick house by dipping rhythm sticks (or other wooden sticks) into brown tempera paint and pressing them onto the sides of the box. Have the remaining group use rectangular sponges and red paint to methodically sponge print "bricks" on the sides of their box. When the paint is dry, have groups decorate and furnish their houses in preparation for the role-playing activity described in "Peekaboo Piggies."

Peekaboo Piggies

Using these masks, eager actors-to-be can take turns reenacting several versions of the pig's tale. To make pig masks, glue a nut-cup snout to the bottom of each of three paper plates. Glue on triangular tagboard ears and bend the tips downward. Cut two eyeholes in each plate; then spray the plate bottoms (and snouts) with pink paint. When the plates are dry, use markers to add nostrils and grins. Glue a tongue depressor to the back of the chin area of each mask. Make a wolf mask in a similar manner by attaching a paper-cup snout and larger tagboard triangles for ears. Spray paint this puppet with brown or gray paint. Add paper teeth and whiskers for dramatic effects, and a tongue-depressor handle. For loads of chinny-chin-chin fun, have students take turns dramatizing several versions of *The Three Little Pigs.*

A Contemporary Companion

Delight your youngsters with "A. Wolf's" entertaining rebuttal to the tale of *The Three Little Pigs.*

The True Story Of The 3 Little Pigs! By A. Wolf as told to Jon Scieszka

This whimsical, contemporary takeoff will tickle your youngsters' fancy. Long misunderstood, the wolf finally tells his side of the story. As you begin this amusing account, it's best to remember there are always two sides to every story!

- Discuss the dramatic contrasts between the traditional *Three Little Pigs* and A. Wolf's version. Have your youngsters assess the wolf's claims and determine if the story could have really happened this way. Help students understand that most situations can be viewed in different ways. To further explain, have students share situations (such as instances on the school playground or in their homes) when their points of view have differed from the perspectives of others.
- If the wolf was wrongly accused on this account, isn't it possible that he has been misjudged on other accounts as well? Challenge youngsters to create the wolf's versions of *Little Red Riding Hood* and *Lon Po Po.* Also have students consider how the giant in *Jack And The Beanstalk* and the stepsisters in *Cinderella* would retell their stories.

Name ______________________________ Story mapping

Once Upon A Time

Note To Teacher: Use this worksheet to reinforce basic story elements.

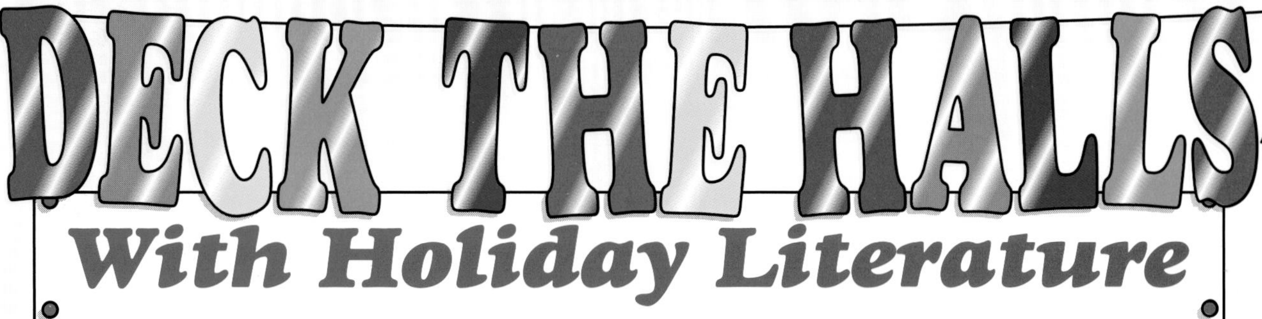

Deck the Halls With Holiday Literature

Share the joys of the holiday season with this collection of children's stories and their accompanying hands-on activities. You'll find all the ingredients you need for a season full of reading pleasure!

by Pamela Fulton

The Chanukkah Guest

by Eric Kimmel • illustrated by Giora Carmi
Published by Holiday House

Bubba Brayna is very old. She doesn't see or hear as well as she used to, but she still makes the best potato latkes in the village! On this first night of Chanukkah, Bubba has prepared a special batch of latkes for the rabbi, who is coming to pay her a visit. And even though her "guest" arrives a little early, Bubba's evening goes as planned—that is, until the *real* rabbi knocks on her door!

Just like the old bear, your youngsters will enjoy a feast of latkes and jam. If desired, have adult volunteers prepare the latkes in your school kitchen. While the latkes are being made, have each youngster measure and mix a single portion of cranberry jam in a small paper cup. Yummy!

Bubba's Potato Latkes

6 medium potatoes, peeled and grated (pour off extra liquid)
1 onion, grated
2 eggs
2 Tbsp. unsweetened cracker crumbs
1 tsp. salt
1/8 tsp. pepper
1/2 cup vegetable oil (for frying)

In a large mixing bowl, combine the potatoes, onion, eggs, cracker crumbs, salt, and pepper. Stir until well mixed. Heat a desired amount of vegetable oil in an electric skillet. When the oil sizzles, carefully drop the batter into the skillet by tablespoonfuls. Use a spatula to flatten the batter into pancakes. Turn the pancakes when they are golden brown; then continue frying them until they are brown and crisp. Remove the pancakes and place them atop a platter layered with paper towels. Allow the excess oil to drain from the pancakes before serving.

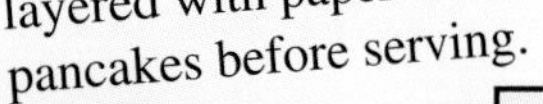

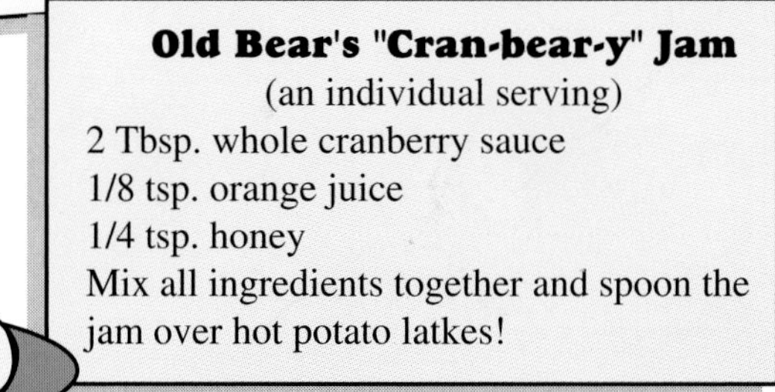

Old Bear's "Cran-bear-y" Jam

(an individual serving)
2 Tbsp. whole cranberry sauce
1/8 tsp. orange juice
1/4 tsp. honey
Mix all ingredients together and spoon the jam over hot potato latkes!

Hershel And The Hanukkah Goblins

by Eric Kimmel • illustrated by Trina Schart Hyman
Published by Scholastic Inc.

Hershel of Ostropol was expecting to find bright candles, merry songs, and platters of latkes awaiting him in the next village. After all, it was the first night of Hanukkah. But instead, he found a village that no longer celebrated Hanukkah. So Hershel agreed to spend the next eight nights in the village's "haunted" synagogue to break the power of the wicked goblins residing there. Your youngsters will hang onto your every word and the edges of their seats as this lively story unfolds.

For a fun follow-up to Hershel's adventure, have students make these edible menorahs. Simply spread a layer of cream cheese atop a slice of bread; then arrange eight pretzel sticks and a carrot stick shammes to form a menorah. Top each "candle" with a candy corn "flame."

My Prairie Christmas

by Brett Harvey • illustrated by Deborah Kogan Ray
Published by Holiday House

Elenore and her family knew their first Christmas on the prairie would be very different from the Christmases they'd spent in Maine with their relatives. Many of the past traditions such as decorating a big evergreen Christmas tree, baking cookies, and stringing cranberries would be missed. Still, Mama had lots of good ideas. Papa did, too. He was hiking "outside of Britton" to find a cedar tree for his family's Christmas. But when a blizzard hit and Papa didn't return as expected, hopes for a merry Christmas seemed *almost* impossible.

Here's a tasty holiday treat that's perfect for a prairie Christmas! Make a batch for sampling and another for gift giving. Have youngsters help prepare the peppermint popcorn on jelly roll pans. When the popcorn has cooled, have students measure one-cup servings into coffee filters for snacking and into small plastic bags for gift giving. Tie each bag with a length of red or green curling ribbon.

Peppermint Popcorn

- 16 cups freshly popped corn
- 3/4 cup butter or margarine
- 1 1/2 cups sugar
- 3/4 tsp. salt
- 1/2 cup light corn syrup
- 1/4 tsp. peppermint extract
- 1/4 tsp. red food coloring

Spread popped corn in jelly roll pans. Over medium heat, melt butter in a saucepan; then stir in sugar, salt, and corn syrup. Stir continuously until boiling; then boil for five minutes without stirring. Remove from heat and add peppermint extract and food coloring. Pour mixture over popped corn. Gently stir the corn until it is well coated. Bake in a 250° oven for one hour, stirring every 15 minutes. Cool completely.

The Year Of The Perfect Christmas Tree

by Gloria Houston • illustrated by Barbara Cooney
Published by Dial Books For Young Readers

Take your young'uns to a simpler time and place, where the spirit of Christmas was handmade—yet heavenly, nonetheless. Journey to Pine Grove, a village in the Appalachian Mountains, where some folks mistook a mother and daughter for angels as they delivered the perfect Christmas tree.

Your children will enjoy making these handmade holiday gifts. Working atop a paper plate, make a pomander ball by inserting two heaping tablespoons of whole cloves into the peel of an orange. To prevent the cloves from breaking, use a toothpick to gently pierce the orange peel before inserting each clove. Next measure and cut two, one-foot lengths of red ribbon. Wrap and tie each ribbon length around the orange as shown; then fashion a bow from the ribbon ends. Place each pomander ball in a resealable plastic bag.

For a festive finish, sponge-paint or stencil a "perfect" Christmas tree on each side of a brown lunch sack. After placing the sealed pomander ball inside the "Christmas poke," fold down the top of the bag and punch two holes near the center of the folded portion. Next thread the ends of a curling ribbon length through the holes; then tie and curl the ribbon ends.

The Christmas Day Kitten

by James Herriot • illustrated by Ruth Brown
Published by St. Martin's Press

Here is a heartwarming story that will touch the hearts of both young and old. Debbie, an independent-minded stray cat, is a regular visitor to Mrs. Pickering's house. It is here that Debbie can count on a bite to eat and, if she desires, a few minutes in front of the fire with Mrs. Pickering's three basset hounds. Youngsters won't soon forget this emotional tale of how, one snowy winter, Debbie gave Mrs. Pickering the best Christmas present she's ever had.

Invite each youngster to share his most heartwarming tale about a pet or a memorable Christmas. As classmates take their turns, students will enjoy sipping on cups of hot cocoa and munching on Paws (Chee•tos® paw-shaped cheese-flavored snacks) as they listen. Now that's a "purr-fect" follow-up activity!

A Christmas Promise

written and illustrated by Lark Carrier
Published by Picture Book Studio

Amy had insisted that each animal living in or around her special tree make her a promise—a promise to be moved out before Christmas. How else could the tree be brought indoors and decorated? But when the animals have departed, Amy is overcome by the silence which surrounds the tree and the loneliness she feels. Your youngsters will cheer when Amy makes her own Christmas promise, a wise and generous one which assures a very happy ending.

After listening to Amy's Christmas experience, your youngsters will be eager to make special treats for their fine-feathered neighbors. Give each student one cup of Cheerios and two 18" lengths of yarn. Have each student string one-half of his cereal onto one yarn length, then bring together and knot the loose yarn ends to create a loop for hanging. Have each youngster repeat the activity using his second yarn length and remaining cereal. Invite each student to suspend one treat from a tree on the school grounds and one on a tree near his home.

The Cobweb Christmas

by Shirley Climo • illustrated by Joe Lasker
Published by Thomas Y. Crowell

This is a story of Tante, a kindly old woman who lived in a tiny cottage at the edge of a thick forest. Each year Tante cleaned, baked, and decorated for Christmas. And each year she shared her celebration with the village children and all the animals from near and far. But Tante had never been given what she wanted for Christmas. All of her life she had wished for some Christmas magic, that special kind of unexplainable magic that she couldn't make herself. This year, Tante's wish comes true!

Stir up a batch of your own Christmas "magic" in honor of Tante's Christmas visitors. These chocolate-covered critters are certain to bring shrieks of delight! Have each child, working atop his own sheet of waxed paper, insert eight crunchy Chinese-noodle "legs" into a large marshmallow "body." Then have him spoon approximately three teaspoons of melted chocolate chips over his creation. Set the critters aside to let the chocolate harden; then indulge!

The Christmas Train

written and illustrated by Ivan Gantschev
Published by Little, Brown and Company

Malina's father, the stationmaster, had told her how to warn an oncoming train of danger. When Malina hears the sound of falling rock near the tracks, she knows she must act fast! The Express train is due any minute and her father is away. Thinking only of the safety of the train's passengers and crew, Malina grabs her decorated Christmas tree and makes an unselfish sacrifice.

These Christmas tree jiggles are fun to make and will initiate a lively discussion of Malina's courageous act. (Be sure to tell youngsters that Malina's tale is a true story!) Prepare the gelatin in advance using the recipe shown. Then have each youngster use a tree-shaped cookie cutter to cut his Christmas tree jiggle.

Christmas Tree Jiggles

6 envelopes of unflavored gelatin
3 (6-oz.) packages of lime gelatin
6 cups of water
vegetable cooking spray
18 ice cubes

Lightly spray three 13" x 9" x 2" pans with vegetable oil; then set aside. In a medium bowl, combine the unflavored gelatin with three cups of water. Stir until partially dissolved; then set aside. In a large saucepan bring three cups of water to a boil. Stir the lime gelatin into the boiling water. Continue stirring the mixture until it boils a second time; then remove it from heat. Pour the contents of the medium bowl into the saucepan along with the ice cubes. Stir until the ice cubes have melted; then pour an equal amount of the mixture into each of the prepared pans. Refrigerate approximately three hours until firm.

Apple Tree Christmas

written and illustrated by Trinka Hakes Noble
Published by Dial Books For Young Readers

This year, because of everything that has happened to the old apple tree, Katrina wants nothing to do with Christmas. When an ice storm left the tree in ruins, Katrina was heartbroken. But when Papa chopped down the remainder of the old tree, Katrina was devastated. Not only were the apples gone for good, but Katrina's drawing studio, nestled in one branch of the tree, had been destroyed as well. How could Papa have done such a thing? Didn't he know she couldn't draw unless she was in the apple tree? But what Katrina didn't know was that Papa did know. And, unbeknownst to Katrina, she has a very special Christmas awaiting her.

Appeal to your youngsters' "apple-tites" with homemade applesauce. On the day you read *Apple Tree Christmas,* arrange to have each youngster bring a cooking apple to school. At the completion of the story, have students use plastic knives to cut their apples into sixths. Place the apple sections in a large cooking pot. Add approximately 2 1/2 cups of water to the apples; then cover and cook over low heat until tender (about 45 minutes). Let the apples cool. Have each student use a wooden spoon and a strainer to press one-half cup of cooked apples into a small container. Then have him measure and stir one to two teaspoons of honey and a pinch of cinnamon into his portion before eating. Yummy!

A Candle For Christmas

by Jean Speare • illustrated by Ann Blades
Published by Margaret K. McElderry Books

It was Christmas Eve and Tomas was missing his parents. They'd been away from the reservation for almost two weeks. And although Nurse Roberta assured Tomas his parents would return for Christmas, Tomas was certain they would not. But a candle, a dream, and a whole lot of love made what seemed impossible come true!

Students will "ooohh" and "aaahh" as these glistening candles unfold. To make a candle, use a template to draw the shape shown on a folded paper plate. Then cut on the lines and unfold the paper plate. Fill the resulting candle and flame with one-inch tissue paper squares that have been wrapped around the end of a pencil and dipped in glue. Using liquid starch and a paintbrush, "paint" yellow tissue paper squares onto the outer rim of the paper plate. While still damp, sprinkle the rim with clear glitter for added sparkle. When dry, trim the tissue paper from inside and outside the rim as needed.

The Christmas Box

by Eve Merriam • illustrated by David Small
Published by William Morrow and Company, Inc.

Christmas is a time for surprises. And this Christmas the whole family—Grandmother, Grandfather, Mother, Father, Aunt Elma, Jasper, Belinda, Louis, the twins Waldo and Wilma, the baby, and even Whiskers the cat—is in for one very thin and very long surprise. What could Santa have been thinking? Your youngsters are sure to enjoy this delightful tale of a very surprising Christmas.

Your youngsters will delight in creating surprise Christmas boxes for their families. To make a surprise box, cover the box and lid portions of a shoe box with construction paper. Next draw, cut out, and personalize one construction-paper gift for each family member. Using a hole punch, punch a hole in both ends of each cutout; then tie the cutouts together using lengths of red curling ribbon or yarn. Place the "string of gifts" inside the box, and tie the box with ribbon or yarn. To complete the gift, attach a bow and a personalized Christmas tag. Merry Christmas!

This classic tale by Richard and Florence Atwater will keep your students delightfully entertained right down to the last sentence! Filled with impossible situations, hilarious outcomes, and Mr. Popper's abundance of goodwill, it's a story that won't soon be forgotten!

by Pamela L. Fulton

About The Authors

Richard and Florence Atwater met while Richard was teaching Greek at the University of Chicago. A student in one of his classes, Florence eventually became Richard's wife. After writing a column for the Chicago *Evening Post* and two books, Richard was inspired to write the story by his daughter's objection to the amount of historical background present in the books she was reading. Florence joined the writing force when Richard became ill and is given credit for completing the book. *Mr. Popper's Penguins* was first published in 1938 and quickly became a best-seller. It has since been translated into numerous languages including German, Japanese, Italian, and Spanish.

Shhh! It's A Secret!

Spark interest in *Mr. Popper's Penguins* before introducing the read-aloud to your students. Fold and staple a sheet of construction paper to make a pocket. Label the pocket "Top Secret," and place a picture of a penguin inside. Challenge students to ask questions that can be answered with a *yes* or *no* to determine the identity of the hidden character. To add to the intrigue, provide three clues to the character's identity: It's very fancy, it likes to dive, it will make you laugh. Won't they be surprised!

Popper's Penguins

Way Down South

Using a globe, point out the continent Mr. Popper dreamed of one day visiting. Amaze students with the facts that cold temperatures exist year-round at the South Pole and that the continent of Antarctica is buried beneath an icecap. Invite students to visit the media center or library to discover additional facts about this chilly place.

Provide student pairs with sets of letter cards spelling the word Antarctica. Students work together to list words made using only the letters on their cards. Enlarge and label the outline of Antarctica on a sheet of white bulletin board paper. Record a class word list within the outline using colorful markers. Admiral Drake would be so proud!

(Possible words include: ant, tar, cat, car, art, tin, ran, cart, rat, can, tart, an, it, at, act.)

Special Delivery

The morning after your students learn of Mr. Popper's special delivery, arrange for your school custodian to deliver a large box bearing your school address, room number, and several warnings (Keep Cool, Unpack Carefully, Please Do Not Touch). Fold 3" x 6" sheets of brown construction paper in half; then attach to students' desks. Each student labels the outside of his construction paper "box" with a warning, then opens his box and draws a picture to show what might be inside the classroom box. Later in the day, have students share their expectations and unveil the contents of the box. What's inside the box? How about a penguin stuffed toy and directions that lead your students to a container of ice cream treats?

Dear Mr. Popper

Build suspense among listeners by halting your reading in chapter ten just prior to Dr. Smith's response concerning Captain Cook's illness. Though students may think the situation is hopeless, have each compose a letter to Mr. Popper giving his diagnosis of Captain Cook's ailment along with a prescription for a remedy. Have students complete envelopes using their home address (as return addresses) and Mr. Popper's address: 432 Proudfoot Avenue, Stillwater, USA. Conclude the activity by completing the chapter. Won't your audience be pleasantly surprised to find that Captain Cook has a simple case of loneliness?

Pinching Pennies

Soon after Greta's arrival, ten baby penguins arrive. Though the Poppers are thrilled with the newcomers, they are faced with the fact that money is tight. Sharpen your students' money skills with this activity. Label each of ten penguin cutouts with a coin value appropriate to your grade level. Label each of ten egg cutouts with coins to match. Students pair the egg and penguin cutouts by matching the money amounts. For self-checking, label the penguin cutouts and the backs of the egg cutouts with the names of the penguin children.

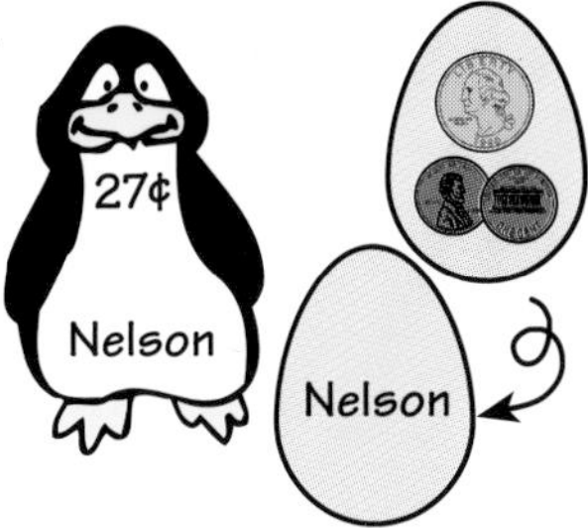

Where In The World Are They?

Popper's Performing Penguins made their first performance at the Palace Theatre in Stillwater. Little did they know they would soon be on the road to fame. Track the performances of Popper's penguins on a map of the United States. Use colored pushpins to mark each city where the penguins perform. *Since an exact location for Stillwater is not provided, you may wish to have students nominate a state to house the city for this activity.

Performance stops: *Stillwater, Seattle, Minneapolis, Milwaukee, Chicago, Detroit, Cleveland, Philadelphia, Boston, New York

Bon Voyage!

As a cooperative learning activity, plan a bon voyage party for Mr. Popper and his penguins! Group students; then assign each group a specific assignment. Assignments might include:

— **Games to play.** Have students keep in mind that both people and penguins will be playing games. What games could people and penguins play together? Or should they play separately?

— **Refreshments.** Students must plan for adults, children, and 12 penguins!

— **Invitations.** Students should consider how Mr. Popper would like these invitations to be designed. (Remember Mr. Popper's first two loves!)

— **Guest list.** Help students recall that though the penguins stole the hearts of many, there were others' hearts they did not steal. Who should be invited?

— **Decorations.** Students need to decide the color scheme and the necessary decorations. Will this be a formal affair?

When the party plans are complete, enlist the help of your students in altering the plans just enough so you might have a classroom bon voyage party. Won't that be fun?

Name ____________________

Pondering Popper's Penguins

Read each sentence.
Decide if it could happen in real life or if it is make-believe.
Circle the letter in the matching column.

Sentence	It could happen in real life.	It is make-believe.
1. Captain Cook lived in the Poppers' refrigerator.	1. U	S
2. Mr. Popper dreamed about penguins.	2. T	M
3. The Poppers had snowdrifts in their living room.	3. R	I
4. Mr. Popper liked to read about Admiral Drake.	4. O	B
5. Mrs. Popper liked to keep her house tidy.	5. N	L
6. Captain Cook acted like he was hungry.	6. G	O
7. A freezing plant was installed in the Popper basement.	7. S	A
8. The penguins and Mr. Popper spent a week in jail.	8. P	T
9. Mr. Popper and Captain Cook were pictured in the newspaper.	9. U	O
10. Mr. Popper kept 12 performing penguins one winter.	10. H	N

What word might describe Mr. Popper's penguins?
To find out, write each circled answer in a matching box.
Do you agree?

Gork!

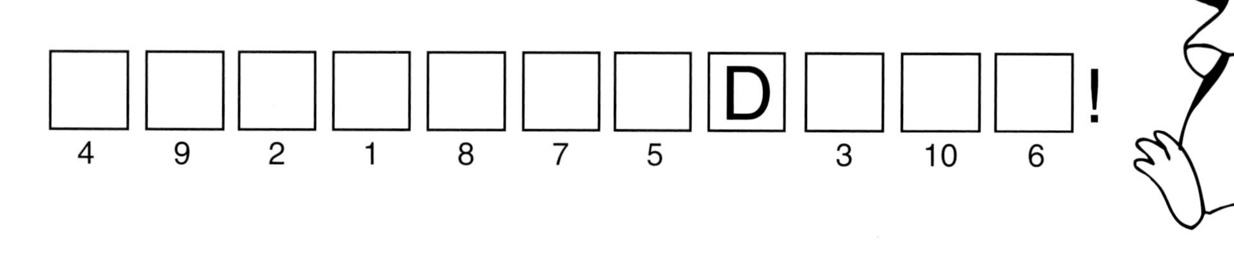

Bonus Box: Authors often combine real facts with make-believe ideas to make their stories more interesting. On the back of this sheet write your own make-believe idea to add to the story about Mr. Popper and his penguins. Draw a picture to go with your idea.

Name ______________________________

Life With The Poppers!

The Popper family had an exciting winter.
Cut and paste the events in order.

The house filled with snow!
The penguins performed in Stillwater.
Captain Cook arrived.
The penguins grew too big for the refrigerator.
Mr. Popper and his penguins left for the North Pole.
Greta arrived to keep Captain Cook company.
Mr. Popper put his paint-brushes away.
Mr. Popper decided to train the penguins.
There are now 12 penguins to feed.
Mr. Popper and his penguins spent a week in jail.

Bonus Box: Pretend you could have any kind of pet for one month. On another piece of paper draw a picture of the pet you would like to have. Write a story about an adventure you might have with your new pet.

Stone Fox

by John Reynolds Gardiner

This fast-paced, emotional tale will have your young listeners perched on the edges of their chairs—and with good reason. Based on a Rocky Mountain legend, the story describes the fearless efforts of its young ten-year-old hero as he and his dog desperately try to save his ailing grandfather's farm. It's a read-aloud that is simply too good to miss!

A Rocky Mountain Legend

Stone Fox is based on a legend its author, John Reynolds Gardiner, was told over a cup of coffee in Idaho Falls, Idaho. Though Stone Fox and the other characters are purely fictitious, the tragic ending to the story reportedly happened. Like most legends, Gardiner's story includes a heroic character. And, after reading *Stone Fox,* you might find that this story has more than one. Before reading aloud the story, use a wipe-off marker to circle Idaho Falls, Idaho, and the Rocky Mountains (the acclaimed source of the legend) on a map of the United States. Then, as the story unfolds, locate and circle the setting of the story (Jackson, Wyoming) and other geographic features as they are mentioned.

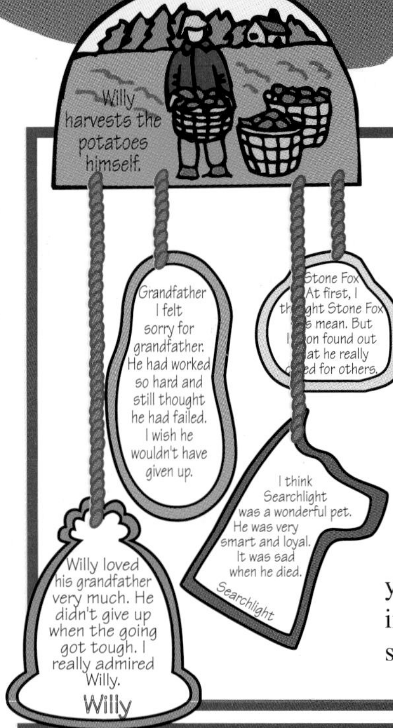

A Cast Of Characters

Here's a fun way for students to express their opinions about four story characters. Have each student illustrate and label his favorite scene from the story on one side of a poster board semicircle and then personalize the opposite side of the cutout with his name. Next have each student write his opinions about the characters on duplicated copies of page 120 before coloring and cutting out the patterns. Mount the duplicated cutouts on colored construction paper and cut around the shapes, leaving narrow construction paper borders. To complete the mobiles, have students punch holes in the cutouts, then suspend the cutouts from lengths of yarn or curling ribbon as shown. Display the completed mobiles in your media center to stimulate interest in this superb piece of storytelling.

Thinking About The Story

Challenge your students' thinking skills with these thought-provoking questions:

- Do you think if Grandfather had wanted to, he could have gotten better? Why or why not?
- Do you think Willy made a smart decision when he used his college money to enter the race? Why or why not?
- Why do you think Stone Fox hit Willy? Do you think Stone Fox knew it was Willy? Why or why not?
- Even though Stone Fox had never lost a race, little Willy felt confident that he and Searchlight could win this race. Do you think you would have felt the same? Why or why not?
- Why do you think Stone Fox made certain that Willy finished the race first? Do you think he would have done the same thing if he had not known why Willy entered the race?
- Grandfather once told Willy that there were certain things in this world worth dying for. How do you think Willy will feel about his grandfather's words after the death of his dog Searchlight?
- What does the saying "Where there's a will, there's a way" mean to you? Do you believe in this saying? Why or why not?

Giving Up

Grandfather was so discouraged with his life that he became physically ill. If it hadn't been for Willy's love and determination, Grandfather might not have recovered from his illness. Ask students to tell how they feel when they become discouraged with themselves and discuss why they think these feelings of discouragement occur. Then have students share how they overcome these feelings. Compile their suggestions on a large smiley face poster board cutout. Display the cutout and encourage students to refer to it whenever feelings of discouragement begin to surface.

Trading Places

Willy's life-style differed from the life-style children experience today. Ask students to consider what they would like the best and the least about trading places with Willy. Next have students consider what Willy might like the best and the least about trading places with them. Have each student fold a sheet of drawing paper in half, then unfold the sheet and label one half for Willy and the other half for himself. Have students illustrate the labeled portions of their papers to show the things they think each person would enjoy about such a trade.

Tracking Down Answers

Grandfather told Willy he could learn a lot by asking questions. But sometimes Willy's teacher and other adults felt Willy asked too many questions. Ask your students if they have ever been accused of asking too many questions; then discuss why this can happen and what they can do when it does. Next have each student write a question he would like to have answered on a sheet of paper. Then have students, working individually or in pairs, track down and write the answers to their questions. Mount the completed papers atop 9" x 12" sheets of construction paper. Laminate the papers for durability if desired; then punch with holes and place in a three-ring binder labeled "Questions And Answers." Place the binder in your classroom library. Encourage students to continue to add questions and answers to the binder throughout the remainder of the year. At the year's end, have each student sign the binder before wrapping it with gift wrap. Your next-year's class will be tickled with this unusual gift!

An Awesome Mountain Man

Stone Fox was a man who was admired and feared. He was admired because of his determination and intelligence, and he was feared because of his size, strength, and mystique. Ask students how their feelings about Stone Fox changed as the story progressed, what they most admired about the man, and what more they would like to know about him. In partners, have students create and practice telling original tales about this awesome mountain man. Then gather students together in a large circle for an oral storytelling session. Partners may elect to tell their tales by alternating speaking roles, or by having one student tell the tale while the other student engages in role-play.

What Now?

The tragic conclusion of this story will shock your listeners and tear at their hearts. Take time to evaluate both the sorrow and the triumph that occur at the finish line. Reassure students that Searchlight died instantly in her quest, evaluate Willy's loss and his gain, and analyze the actions of a man whose compassion was compared to that of a stone. Then contemplate what effect these events will have on Willy, Grandfather, Stone Fox, and the people of Jackson, Wyoming. Summarize the feelings of your students in a written epilogue. Have students illustrate the epilogue on sheets of drawing paper, then post the drawings and the epilogue on a bulletin board for all to see.

Use patterns with "A Cast Of Characters" on page 118.

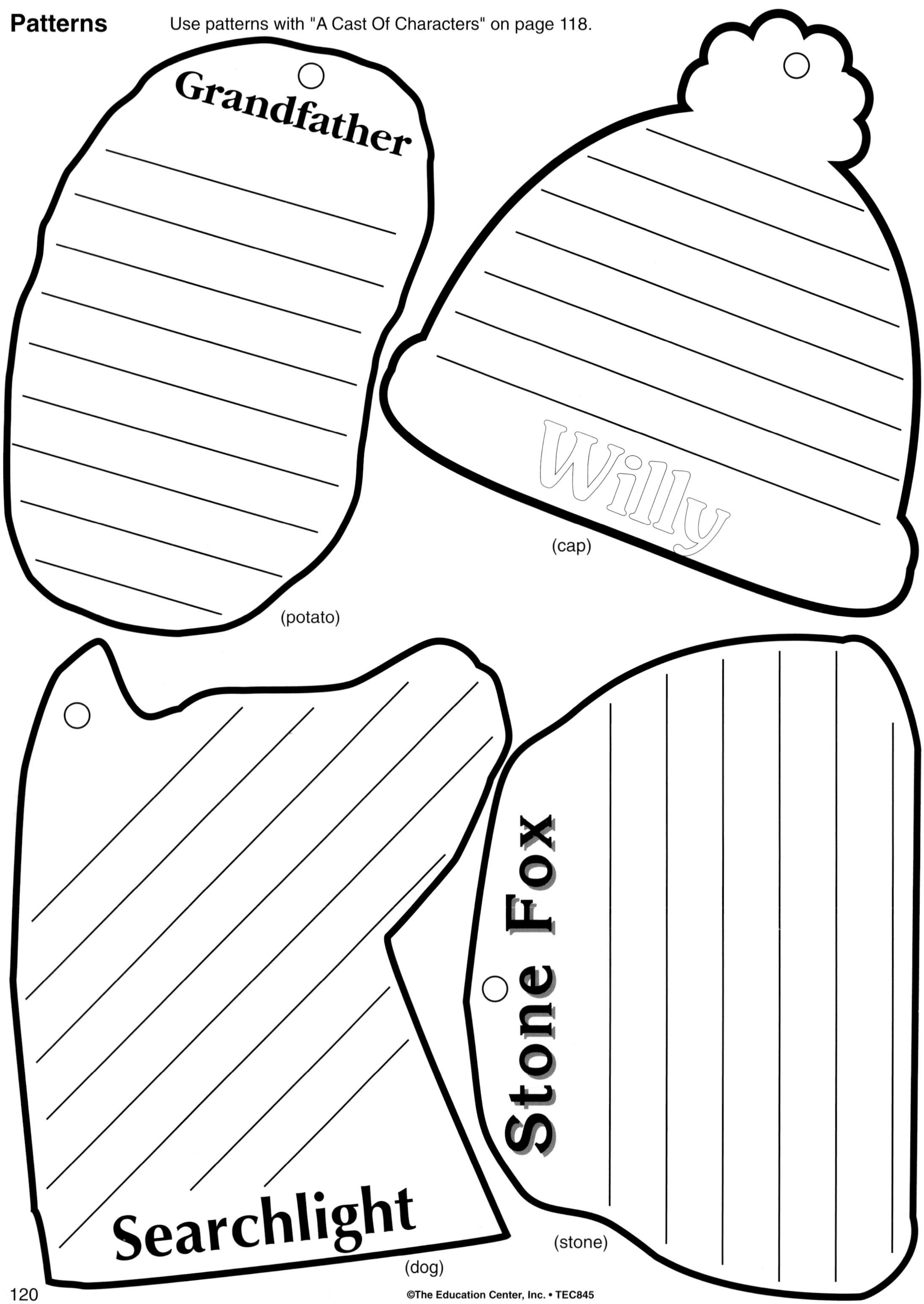

(potato)

(cap)

(dog)

(stone)

Stone Fox

by
John Reynolds Gardiner

Name ______________________________

The best part was

The funniest part was

The scariest part was

The saddest part was

Note To Teacher: Duplicate on white construction paper. Have students illustrate and complete each section, then cut on the bold lines and staple pages to form booklets. To program for another book selection, white out the title and author on a duplicated copy and reprogram as desired.

A Treasury Of Chris Van Allsburg Collectibles

Extraordinary and exquisite. Beautiful and bizarre. Unique and unusual. Strong and surreal. The works of author and illustrator Chris Van Allsburg are all of these and much more. Select from the following books and ideas to introduce your youngsters to the unique style and timeless appeal of Chris Van Allsburg's books.

Jumanji

(Houghton Mifflin Company, 1981)

The game under the tree looked like many others Peter and Judy had at home. Little did they know that when they unfolded its ordinary playing board they would be in for the most exciting and bizarre adventure of their lives.

At Home Alone

Ask your youngsters what they think are the most exciting aspects of staying at home alone (or with older siblings or baby-sitters). Then have each student write and illustrate a story about his most memorable "at-home-alone" experience.

Jumanji Strikes Again

For a fun follow-up writing activity, challenge each of your youngsters to write and illustrate a sequel to Van Allsburg's delightful story. Before students begin to create, reread the final page of *Jumanji* and discuss the habits of the Budwing brothers. Find out what your youngsters think might happen when these two boys begin to play Jumanji. Also ask your youngsters what Mrs. Budwing might find when she returns home. Your youngsters are sure to be filled with ideas when they embark on this writing assignment!

Group Gameboards

This cooperative task results in several jungle gameboards. Divide students into small groups. Give each group a large square of tagboard, pencils, a supply of markers or crayons, a die, and a sheet of writing paper. Challenge each group to design and decorate a gameboard. Then have each group compose a complete set of playing directions. Have one member of each group write the directions on the writing paper and attach the paper to the back of the gameboard. Laminate the gameboards for durability if desired. Store the gameboards and a supply of dice and pawns at a center.

Jumbo Jumanji

Creating a classroom-size jungle gameboard may be the project your youngsters deem the most memorable of the past year! To begin, create a student-generated list of jungle elements. Divide students into groups of three. Have each group choose a different element, create a related gameboard scenario, and then write a description of the scenario on a 9" x 12" sheet of construction paper. Randomly place the resulting gameboard spaces atop your students' desks. On the remaining desktops, place blank 9" x 12" sheets of construction paper. Label the first and last spaces "Start" and "City Of Gold" respectively. Then, with your youngsters' input, randomly label several sheets with instructions such as "Go ahead two spaces" and "Lose one turn."

To play, select two student players and one student to roll a die. Both players begin at Start. All other students are seated. For each turn, a player walks to the appropriate gameboard space; then he listens for the student seated there to read his instructions. (If the desk is vacant, the player completes this step.) Play continues in this manner until one player reaches the City Of Gold and declares, "Jumanji!" To play again, redistribute the gameboard spaces and choose new players. For added fun, invite seated students to perform sound effects during the scenarios that they created.

Journal Writing Topics

Give daily journal writing an unusual twist by having students write their opinions about the story. If desired, use the following suggestions:

- Explain what the name *Jumanji* means and where you think the name originated.
- Tell who you think wrote the note that was taped to the bottom of the game box. Also tell why you think that person wrote it.
- Write how you think Mother and Father would have reacted if they had come home while Peter and Judy were playing the game.
- Tell why you think Chris Van Allsburg wrote this book.

The Stranger

(Houghton Mifflin Company, 1986)

This delightfully mysterious tale is filled with clues, but no solution. It is late summer when Farmer Bailey accidentally hits a man with his truck. The strange man can remember nothing after the accident, so Farmer Bailey takes him to his home to recuperate.

A Key Clue

Clarify a key clue from the story with this simple demonstration. In advance, cut out two matching leaf shapes: one from green construction paper and one from orange construction paper. Glue one cutout atop the other, aligning the edges. Keep the cutout concealed as you begin your story presentation. After the stranger plucks the green leaf from the tree and blows on it with all of his might, reveal the green side of the leaf cutout. Next ask a student to blow on the cutout just as the stranger had blown on the leaf. At this point, slowly turn the cutout so that the orange side can be seen by your youngsters. Who was that stranger, anyway?

The Wreck Of The Zephyr

(Houghton Mifflin Company, 1983)

In this intriguing tale, an old man recounts a young boy's sailing adventure.

Sailing Scenes

Have your youngsters man the sails during this follow-up activity! Give each youngster a large sailboat pattern and a length of white bulletin board paper. First have each student color and cut out his sailboat. Then instruct each youngster to mount his cutout atop his larger paper (however he desires) and create a colorful sailboat scene. Invite students to share their completed projects with their classmates.

Just A Dream

(Houghton Mifflin Company, 1990)

A frightful look at the future convinces a young boy to do everything that he can to preserve the earth's environment.

Cooperative Issues

Increase your youngsters' environmental awareness by using this cooperative learning project. Divide students into small groups; then have each group choose a different dream episode from the story. Have each group discuss reasons why its episode occurred and how this situation might have been prevented. Then have each group design an awareness poster about its particular environmental issue.

The Mysteries Of Harris Burdick

(Houghton Mifflin Company, 1984)

Unsolved mysteries lurk within the covers of this unique picture book. And the solution to each one is not found in the book, but instead in one's own imagination.

Creative Interpretations

Using the information found in the book's preface, share the strange disappearance of Harris Burdick and the mystery of his drawings. Then examine each picture carefully and discuss its title and caption. During the next few weeks, present the pictures as topics for creative writing. Have students write stories independently, with partners, in small groups, or as a large group. Or have students give oral story presentations. Whatever you choose, you can count on a wealth of student creativity!

The Garden Of Abdul Gasazi

(Houghton Mifflin Company, 1979)

The sign read: "Absolutely, positively no dogs allowed in this garden. At the bottom it was signed: Abdul Gasazi, retired magician." So when the dog Alan is caring for escapes into the garden, Alan races after it. Can he save the dog from the magician's magical spell?

Maze Makers

This follow-up activity is "a-maze-ingly" fun! First have each student create a garden maze. To do this, a student draws Alan in the top left-hand corner of a sheet of drawing paper. Then he draws Fritz the dog in the lower right-hand corner. He then draws a series of garden passageways from Alan to Fritz, making certain that only one of the passageways actually connects the two. When the mazes are complete, pair students and have each student complete his partner's puzzle.

The Garden Of Whom?

You'll have gardens galore when this writing activity is completed. After reading the story aloud, invite each youngster to write and illustrate a story that tells about his own magical garden.

Two Bad Ants

(Houghton Mifflin Company, 1988)

A dangerous adventure teaches two tiny ants a valuable lesson about their home and family.

Aspiring Authors

Once students have heard and discussed the tale of the two bad ants, they'll be ready to create their own "bad" tales. Have each youngster entitle his story *Two Bad* _______. Encourage students to write from the perspectives of their chosen characters, just as Chris Van Allsburg has done. Then have each youngster illustrate his story and, if he desires, share it with his classmates.

Keeping The Perspective

For a fun first reading of the story, read aloud the text without revealing any of Van Allsburg's delightful illustrations. At the completion of the story, give each youngster a sheet of drawing paper. Have each student pretend that he is an ant in the story and draw a picture of one thing that he saw. When the drawings are completed, reread the story and invite your youngsters to share their pictures at the appropriate times during the story. Finally share the story again by displaying only Van Allsburg's illustrations.

Those Ants!

Those ants are at it again! Tell your youngsters that the two bad ants are ready for another adventure. Ask your youngsters where the ants should visit; then write their ideas on the chalkboard. Next have each youngster write and illustrate a story about the ants' next adventure. Challenge each student to write and draw from the perspective of an ant.

The ants struggled upward. Their legs felt weak. Then they reached the ledge. The white powder along the ledge stuck to the ants' feet.

Dear Ants,...

For a fun letter-writing activity, have each student write a letter to the two bad ants. Invite students to write a variety of messages in their letters. For instance, a student may congratulate the ants for returning to their home, give them precautionary measures about other dangers that lie outside their home, or give them instructions on how to take another safe, yet exciting, adventure. Write on!

A Class "Ant-thology"

Create an unusual collection of "antwork"! Challenge each youngster to illustrate an ant in a very perplexing predicament. When his illustration is complete, have him write a story about his artwork. Each youngster's story must tell where his ant is, how it got there, and how it will get out. Bind the stories and illustrations in a class booklet entitled *Our Class "Ant-thology."*

Our Class "Ant-thology"

The Z Was Zapped

(Houghton Mifflin Company, 1987)

This alphabet book stretches one's imagination and vocabulary.

An Alphabet Production

Everyone gets into the act when you transform the contents of this picture book into a class play. If desired, create a backdrop resembling a stage curtain. For props, have youngsters decorate large poster-board letter cutouts. Then, in turn, have your youngsters present the alphabet letters and recite the corresponding mishaps from the book. "The B was badly Bitten."

The Z Was Zonked!

Broken! Crushed! Dropped! Eaten! Brainstorming verbs has never been so much fun! Write the letters of the alphabet on the chalkboard. Beneath each letter, write a student-generated verb beginning with that letter. If desired, repeat the activity using adjectives. Next, on scrap paper, have each youngster write a sentence about one of the alphabet letters. After the sentences have been edited, have each student copy his sentence onto a 9" x 12" sheet of colorful construction paper. Then, using a tagboard tracer, have each youngster trace his assigned letter onto the construction paper. Next have each student decorate his letter using markers, crayons, and/or construction paper scraps to reflect the action described in his sentence. Display the resulting projects in alphabetical order around the classroom.

Or, to create a class booklet, have each youngster copy his edited sentence onto a construction paper sheet. Then have him trace and decorate the corresponding letter on the blank side of the construction paper. Compile the resulting booklet pages in alphabetical order between two construction-paper covers.

The G was grabbed.

Our thanks to the following contributors to this literature feature: **Kimberly Agosta**—Substitute teacher, Raleigh, NC; **Carol Bourgeois**—Gr. 2, Buena Vista Elementary School, Greer, SC; **Tonya Byrd**—Gr. 2, Shaw Air Force Base, SC; **Tara Endris**—Gr. 2, St. Raphael School, Louisville, KY; **V. Gianakopoulos**—Librarian, Smith School Library, East Hanover, NJ; **Dawn Helton**—Gr. 3, Lumberton Primary School, Lumberton, TX; **Marilyn Leiszler**—Gr. 2, Swaney Elementary School, Derby, KS; **Darlene Marshall**—Gr. 1, South Salem School, Salem, VA; **Lynda Neuroth,** Canton, MI; **Debbie Patrick**—Gr. 3, Filbert Street Elementary, Mechanicsburg, PA; **Louise Quynn**—Media Specialist, West Elementary School, Plymouth, MA; **Kim Reding**—Gr. 2, Dallas Center–Grimes Elementary, Grimes, IA; **Judy Skalicky**—Gr. 3, Meadowbrook Elementary, Golden Valley, MN; **Kimberly Spring**—Gr. 2, Lowell Elementary School, Everett, WA; **Abby Tuch,** Oswego, NY; **Jolene Vereecke**—Gr. 1, Grandview Elementary School, Higginsville, MO; **Donna Woods**—Gr. 2, Gulf Breeze Elementary, Gulf Breeze, FL

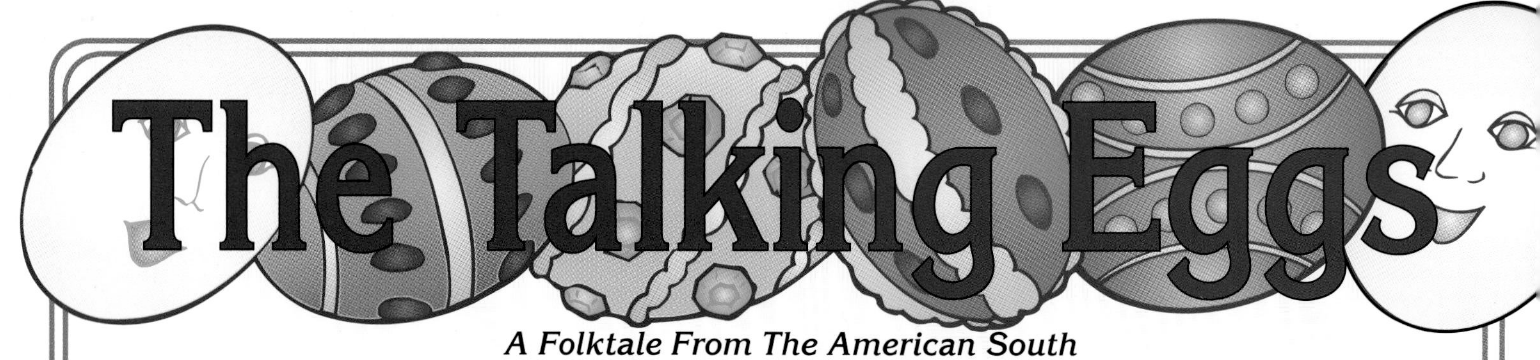

The Talking Eggs

A Folktale From The American South
retold by Robert D. San Souci

Adapted from a Creole folktale, this imaginative read-aloud will capture your listeners' attention. Hearts will be stolen by kindhearted Blanche and angers flared by Rose, her self-centered sister. But in the end, youngsters will learn that kindness and generosity are graciously rewarded.

ideas contributed by Kimberly Spring

A Basket Of Clues

To build interest in this beautifully illustrated tale, prepare a basket of story clues. In a basket suitable for gathering eggs, place a small drinking cup, a comb, a plastic bag containing one grain of rice and/or a beef bone, two egg-shaped cutouts—one resembling a real egg and the other decorated to resemble a jeweled egg, several pieces of costume jewelry, and a rubber snake. Several days before reading the story aloud, display the basket and a copy of *The Talking Eggs*. Invite youngsters to predict how each item relates to the story. List their predictions on the chalkboard; then evaluate the predictions at the completion of the story.

For a fun sequencing activity, remove the items from the basket. Then under your students' direction, arrange the items to show how they appeared in the story. For added fun, take single items from the sequenced collection and have students discuss how the absence of each item could have changed the outcome of the story.

Making Choices

Each sister helped determine her fate by the decisions she made. Blanche, who respected the old woman's requests, was rewarded with riches. Rose, who favored her own desires, remained poor and unhappy. Invite youngsters to tell about choices (wise or unwise) they have made and discuss the consequences of their actions.

Your Opinions, Please

Challenge your students' critical-thinking skills with these thought-provoking questions.

- How was the feeling of trust important in this story?
- Think about the decisions Blanche made. Which decision would have been the most difficult for you to make? Why?
- What did you like most about the old woman?
- Why is it important to have a spirit of "do-right" in your soul?
- What lesson do you think Rose and her mother learned?
- What do you think happened to the old woman and her cabin?

Toe-Tappin' Fun!

Release some wiggles with this toe-tappin' story tie-in. Gather your youngsters in a large open area such as the school gym and play an instrumental square dance or banjo music recording. First have students clap to the beat; then encourage them to clap, stamp, and dance around the large open area until the music stops—just as the bunnies did in the old woman's backyard!

For more bunny fun, stage a cakewalk! In a small container, place slips of paper numbered to correspond to your enrollment. Number large-sized paper squares to match. Attach the squares to the floor in a large circle. To play, have each student stand atop a square. Start the music and instruct students to move clockwise around the circle. Periodically stop the music. Be sure each student is standing on a numbered square; then draw one or more numbers from the container. Call each drawn number and give the student standing atop that number a cupcake cutout. Continue in this manner until all of the numbers have been called. Ask students having more than one cutout to demonstrate Blanche's generosity by giving their extras to those students without cutouts. Back in the classroom, surprise your youngsters with cupcake treats!

Just Like Magic!

These jeweled eggs may not talk, but they're "magical" just the same! To make a magical egg, tint glue with a desired color of food coloring or tempera paint. Mix well; then pour the glue into a squeeze bottle. (If you're short on time, use Elmer's GluColors instead of mixing your own.) Also, in preparation for this project, tape an egg outline beneath a clear sheet of plastic. (Some fast-food restaurants use clear take-out containers that have surfaces that are excellent for this.) Looking through the plastic, squeeze a trail of tinted glue atop the egg outline; then fill the outline with glue. Allow the glue to partially dry; then sprinkle small glittery beads or small sequins atop the egg. When the glue has thoroughly dried, peel the jeweled egg from the plastic! You may attach this peel-and-stick decoration to any slick glass, plastic, or metal surface. Or punch a hole in the dried glue, thread it with ribbon, and wear the jeweled egg.

"Egg-normous" Wishes

Egg on your youngsters' creativity with this writing activity! First have students recall how Blanche received her lovely gifts. Then ask each youngster to choose the gift he would like to have spill out from a magical egg. On the count of three, have each youngster pretend to toss an egg over his left shoulder. Then on egg-shaped writing paper, have the student describe the gift that spilled out and tell how that gift might change his life. To make individual booklet covers, have each youngster cut two slightly larger egg shapes from construction paper, then decorate the covers as desired. Staple the stories between the covers. Invite youngsters to read their stories aloud, or mount the booklets for all to read on a bulletin board entitled "Egg-normous Wishes."

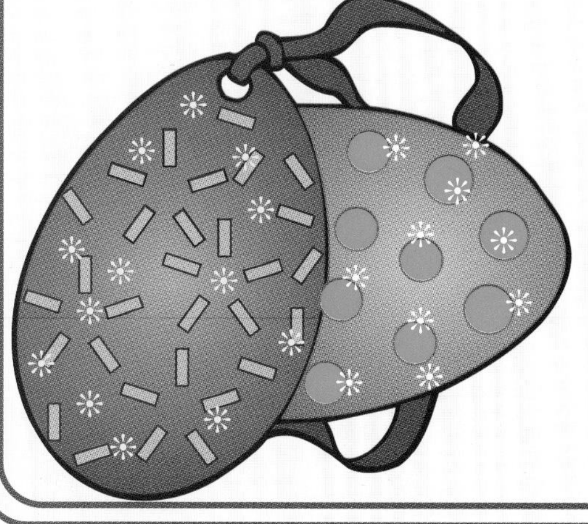

Meet Robert D. San Souci

Robert D. San Souci enjoys writing for both children and adults. He feels that his writing is fresher and more energized when he simultaneously works on projects for both levels. San Souci also enjoys collaborating on projects with his brother Dan. Besides having similar interests, both brothers, two years apart in age, were born on October 10!

Find out who your youngsters would like to share their birthdays with! On a sheet of drawing paper, have each youngster draw and label a self-portrait and a portrait of the person he wishes had the same birthday as himself. Then have each youngster share his drawings with his classmates as he gives one or more reasons for his selection.

Name ______________________

Colorful Characters

Read each word.
Use the code.
Color an egg to show each character the word describes.

Blanche
Mother

Color Code

Blanche	=	purple	Mother	=	blue
Rose	=	red	Old Woman	=	yellow

- ☐ 1. thoughtful ⬭ ⬭ ⬭ ⬭
- ☐ 2. mean ⬭ ⬭ ⬭ ⬭
- ☐ 3. kind ⬭ ⬭ ⬭ ⬭
- ☐ 4. lazy ⬭ ⬭ ⬭ ⬭
- ☐ 5. giving ⬭ ⬭ ⬭ ⬭
- ☐ 6. happy ⬭ ⬭ ⬭ ⬭
- ☐ 7. unhappy ⬭ ⬭ ⬭ ⬭
- ☐ 8. wise ⬭ ⬭ ⬭ ⬭
- ☐ 9. trustworthy ⬭ ⬭ ⬭ ⬭
- ☐ 10. adventurous ⬭ ⬭ ⬭ ⬭
- ☐ 11. friendly ⬭ ⬭ ⬭ ⬭
- ☐ 12. helpful ⬭ ⬭ ⬭ ⬭
- ☐ 13. rude ⬭ ⬭ ⬭ ⬭
- ☐ 14. hardworking ⬭ ⬭ ⬭ ⬭
- ☐ 15. brave ⬭ ⬭ ⬭ ⬭
- ☐ 16. stubborn ⬭ ⬭ ⬭ ⬭

Bonus Box: Read each word again. If the word describes you, color the square green.

Teaching And
Resource
Units

Crazy About

It's time to capitalize on your students' fascination with dinosaurs! Pick and choose from this collection of vocabulary, writing, math, literature, and language arts activities and the reproducibles found on the following pages. Without a doubt, you'll have hit after ENORMOUS hit on your hands! *by Pamela L. Fulton*

Word-O-Saurus

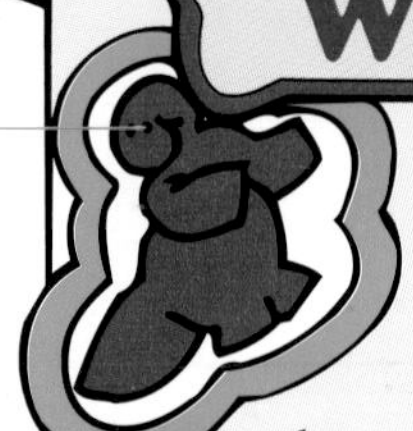

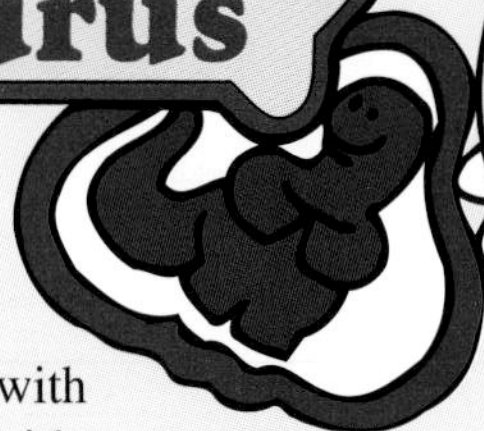

Students will quickly realize that even though dinosaurs are extinct, the vocabulary words associated with them are not. Decorate a large box with dinosaur gift wrap or stickers, and label the box "Word-O-Saurus." Next duplicate and cut out several dinosaur cards (pattern on page 134). Each time a new dinosaur word is introduced (such as in a book you're reading aloud or a movie you're viewing), label a dinosaur card with the word and deposit it in the Word-O-Saurus box. Encourage students to introduce and add new dinosaur words to the Word-O-Saurus, too. Each morning, review the meanings of two or three words chosen from the box. Or use selected words at a center for a variety of activities such as alphabetizing, defining, or illustrating.

Once Upon A Dinosaur Hunt

Tap into your students' creativity with this writing activity. Duplicate an enlarged version of the egg pattern (page 134) onto white construction paper—two copies per student. Have each student decorate and cut out one egg shape, then write a story explaining how he found this egg while on a dinosaur hunt. Next have each student cut out a second egg shape and draw what he thinks is inside his egg. Staple the decorated egg at both ends atop the illustrated egg; then carefully "crack open" the decorated cutout by cutting it in half as shown. Have students complete their stories by describing when and where their eggs hatched and what "dinosaur surprises" awaited them. Mount the completed stories and egg cutouts side by side on a display entitled "Once Upon A Dinosaur Hunt."

Pam Crane

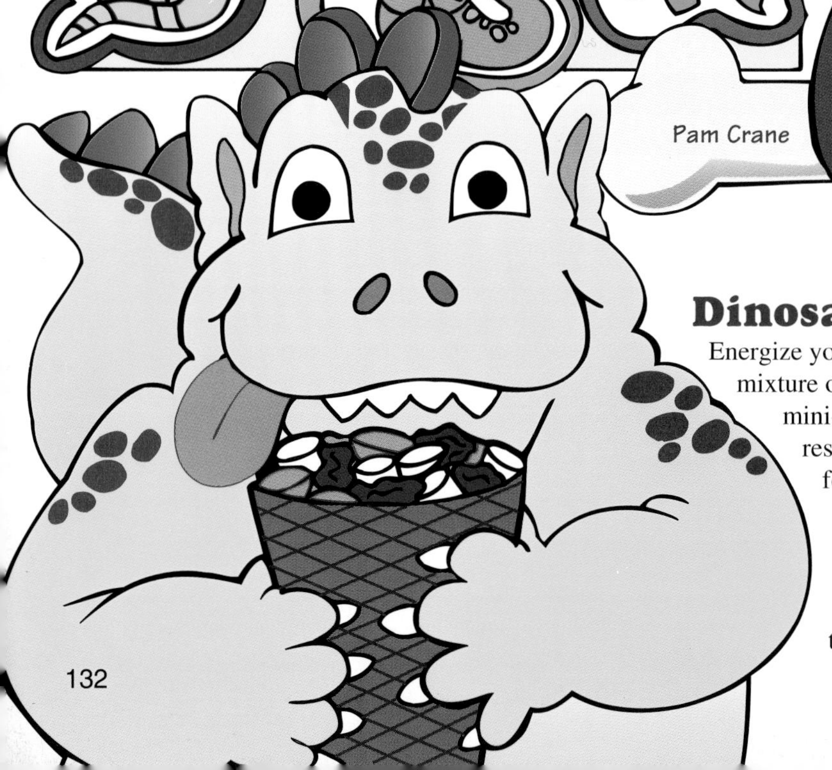

Dinosaur Delight

Energize your dinosaur lovers with this "tree-rific" dinosaur snack. Serve a mixture of trail mix (representing leaves, roots, dirt, and pebbles) and mini-marshmallows (representing stones) in brown sugar cones (representing tree limbs). As students munch on this meal appropriate for plant-eating dinosaurs, explain that scientists believe large dinosaurs such as the apatosaurus ate all day long and didn't even stop to chew their food! The whole leaves and small branches they ate were ground up in their stomachs by stones they swallowed. Then have students discuss why humans must take care to chew their foods thoroughly.

DINOSAURS!

An "Eggs-ellent" Choice!

If your students are having difficulty counting coin amounts, fear not! These mighty stegosauruses will provide plenty of motivational practice. Duplicate several construction paper copies of the stegosaurus and egg patterns on page 134. Using stamps or cutouts, program the plates of each stegosaurus with coin amounts. (Sequentially program the plates from left to right showing the largest coin amounts to the left.) Label the egg shapes with the total coin amounts shown on the dinosaurs. Laminate and cut out all pieces. If desired, use a permanent marker to label the backs of the cutouts for self-checking. Store the cutouts in a resealable plastic bag at a center. A student matches the stegosaurus and egg cutouts by counting the coin amounts.

Tonya Byrd—Gr. 2, Shaw AFB, SC

18¢

"Dino-mite" Contractions

This easy-to-make matching center is perfect for contraction practice. And when the color-coded answer key is used, immediate student reinforcement is guaranteed! Cut four stegosaurus shapes from green construction paper (pattern—page 134). Number each dinosaur shape; then program each of its plates with a different contraction. Make a tagboard tracer using the plate pattern on page 134; then trace and cut out 20 construction paper plates (four plates from each of five different colors). Match one plate of each color to every dinosaur shape. Program the plates for each stegosaurus by labeling each cutout with the two words needed to form one of its contractions. Make the color-coded answer key by duplicating four stegosaurus cards (page 134) onto white construction paper. Number the cards; then color the plates on each stegosaurus card to show the correct responses for the matching stegosaurus cutout. Laminate all pieces for durability if desired; then store in a resealable plastic bag.

Annette Roybal—Gr. 2, Monte Vista Elementary, Monte Vista, CO

1.
won't
can't
isn't
will not
can not
shouldn't
couldn't
could not
1.

A Pet Dinosaur?

Students will enjoy discussing the advantages and disadvantages of having pet dinosaurs. Follow up the discussion by reading aloud *Danny And The Dinosaur* by Syd Hoff. After students hear about the adventures Danny and his pet dinosaur experienced, have them consider other adventures this unusual twosome might enjoy. Have each student design a page of dinosaur stationery and write a letter to Danny. Encourage students to include one or more adventure suggestions in their letters.

Dinosaur Bob And His Adventures With The Family Lazardo by William Joyce is another exciting dinosaur tale your students will enjoy. The Lazardos adopt the dinosaur their son Scotty finds on an African safari and take home all the pleasures and problems that come with keeping such an oversized pet. It's a must for your dinosaur literature collection!

How Would You Do It?

There will be plenty of giggles as students prepare and share their written advice for these unusual tasks. Write each of the following questions on individual construction paper strips; then place each strip inside a plastic egg-shaped container at a center. Each student "cracks open" a plastic egg, then writes the steps (in the order they must be done) to accomplish the task he chose. Remind students to place the paper slips back in the eggs before leaving the center.

How would you give a dinosaur a bath?
How would you feed a dinosaur?
How would you hide a dinosaur?
How would you brush a dinosaur's teeth?
How would you help a dinosaur get rid of the hiccups?

Patterns

Enlarge the stegosaurus and plate patterns as desired.

Use the stegosaurus pattern with "An 'Eggs-ellent' Choice!" on page 133.

Use the stegosaurus and plate patterns with "'Dino-mite' Contractions" on page 133.

Use the egg pattern with "Once Upon A Dinosaur Hunt" on page 132 and "An 'Eggs-ellent' Choice!" on page 133.

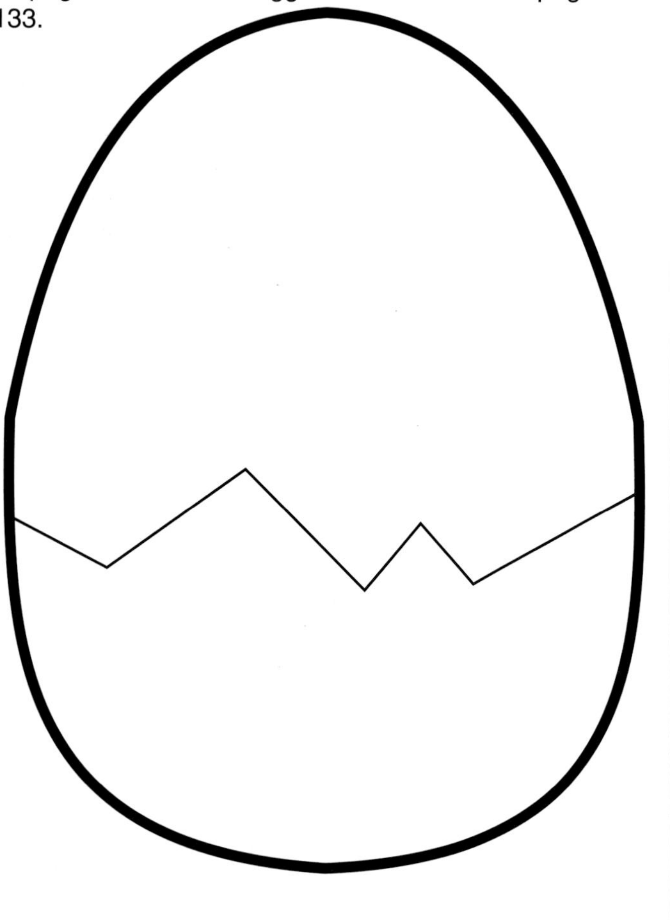

Use the dinosaur card with "Word-O-Saurus" on page 132 and "'Dino-mite' Contractions" on page 133.

Name ____ Fun

Shape-O-Saurus

Find the dinosaur name that matches each shape.
Fill in the boxes.

Example:

B r a c h i o s a u r u s

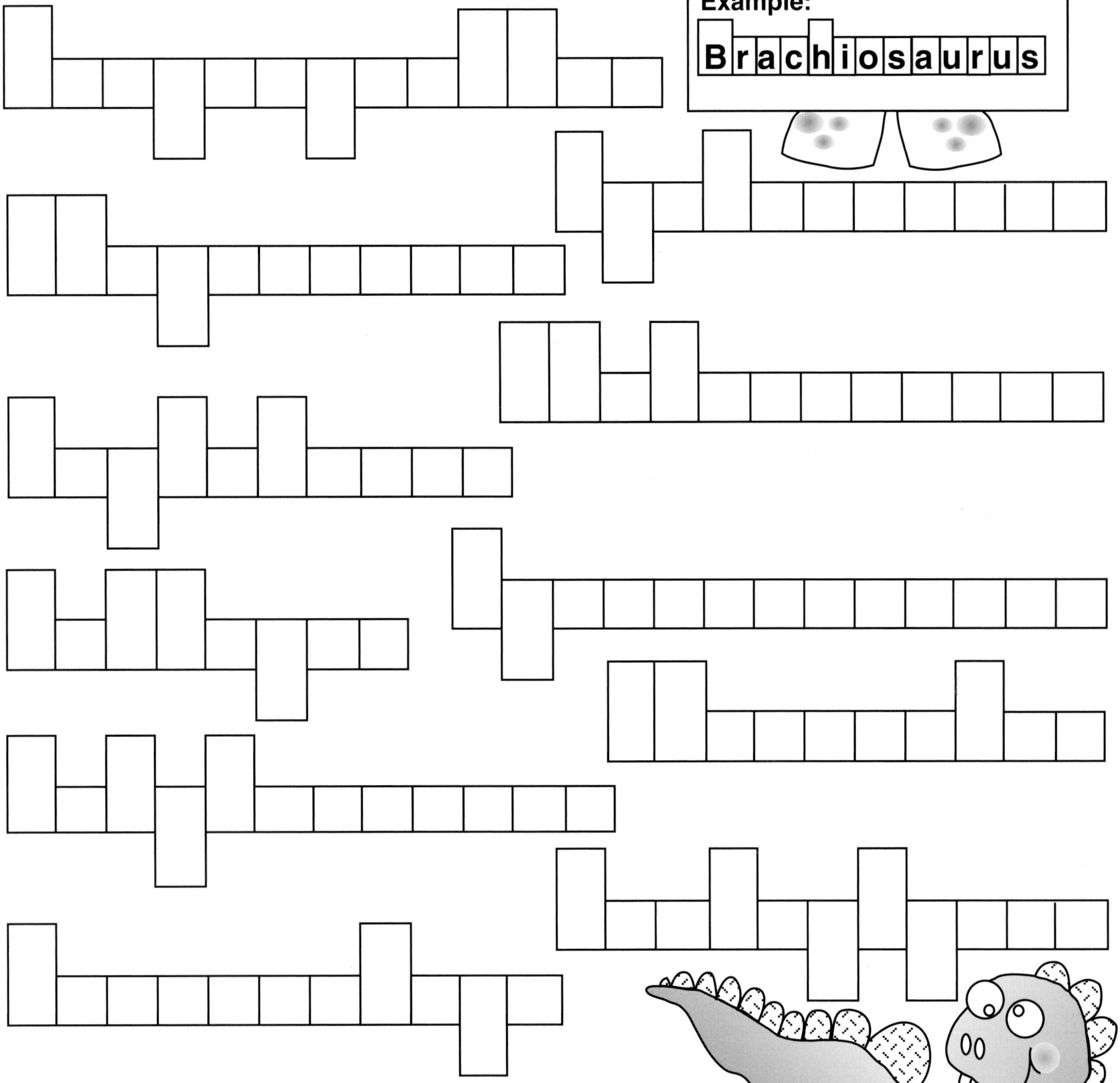

Dinosaur Names

Triceratops	Diplodocus	Ankylosaurus
Stegosaurus	Pteranodon	Tyrannosaurus
~~Brachiosaurus~~	Apatosaurus	Compsognathus
Saltopus	Plateosaurus	Coelophysis

Building Cooperation

Design a cooperative-learning blueprint for your crew using these teacher-tested ideas. You'll take learning to new heights!

Job Necklaces

Help students identify their roles in cooperative learning groups with job necklaces. For each group, program a set of four-inch tagboard circles with the jobs and illustrations shown. Laminate the circles for durability. Next punch a hole in the top of each circle; then thread and tie a yarn length through each hole. Have group members wear these job necklaces before beginning each cooperative learning project.

job	illustration
writer	a pencil
listener	an ear
question asker	a question mark
speaker	a mouth
supply person	crayons, glue, and/or scissors
reader	a book

Math Trios

These cooperative trios make math practice more fun. Divide students into groups of three. Provide students with identical math worksheets. Have the students solve the first problem independently, then compare their answers with their fellow group members. When one student's answer does not match, the other two members show him how they arrived at their answers. When all three members calculate different answers, the students rework the problem until a correct answer is determined. Students continue in this manner until their worksheets are completed. *Three* heads really are better than one!

Spelling Partners

In this partner activity, challenge students to construct well-built sentences using their spelling words. One student says a sentence that contains a word from the weekly spelling list. His partner either approves the sentence or makes suggestions to improve it. The student then writes the agreed upon sentence on a sheet of paper. After his partner proofreads the sentence, the student makes any necessary changes. Then the student and his partner switch roles and repeat the procedure using another spelling word. The student pair continues in this manner until a sentence has been written for each spelling word.

Newsworthy Cooperation

The news is out! Weekly classroom newspapers (such as *Weekly Reader* and *Scholastic News)* provide creative opportunities for cooperative learning. Divide students into groups. Distribute student copies of your classroom newspaper and assign each group one section or article. Then have each group determine a method for "teaching" its assigned information. Follow up each group's presentation with a brief discussion. As a variation, try this group approach to teaching lessons from your youngsters' science, social studies, or health textbooks.

Words Of Encouragement

Help students remember to encourage one another during cooperative learning activities with this idea. As a large group activity, have students brainstorm encouraging words and phrases. List the words and phrases on a large sunshine cutout; then display the cutout in a prominent location. Before beginning a cooperative learning activity, place a small container in the center of each group and give each student several small construction-paper squares. Ask students to place one square in the container each time they encourage a group member. (Students may choose their own words of encouragement or use those displayed on the cutout.) Students will soon be encouraging one another with ease!

Great idea!

Book Characters' Hall Of Fame

Bring favorite book characters to life with this cooperative learning project. Have each group choose a book to read and discuss. Then have each group identify its favorite character from the book and brainstorm a list of words to describe that character. Next have each group draw, color, cut out, and stuff a life-size resemblance of its character. Display the completed characters in a Book Characters' Hall Of Fame. These realistic characters will inspire students to read and reread favorite books throughout the year.

Team Paragraphs

Once you've introduced the mechanics of writing paragraphs and have written a number of simple paragraphs with your students, try this cooperative writing assignment. Begin by having students brainstorm topic sentences as you list them on the chalkboard. Then divide students into groups of four and assign each group member a job from the list shown. When a group has decided upon a topic sentence, have the group members work together to write and edit a paragraph. Conclude the activity by having the groups present their paragraphs to their classmates. Repeat the activity several times so students can experience each of the group jobs and become confident of their writing skills. You'll be amazed at the quality work your students will produce!

job	role
gatekeeper	makes sure all team members have an opportunity to participate
team writer	writes ideas on paper
proofreader	checks and corrects proper paragraph form, capitalization, punctuation, and spelling
reporter	presents the paragraph

Poetry Presentations

Youngsters will enjoy presenting poetry to their classmates using this cooperative learning strategy. Each group of students chooses one poem to present. After practicing its poem, the group then brainstorms and collects several small items related to its poem. When a group is ready to rehearse its presentation, each group member dons a colorful apron and tucks one or two of the collected items in his apron pockets. Then as the group reads or recites the poem, the group members reveal their hidden objects at the appropriate times. When the groups are rehearsed and ready, have them share their poetry presentations with their classmates.

The Quiet Signal

Introduce this quiet signal for cooperative learning success. To quietly signal your youngsters' attention, stand with your hand raised above your head. Tell students that the signal means they must complete their sentences, then quietly face you and return the signal. When all students are focused on you, say "hands down" and give the necessary instructions or information. For a fun variation, invite students to use this signal when they feel the noise level of the classroom is too high.

Cooperative Color Words

Try this colorful activity to introduce younger students to cooperative learning. For each group, program a manila folder with a different color word. Next challenge the students to cut pictures and words of this color from magazines. At the end of a predetermined length of time, have each group of youngsters evaluate the pictures and words it has collected and determine which cutouts should be glued inside its folder. When the folders are finished, have a chosen leader from each group present its project.

Blue

Purple

Making Maps

Cooperative learning takes direction with this group project. As a follow-up to a map skills unit, divide students into small groups. Assign each group a special area of the school such as the library, gym, cafeteria, or office. Have each group work cooperatively to design and color a map (with a corresponding map key) of its designated area. When the maps are completed, display them in your school's main hall. They'll be great visual references for visitors, parents, and new students!

"Boo-Boo" Math

Partners heal math boo-boos during this fun activity. Before duplication, program a math worksheet with correct and incorrect answers. Then give each student pair a supply of Band-Aids which have been cut in half and a duplicated worksheet. Working together, each pair locates the incorrect answers on its worksheet, then attaches a Band-Aid half atop each boo-boo. Check each pair's work for accuracy; then have the students write the correct answers atop the Band-Aid halves.

Cooperative Categorizing

Give vocabulary skills a new twist with cooperative categorizing. Give each group of students a sheet of chart paper programmed with a category name such as *school, pets, food,* or *feelings.* Then, working cooperatively, each group searches through newspapers and magazines to find words appropriate for its category. When a student locates a potential word, he reads the word to his group. If his group agrees that the word fits the category, the student cuts out the word and glues it onto the chart paper. Have each group share several of its favorite words with its classmates; then display the completed projects on a bulletin board for student reference.

Cooperative Literature

Follow up your youngsters' favorite read-alouds with one of these cooperative learning suggestions. Have each group of youngsters

- write a different ending for the story
- act out its favorite part of the story
- compare elements of the story (such as plot, setting, character traits) with those of a previously read story
- rewrite an event from the story as a newspaper article

Then have each group give an oral presentation of its work. After each presentation, invite the audience to share their positive comments.

Charting Cooperative Learning

With this handy chart, a student can tell at a glance which cooperative learning team he is a member of and what his group role will be. On poster board, draw and program a grid with cooperative learning roles and colored symbols similar to the ones shown. Laminate the grid for durability. Then, using a wipe-off pen, write each youngster's name on the grid. When it's time to assign new jobs or create new teams, simply wipe off the programming and reprogram the chart as desired.

Cooperative Learning Teams

Leader	Supply Clerk	Recorder	Reporter
Amy	Heather	Landon	Lyndsey
Matt	Josh	Rashida	Isaiah
Lauren	Jessica	Ryan	Steven
Mary	John	Betsy	Mark

Group Research Reports

This cooperative research method lets students find answers to questions they have asked. As a large group, have your youngsters determine a topic to research and brainstorm questions they have about the selected topic. List the questions on a length of bulletin board paper. Next divide students into small groups and assign each group several questions from the list. Challenge the groups to research the topic to find the answers. Later invite each group to share the answers it has found. List these answers on another sheet of bulletin board paper placed alongside the displayed questions. Conclude the research by having each group use the recorded facts to write and illustrate a report. Inquiring minds want to know!

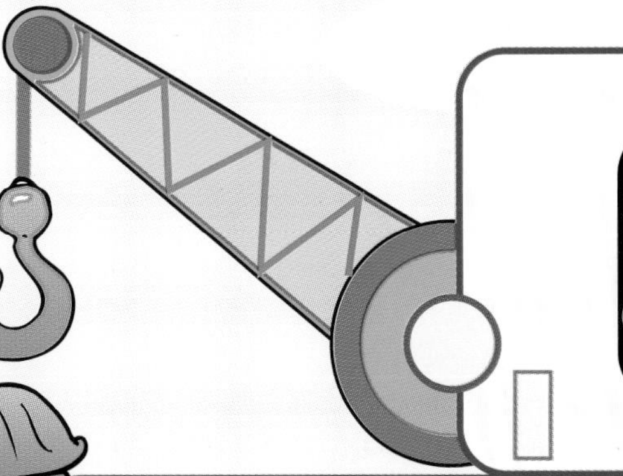

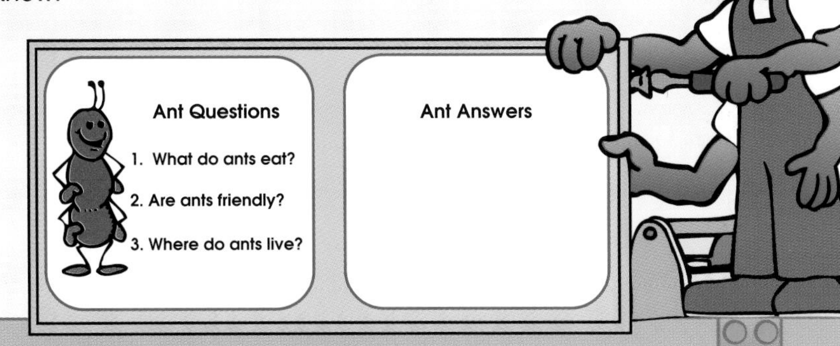

Phonics Cut-up

Snip! Snip! Snip! Phonics has never been so much fun! Give each group of students a length of bulletin board paper labeled with a beginning consonant sound and a supply of magazines, newspapers, markers, scissors, and glue. Then have each group work cooperatively to decorate its paper with corresponding picture cutouts and illustrations. Have students label the pictures and illustrations if desired. Now that's fun phonics!

"Weigh-out" Measurement

This cooperative learning project carries its own weight. Give each group of four students a collection of objects to be weighed and a scale. To begin, have each group member list the objects and an estimated weight for each on his paper. Next have each group member assume one of the following roles: item selector (places each item on the scale), scale reader (reads the scale to determine each object's weight), scale checker (verifies the weight of each object), or recorder (records the weight of each object). When all objects have been weighed, have each group member list the actual weights on his paper. Then have the members of the group critique the weight estimations they made.

Winding It Up

Before creating new cooperative learning teams, have the members of each team participate in one of these parting activities.

- Photograph each team with a special team project and place the photo in a cooperative learning album or scrapbook.
- Have each team write a paragraph entitled "What We Have Learned Together."
- Have each team member recognize another team member by completing one of these sentences: "One thing I learned from ____ is..." or "I liked working with ____ because..."
- Have each student write a short message to another teammate telling him why he enjoyed working with him or what he has learned from him.

Our thanks to the following contributors to this cooperative learning unit:
Charmaine Allen—Gr. 2, Judd School, North Brunswick, NJ; **Susan Beeson**—Gr. 2, Townsend Elementary, Townsend, DE; **Sally Bivins**—Gr. 1, Apache Elementary, Peoria, AZ; **Faith Bonadonna**, Cornwell Avenue Elementary School, West Hempstead, NY; **Elizabeth M. Bringle**—Special Education, Holly Hall Elementary, Elkton, MD; **Sarah A. Daniels**—Gr. 3, George's Creek Elementary, Lonaconing, MD; **Susan Ezzell**—Gr. 1, Bethel Grove Elementary, Memphis, TN; **Mary Finney**—Gr. 3, St. Mary's School, Flint, MI; **Kathleen M. McCann**—Gr. 1, McMillan School, Detroit, MI; **Lynn Morrison**—Gr. 2, University Laboratory School, Baton Rouge, LA; **Jennifer Overend**—Gr. 3, Ash Fork School, Ash Fork, AZ; **Gina Parisi**—Gr. 2, Demarest School, Bloomfield, NJ; **Rebecca Peacock**—Special Education, Cecilton Elementary School, Cecilton, MD; **Joyce Swan**—Gr. 2, Prairie View School, Hager City, WI; **Diane Vogel**—Gr. 3, W. B. Redding School, Lizella, GA; **Lois Waxman**—Gr. 1, Wheeler Avenue Elementary School, Valley Stream, NY; **Barbara Williams**—Gr. 3, Bel Air Elementary, Evans, GA; **Nancy Wojcik**—Gr. 1, Big Shanty Elementary School, Kennesaw, GA; **Donna Woods**, Holley-Navarre Elementary School, Navarre, FL

Awards

Duplicate and present these awards to students during any cooperative learning activity.

Calling The Plays

For Good Study Habits

Hut one! Hut two! Enhance your study-habit game plan with the following activities and reproducibles. They could be just the plays you'll need to score the victory touchdown! Hut! Hut!! *ideas contributed by Mary Anne Haffner and Sue Ireland*

Positive Chart
I can do this!
I'm learning!
Every little bit counts!
Learning takes time!
I'm proud I'm trying!

Training Camp

Believing in oneself is an important part of a good study habit plan. Discuss with your students how they feel when they are discouraged with their schoolwork. On chart paper, brainstorm a list of "discouraged" thoughts such as "I can't do this" and "I'll never understand this stuff!"

Help students realize that these thoughts only make them feel more discouraged. On a second sheet of chart paper, reword the thoughts to create positive phrases such as "I can do this" or "I can learn this stuff!" Discuss how these phrases encourage a person to keep trying.

End this activity by getting rid of those discouraging thoughts. Have each student tear off a piece of the first chart to throw in the wastebasket, where it belongs! Display the second chart for students to refer to the next time they begin to feel discouraged.

Listening To The Coach

Learning to carefully listen to and follow directions is an important study habit. Group students into four teams. Have each team form a huddle by sitting together at a large table or arranging their desks in a circle. Each team member needs drawing paper and crayons. Acting as the coach, call together one member from each team. Give these four students a direction such as "Draw a blue dot in the top right-hand corner of each of your papers." The four students then deliver the direction to their teammates. Encourage each team to discuss and agree upon the meaning of the delivered direction before completing it. Continue in this manner until each team member has delivered a "play" from the coach. Discuss and compare the completed team projects.

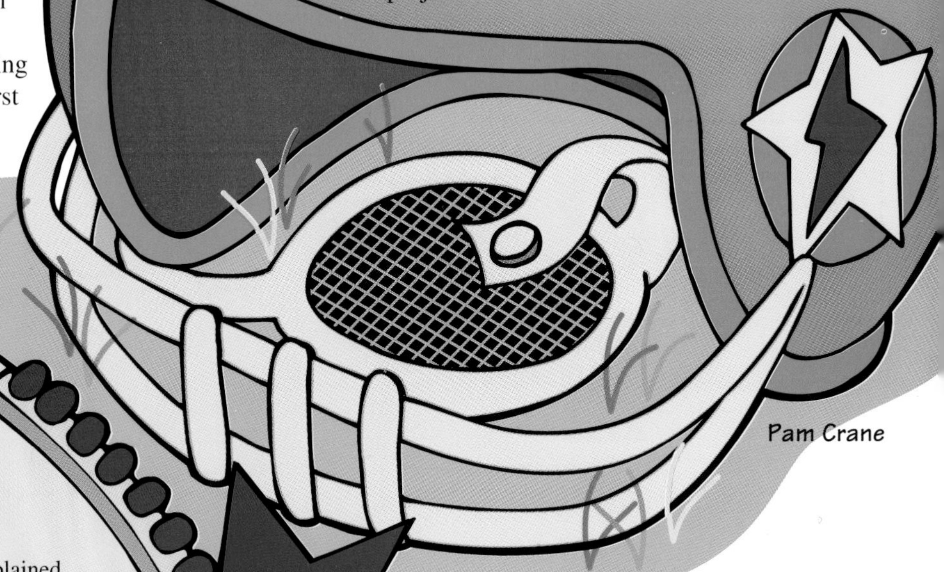

Pam Crane

Calling The Play

Challenge your students to put their study-habit knowledge into play by brainstorming solutions for the following situations. Then invite students to create additional situations to discuss.

- Jordy is confused. She listened when Mrs. Nelson explained the math worksheet, but Jordy isn't sure she understood what Mrs. Nelson meant. Now Mrs. Nelson is working with another group of kids. What do you think Jordy should do?
- Mark's best friend is having difficulty learning his basic addition facts. How do you think Mark can help his friend?
- For homework, Susan must write each of her ten spelling words in a sentence. As soon as she sits down to do her assignment, Susan realizes she left her spelling book at school. What do you think Susan should do?
- Bobby has a science test tomorrow. He is planning on studying for the test as soon as he gets home. Five minutes after Bobby is home, a friend calls. Bobby's friend invites him to play video games until dinnertime. What do you think Bobby should do?

Being A Star Player

Every student has the opportunity to be a star player during this goal-setting and monitoring activity. Duplicate student copies of "A Star Player" on page 143.

Have students write study-habit goals for the day or week (giving assistance as needed) on the lines. Each time a student meets his goal, he colors a star on his paper. When all the stars are colored, the student officially becomes a star player! Reward each star player with a special stamp or sticker. Use the activity daily or weekly, with every student or with individual students, as a means to improve study habits and student self-esteem.

Setting Goals

This eye-catching display creates a great visual reminder of the long-range goals students are working to achieve. For every student, cut out, label, laminate, and mount a goalpost cutout on a bulletin board entitled "We Set Goals." Brainstorm a list of things your students would like to achieve in school during the next six weeks. Then have each student write a goal for himself on a football cutout and tape it to his personalized goalpost.

Periodically mention the goals and encourage students to share their successes and frustrations. Be sure to emphasize that sometimes reaching a goal can take longer than a person anticipates. At the end of six weeks, individually meet with students to discuss their goals. Students may make new goals or choose to continue working on their present ones. Setting goals provides students with added motivation, and reaching the goals is great for the students' self-esteem!

Pat McKinnon—Gr. 3
Travis Elementary, San Marcos, TX

Three Cheers For You!

Students can improve their study habits by evaluating their personal efforts. Periodically distribute duplicated copies of "Three Cheers For You!" (on page 143) to students at the end of a day or after a test or challenging assignment. Emphasize that the forms will not be graded. Discuss the completed forms individually or as a group.

Choosing A Daily Opponent

Reinforce positive study habits with the following game strategy. For this activity, your students will need a team name. Decorate, label, and display a tagboard pennant for your students' team and each of the following teams: the Satisfied On-Time Tigers, the Neat-Hawks, the Careful Cowboys, the Name-Packers. Each morning inform students who their opponent is for the day. For example, if your students need to concentrate on the neatness of their completed work, choose the Neat-Hawks as their opponent. During the day evaluate all work for neatness. If a paper is neat, award the student team one point. If a paper lacks in neatness, award the Neat-Hawks one point. Keep a tally of the points on the chalkboard. Students will enjoy this extra motivation. At the end of the day, say a cheer for the winning team.

Have students play the Careful Cowboys to reinforce accuracy, the Satisfied On-Time Tigers to reinforce completing satisfactory work on time, and the Name-Packers to reinforce writing names on completed papers. Create additional opponents and pennants as needed.

Suiting Up For Action

These student-decorated "jerseys" are sure to enhance your students' concentration and determination. Have each student use Paint Writers (available at craft stores) or permanent markers to write his name and encouraging phrases on an oversized cotton T-shirt. Have students "suit up" for skill reviews, tests, and spelling bees or to complete challenging assignments. The jerseys can also be worn home to remind students to study for a test on the following day. Whatever the occasion, the jerseys are a terrific way to help students keep their study habits positively focused.

Name ____________________ 

Study habits: self-evaluation form

Three Cheers For You!

What kind of a day did you have?

Color the (football) if the sentence is true.

- I finished my work.
- I finished my work on time.
- I understood my work.
- I did my very best work.
- My day was great!
- My day could have been better.

Name ____________________ Study habits: monitoring a goal

A Star Player

My goal is to ______________________________

____

I will color one ☆ each time I meet my goal.

☆ ☆ ☆ ☆ ☆

Relocating to a new school can be a scary, traumatic, and overwhelming experience! Help newcomers make a smooth adjustment to your classroom using these tips from our subscribers, along with the reproducibles on page 147.

Welcome Pad

Welcome a new student with a small pad of paper bearing a positive message. Buy or make a small pad of paper. Attach a colorful sticker and write a "Welcome To _____ Grade" message on the cover. Include your name on the cover of the pad as a helpful reminder of the "new" teacher's name!

Vivian Campbell—Gr. 1
Grandview School, Piscataway, NJ

Supply Bag

For students who enroll unexpectedly, have bags of supplies ready. In a plastic bag, drop a sharpened pencil, crayons, an animal-shaped eraser, and any other items a student is likely to need in order to complete his work during a typical school day. Having a few supply bags on hand will help newcomers get under way with their tasks without the inconvenience involved in rounding up supplies at the last minute.

Gloria Wisniewski—Gr. 1, Dr. Martin Luther King School, Buffalo, NY

Our Album

If you're a camera bug, you'll have no problem filling a photo album with pictures of your students in action. Place photos in an album with corresponding captions which include the names of the students pictured. Keep this album in your reading center. When a new student joins your class, encourage him to take the album home to share with his family. By discussing the pictures with his parents and siblings he can quickly learn his new classmates' names. Continue to add photographs to the album throughout the year.

Bonnie Lanier, Swainsboro Elementary School, Swainsboro, GA

Welcome Banner

Surprise a newcomer with a large banner in his honor. In advance, tape a large piece of bulletin board paper to the chalkboard. Allow each student to use a colored marker to write a personal welcome message. Display the informal, graffiti-like banner on the newcomer's first day! Now that's a grand welcome!

Janice Bradley, Flossmoor, IL

Friendship Chain

A new student will feel instantly welcomed when he receives this rainbow-colored gift from your students. Provide a variety of 1" x 12" strips of construction paper in rainbow colors. Using colorful markers, each student writes his name and one sentence about himself on a strip. Glue the strips together to form a traditional paper chain. The friendship chain provides a warm welcome and a way for the new enrollee to learn about his classmates.

Janice Bradley

New Student Folders

Be prepared for new enrollees with these easy-to-make folders. Inside each construction paper folder place a "Welcome To Our Class" certificate that has been signed by you, a "Welcome To Our Class" card that has been signed by the students, a class schedule, a supply list, a blank name tag, and other items that will need to be labeled (such as a candle cutout for the class birthday cake or a name card for the helper chart). This folder provides a newcomer and his unsuspecting teacher with smooth beginnings!

Denise Capozzi—Resource Room, Cady Stanton School, Seneca Falls, NY

Class Friend

My students pick a new job responsibility for each grading period. One job that is always in demand is "class friend." The responsibility of this student is to be a special friend to a classmate in need and to be a special friend to a new student. The class friend shows a newcomer our school, makes introductions, explains procedures, and helps the new student feel at home in his new classroom.

Kay Trout—Gr. 3, Triad Elementary,
North Lewisburg, OH

Special Jobs

Encourage a new student to make friends, and boost his self-esteem by asking him to complete special jobs for you. For each job, select another classmate to be his assistant. The new student will have several opportunities to talk, work, and nurture friendships with his classmates.

Tina Bassett, Auburn, IN

Who Am I?

Here's a welcoming activity that's fun for all. Each student writes a riddle about himself. He includes clues about his physical characteristics, hobbies, and favorite things; he then signs and illustrates his riddle. Riddles are read by the teacher or volunteer students other than the authors themselves. The new student attempts to identify each mystery classmate. Encourage students to write thorough clues for easy identification. It's a great icebreaker.

Kari S. Greiner—Gr. 2
Paul Banks Elementary School
Homer, AK

New Student Packets

Inform a new enrollee about classroom guidelines, classroom procedures, and his new classmates with a handy "new student packet." In advance, have each student prepare a page for a "class directory." This page could include a self-portrait, personal facts, and special interests. Compile; then place the class directory inside a large decorated manila envelope, along with a duplicated copy of classroom guidelines, procedures, and other desired items.

Karen Frandsen
McLendon Elementary
Decatur, GA

My New Friends

Your newcomer will enjoy having a booklet made by his classmates that tells something about each of them. On provided paper, each child draws a picture of himself and a few of the things he enjoys. He then writes his name, age, address, and a sentence about himself. Compile the completed pages into a large booklet for the student to take home and share with his family. This booklet helps the newcomer learn his classmates' names and interests, and it informs parents of potential after-school playmates who live nearby.

Karen J. Mardin—Gr. 1, Woodland Heights Elementary, Greenville, OH

Classroom Booklet

Not knowing what to expect in a new classroom can be worrisome to a newcomer. This student-made classroom booklet can minimize those worries and provide a newcomer with an assortment of activities to anticipate. Brainstorm a class list of daily, weekly, and monthly classroom events. On provided paper, have each student illustrate and label one event. Compile the completed papers and a construction paper cover into booklet form before presenting it to the newcomer. This project can be completed in anticipation of a new student or after a new student has arrived.

Jane Yarbrough, Oak Grove Elementary, Peachtree City, GA

Student Host Program

My school has adopted a student host program to help new enrollees feel at ease in their new classrooms, make new friends, and learn new procedures. Two student volunteers from each classroom are selected to serve as ambassadors to the program each semester. After receiving each student's commitment and his parent's approval, the student ambassador is given special training. Training involves learning proper introduction procedures, discussing and understanding the feelings of newcomers, and studying the specific duties of a student ambassador. Students serving as ambassadors are awarded with certificates and given special recognition for their responsibility and dependability by our school principal. This program provides new enrollees with well-planned transitions and boosts the self-esteem of student ambassadors.

Tommie Webb—Counselor, Marion, AR
Hazel Skaggs—Counselor, Bentonville, AR
Sue Hull—Counselor, Wynne, AR

It's In The Bag!

Here's a fun way for new students to introduce themselves to their classmates. You will need a small tote bag labeled "All About Me." Send the bag home with each newcomer. (You may wish to attach a parent note to the bag that explains this activity.) The student, with parental guidance, fills the bag with items that represent his likes, dislikes, family, pets, and hobbies. Plan a special time the following day for the new student to share this bag of introductions. The newcomer can enjoy the spotlight while his new classmates learn all about him!

Karen W. Ponder, Raleigh, NC

Meet Our New Student

On a small bulletin board or wall space, spotlight a new enrollee. Help the student list his favorite television show, song, food, sport, hobby, and subject on individual construction paper strips. Display these strips along with a photograph of the student. Encourage the new enrollee to also bring in additional pictures and small items to pin to the display to indicate his background and other interests. The completed display can be shared by the new student or used for a class writing or graphing project.

Margaret T. Galligan, A.H. Morgan Elementary, Rialto, CA

New Student Interview

When a new student arrives, select a committee of three or four students to conduct an interview with the newcomer. After the interview, each person on the committee is responsible for illustrating one fact from the interview (such as where the new student moved from, his hobbies, or his favorite food). Later that same day the committee presents its information to the rest of the class. In this way, everyone learns about the newcomer, and the newcomer avoids feeling embarrassed or frightened about speaking directly to the large group.

Terriann P. Bonfini, Middle Creek Elementary, Wheeling, WV

Use this certificate and card to welcome new students.

(Have students sign duplicated reward before presenting it to a newcomer.)

A Pilgrim Profile

Set sail for an exciting classroom adventure using the following problem-solving strategies.

ideas by Mary Anne Haffner

Packing For The Trip

Preparing for the *Mayflower* voyage took great planning. Because of minimal storage space, each family was limited to one chest of belongings. Packing just the right items was a big challenge! On a length of bulletin board paper, display the webbing diagram shown. Explain that a family would need items from each category to begin their new life. Based on the needs of a family of two adults and two children, list the items your students agree must be taken. As a follow-up, cut and decorate a box to resemble a chest. Pack the chest with items similar to those listed on the chart. Anything that doesn't fit must be left behind!

Packing For The Mayflower
Clothing
Garden Tools
shovel
Building Tools
hammer
Cooking and Eating Utensils
bowls
Special Needs
rifle
Bedding
4 pillows

Laws For The New Land

In the Great Cabin of the *Mayflower*, the *Mayflower Compact* was agreed upon. This agreement promised fair laws for the new land. It also gave the people the right to choose their own leader. For some firsthand experience in lawmaking, divide students into small groups. Ask each group to propose two laws for the people of Plymouth Colony. When each group has agreed upon its proposals, list them on a chart similar to the one shown. Display the chart and several markers at a center. Ask students to carefully consider each proposal before coloring in spaces to cast their votes. After everyone has voted, have students determine the results and proclaim the new laws.

Proposed Laws		*Votes*
Everyone must learn to read.	Yes	
	No	
Everyone must work hard.	Yes	
	No	
There will be no stealing.	Yes	
	No	
Children may not handle guns.	Yes	
	No	

Reading In Colonial Times

Since there were no storybooks for children, the youngsters of colonial times read or listened to books written for adults. One such book was *Aesop's Fables*. After explaining that a fable is a story that teaches a moral or a lesson, read aloud several of Aesop's fables. (Jack Kent has retold and illustrated two collections appropriate for younger children entitled *Jack Kent's Fables Of Aesop* and *More Fables of Aesop*. Ask your media specialist for assistance in locating other appropriate collections.) Before disclosing the moral of each fable, have students suggest the lessons they think the story taught.

Chores For Children

Ask your youngsters to tell about the chores in their homes for which they are responsible. List the chores on the chalkboard; then as a group prioritize the list from easiest to most difficult. Next have students complete the worksheet on page 150. After the students have identified the chores of colonial children, have them determine where these chores would be included on the prioritized list. Most youngsters will agree that being a child during colonial times was hard work!

Hear Ye! Hear Ye!

Have students explain how people today keep abreast of the news and current events. List their responses; then eliminate from the list any means of news travel that did not exist during colonial times. Point out that the few papers published told mostly colony news rather than local news. Often the local news was heard from a town crier. This person walked through the streets calling out the news he had gathered.

For each of the next three days, enlist a volunteer to act as the "class crier." Have this person gather and report classroom news throughout the day. On the fourth day, review the news of the past three days for accuracy and understanding. Then have students use their experiences to determine possible advantages and disadvantages of relying on a town crier for news.

Minding Your Manners

During colonial times youngsters were expected to mind their table manners. In fact, children were given books of manners to memorize! List and discuss the following colonial manners with your youngsters. Then have each youngster create a manners booklet. To make a four-page booklet, accordion fold a 4 1/2" x 12" strip of drawing paper into fourths. Glue the front and back of the folded paper inside a folded piece of 5" x 6 1/2" construction paper. Have each student illustrate and write in his own words one behavior per page, then decorate his booklet cover as desired. For added fun, have students trade booklets with their classmates, then memorize the manners inside!

Toy Making

Colonial children had very few toys. The girls played mostly with dolls made from rags and cornhusks. Most boys liked to play with a leather ball filled with feathers. Challenge your students' toy-making skills by giving each of several small groups a paper grocery bag containing similar toy-making supplies. Supplies might include scraps of fabric, twigs, yarn, string, glue, and acorns. Have each group create one or more toys or games using its bag of supplies. After the toys and games have been presented, place them at a center. Invite students to play with the items during free time or indoor recesses.

Sit not at thy table.
Eat only with thy fingers.
Speak not, unless spoken to.
Stuff not thy mouth.
Sing not.
Hum not.
Wriggle not.
Make not a noise with thy tongue.
Make not a noise with thy lips.
Make not a noise with thy breath.

Going Back In Time

The following read-alouds will enhance your students' understanding of colonial times.

- *...If You Lived In Colonial Times* by Ann McGovern. This question-and-answer book gives insight into the day-to-day living of our colonial forefathers.
- *...If You Sailed On The Mayflower* by Ann McGovern. Another question-and-answer book that enlightens the reader about the Pilgrims' trip across the Atlantic, settling in Plymouth, and the first Thanksgiving.
- *Oh, What A Thanksgiving!* by Steven Kroll. A young boy who thinks modern Thanksgivings are boring, imagines being at Plymouth Colony and celebrating the first Thanksgiving with the Pilgrims.
- *Sarah Morton's Day: A Day In The Life Of A Pilgrim Girl* by Kate Waters. Text and colored photographs of Plimoth Plantation (an outdoor living museum of seventeenth-century Plymouth, Massachusetts) follow a Pilgrim girl through a typical day.
- *How Many Days To America?* by Eve Bunting. Refugees from a Caribbean island who have embarked on a dangerous boat trip share a special Thanksgiving celebration on their first day in America.

Name ______________________________ Inference

Choosing Chores

Read the chores.
Use the code to color each ☐.

Color Code	
a chore for a colonial child	= purple
a chore for a child of today	= green
a chore for either a colonial child or a child of today	= orange

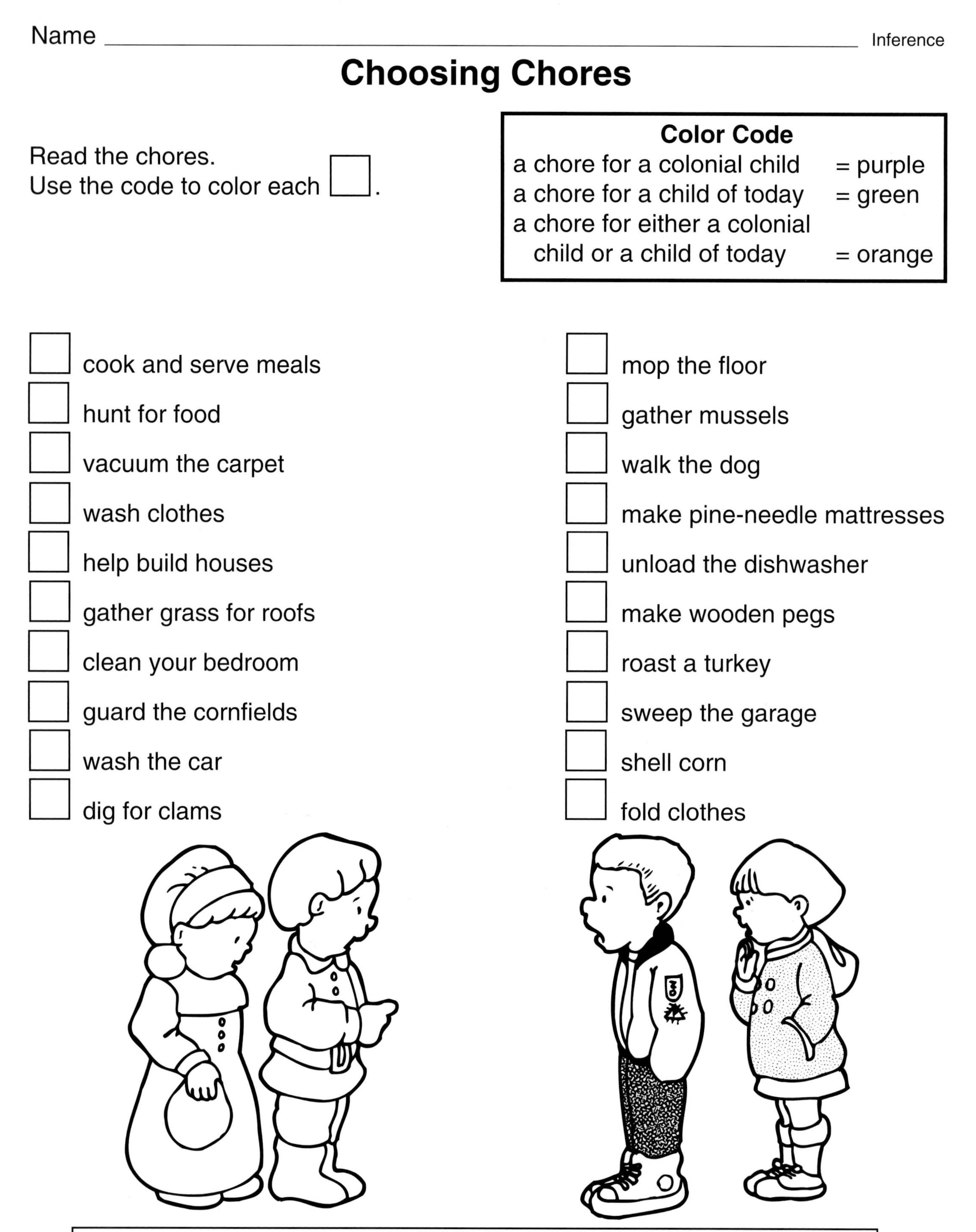

- ☐ cook and serve meals
- ☐ hunt for food
- ☐ vacuum the carpet
- ☐ wash clothes
- ☐ help build houses
- ☐ gather grass for roofs
- ☐ clean your bedroom
- ☐ guard the cornfields
- ☐ wash the car
- ☐ dig for clams
- ☐ mop the floor
- ☐ gather mussels
- ☐ walk the dog
- ☐ make pine-needle mattresses
- ☐ unload the dishwasher
- ☐ make wooden pegs
- ☐ roast a turkey
- ☐ sweep the garage
- ☐ shell corn
- ☐ fold clothes

Bonus Box: On the back of this sheet, draw and color a picture of yourself doing your favorite chore. Write a sentence telling about the chore you're doing.

Swing Into Editing

There's no monkey business in this unit—just practical, classroom-tested ideas for improving students' editing skills. So choose your favorites and go bananas! Editing will be more fun than a barrel of monkeys!

The Daily Edit

Boost students' editing expertise with daily editing practice. Before students arrive each day, write a sentence that contains spelling, punctuation, and/or capitalization errors on the chalkboard. Edit the sentence with your students; then have each student rewrite the sentence correctly in a personalized editing notebook.

Read-aloud Editing

Improve students' editing skills with this sound tip! Each time a student finishes a writing assignment, have him take his paper and pencil to a special read-aloud area. Then have him read his work aloud, stopping to correct any mistakes he finds. Using this method, writing errors and missing words can be discovered quickly.

Wipe-off Editing

This editing method clearly builds writing confidence. When working with individual students, clip a clear sheet of acetate atop a student's paper before beginning the editing process. As you edit the paper with the student, have him use a wipe-off pen to mark all corrections on the acetate. Next instruct the student to write his final draft by referring to his edited work. When his final draft is complete, he can remove the acetate and wipe it clean with a damp sponge. Without editing marks, the student's original draft remains intact, as does his self-confidence!

Editing Table

An editing table is the perfect work area for budding writers. To set up an editing table, tape several laminated editing checklists atop a tabletop. Then place a few dictionaries, junior thesauruses, and/or word lists on the table, along with a supply of colored pens or pencils. Encourage each student to edit his own work at the editing table before scheduling a writer's conference.

Editing Buddies

Editing buddies can help students learn the editing process. Pair each of your students with an editing buddy from an intermediate grade. When a student has a rough draft to edit, his editing buddy can assist him in locating and correcting spelling, capitalization, and punctuation errors. This system gives your students one-on-one editing experience, and it provides intermediate students with additional editing practice, too.

Barry Slate

The Sentence Monitor

Use this proven method to help beginning writers make sense of sentences. Duplicate a supply of editing forms such as the one shown. After writing each sentence of his rough draft, a student checks his sentence against his editing form. He then checks off each item after making any necessary adjustments to the sentence. When he has written and edited five sentences, help the student edit his writing for spelling errors.

Team Editing

A team effort makes editing easier. Divide students into teams. Assign each team a pen color and an editing task (for example, blue/capitalization, red/spelling, green/punctuation). Then give each team several rough drafts. The members of each team work together to find errors in their assigned category. All proofreading marks are made in the appropriate pen color. When a rough draft has been edited, it is passed on to another team. Continue in this manner until all teams have edited each rough draft. Routinely change the teams' tasks so that all students can experience editing different types of errors.

Peer Editing

Editing a peer's work is a great way for students to practice proofreading skills. After writing rough drafts, pair students. Each student edits his partner's draft for proper spelling, capitalization, and punctuation. He then writes his name at the top of the paper. The writer makes the corrections to his rough draft before having a final editing session with the teacher. This method gives students a chance to polish their papers before conferencing with the teacher.

Proofreading "A-peel"

These special proofreading forms have a lot of "a-peel." Duplicate student copies of the proofreading form on page 154. During an individual writing conference, have each student read his rough draft to you. Then have him read it aloud a second time as you assist him in finding three misspelled words. Write the words correctly on a copy of the form; then have the student write each word on a banana. (If desired, the student can add these words to his personal word list.) Next assist the student in finding two sentences that have punctuation and/or capitalization errors. With your help, have the student write the sentences correctly on his form. Staple the completed form to the rough draft. Students gain an awareness about editing without the confusion of editing marks or the frustration of recopying their papers.

Punctuation Edit

This hands-on activity makes editing for punctuation marks "rice" and easy. In advance, use food coloring to tint rice red, blue, green, and yellow. After writing a rough draft, have each student glue a piece of rice atop each punctuation mark according to the code. Piece by piece, students' awareness of proper punctuation will grow.

Punctuation Code

red	=	period
blue	=	comma
green	=	question mark
yellow	=	exclamation mark

Computer Paper Drafts

Computer paper provides the perfect format for writing rough drafts. Have students write their rough drafts on the white spaces, leaving the colored spaces blank. When it's time to edit, students have plenty of room to make corrections in the colored spaces. If the sentence order needs adjusting, it can easily be changed by cutting and pasting. Be sure to recycle the computer paper after the final drafts are written!

Editing Manipulatives

Take a hands-on approach to editing with editing cards. For each student, program a set of four cards with a period, a question mark, an exclamation mark, and a capital *C*. Laminate the cards for durability; then store each set in a Ziploc bag. Before students edit their work, distribute the bags. Have each child remove the period card from his bag, then check his paper for proper use of periods. Repeat the procedure for question marks, exclamation marks, and capital letters. At the end of the editing session, collect the bags of cards and store them for later use.

Writing Workshop Groups

In a workshop group, the input from other group members helps each student fine-tune his writing. Divide students into small groups; then have students share their writing with group members during each step of the writing process. During the editing step, have group members read one another's rough drafts and make oral and/or written comments. After the group edit, a student either writes his final draft or schedules a final editing conference with the teacher.

Monkeying Around With Editing

Mold better editing skills with a little monkey business. As students watch, sculpt a slightly imperfect monkey from clay. When the sculpture is complete, have students critique your work. Then have students make suggestions for improvement like moving the ears, lengthening the tail, or making the head smaller. Then tell students that good writers also "sculpt" their writing by moving words around and adding or taking away words. Finally have student pairs work together to sculpt their own rough drafts. Encourage students to share the improved versions with their classmates.

Chimp's Checklist

Students will swing into editing with this chimp's handy checklist! Duplicate student copies of the checklist on page 154. Have each student attach a copy of the checklist to his rough draft, then evaluate his writing using the checklist criteria. You'll flip over your students' improved editing skills!

Our thanks to the following contributors to this editing article:
Judy Armstrong—Gr. 2, Rib Mt. School, Wausau, WI; **Laura Blevins**—Gr. 3, Wright Elementary School, Wright, KS; **Maggie Diaz**—Gr. 2, Poinciana Elementary, Naples, FL; **Joyce Erickson**—Resource Room, Wisner Elementary School, Wisner, NE; **Arlene Haynes**—Gr. 2, Oak Valley Elementary, Omaha, NE; **Karen Hohner**—Grs. 1 and 2, Manning Elementary, Alberta, Canada; **Kathy Howley**—Gr. 1, Hayshire Elementary School, York, PA; **Patricia Judd**—Gr. 3, Sandy, UT; **Donna Lemorrocco**—Gr. 2, Val Vista Lakes Elementary, Gilbert, AZ; **Norina Nicholson**—Gr. 2, Our Lady Of The Assumption, Toronto, Ontario, Canada; **Gina Parisi**—Gr. 2, Demarest School, Bloomfield, NJ; **Melody Parsons**, Crossroads Elementary, Whitwell, TN; **Denise Quinn**—Gr. 1, Mill Lake School, Spotswood, NJ; **Pam Straub**—Gr. 2, Trinity Lutheran School, Janesville, MN; **Pamela Williams**—Gr. 3, Dixieland Elementary, Lakeland, FL

Name ______________________________

Proofreading "A-peel"

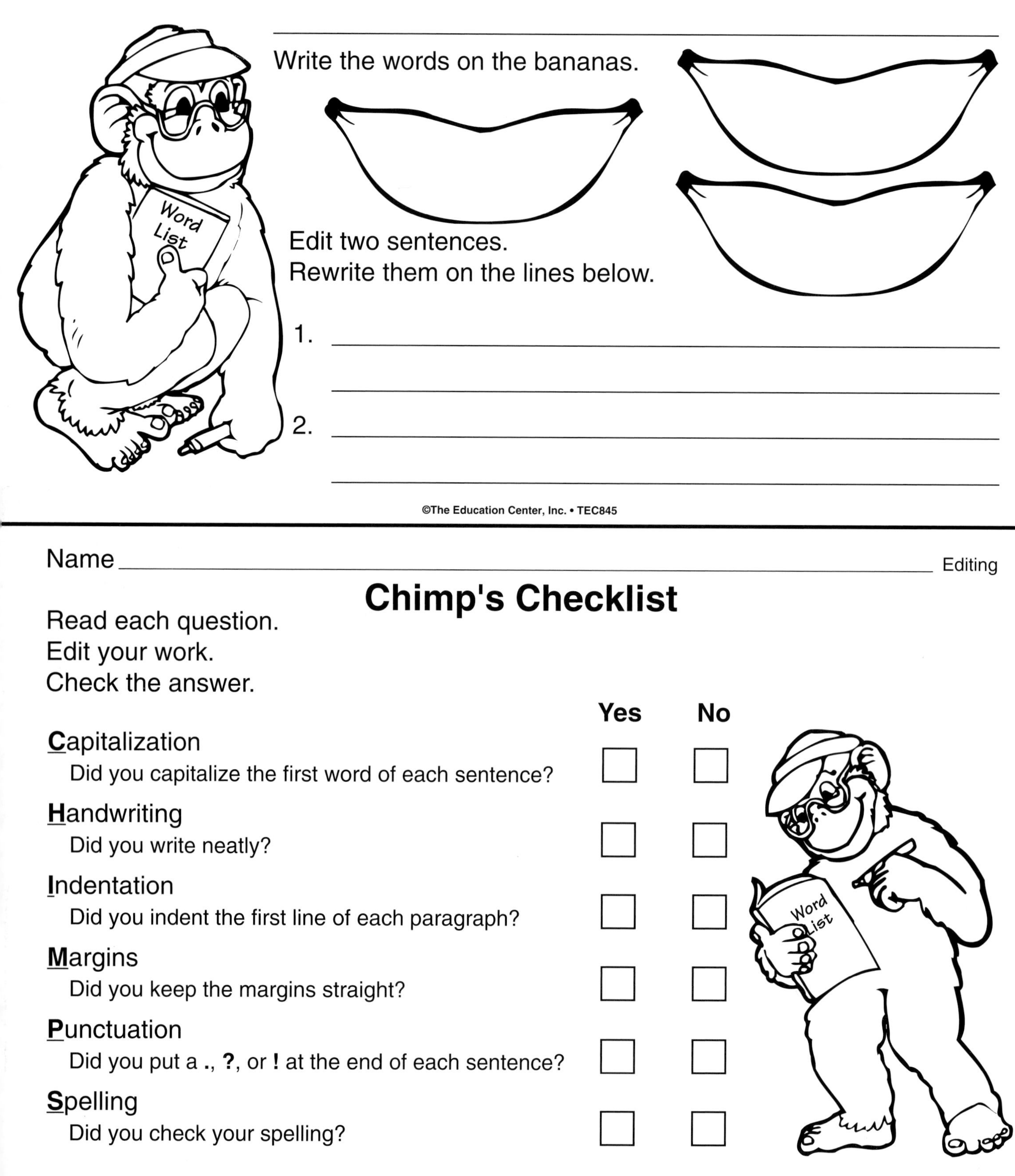

Learn to spell these words: ______________________________

____

Write the words on the bananas.

Edit two sentences.
Rewrite them on the lines below.

1. ______________________________

____

2. ______________________________

____

Name ______________________________

Chimp's Checklist

Read each question.
Edit your work.
Check the answer.

	Yes	No
Capitalization Did you capitalize the first word of each sentence?	☐	☐
Handwriting Did you write neatly?	☐	☐
Indentation Did you indent the first line of each paragraph?	☐	☐
Margins Did you keep the margins straight?	☐	☐
Punctuation Did you put a **.**, **?**, or **!** at the end of each sentence?	☐	☐
Spelling Did you check your spelling?	☐	☐

 Note To Teacher: Use the first reproducible with "Proofreading 'A-peel' " on page 152. Use the second reproducible with "Chimp's Checklist" on page 153.

A Man With A Dream

Every January, America pauses to pay tribute to Dr. Martin Luther King, Jr., and the contributions he made toward achieving peace and racial harmony. Capture student interest in this honorable man with the following activities.

Ha! Ha!
Ha! Ha!
I have a dream that everyone will laugh each day.

Share the following excerpt from one of Dr. King's famous speeches:

"I have a dream that my four little children will one day live in a nation where they will not be judged by the color of their skin but by the content of their character."

Guide students to recognize the importance of Dr. King's dream; then enlist students to create dreams of their own—dreams that could one day provide our world with peace and harmony. Have students complete the sentence starter "I have a dream that...." Students mount their work on large sheets of white construction paper, illustrate their dreams, and trim their completed projects to form cloud shapes. Punch holes and suspend from lengths of colorful yarn or ribbon.

A very peaceful man, Dr. King taught others that changes could be made without the use of violence. Have students propose changes they would like to have happen at home or at school. As a class, determine how these changes could be made without the use of violence. Evaluate each solution and identify the techniques, such as discussion, listening, and understanding, that would be necessary to solve the problem. Point out that these are techniques utilizing the mind and heart rather than the strength of one's body. Conclude the activity by providing each student with a 3-inch construction paper square. Instruct each student to design a "Patch Of Nonviolence" to signal others that he is a peaceful person. When complete, punch a hole in each student's patch; then safety pin it to his clothing.

Even when Martin was a boy he knew that he wanted to help others. At a young age Martin made up his mind to become a minister like his father before him. Brainstorm a class list of service careers such as teachers, policemen, firemen, and doctors. Have each student illustrate and label one career from the list. Compile the illustrations into a class book entitled "Helping Others." For a finishing touch, have each student sign his name on the book cover.

One And The Same: Dr. King believed *all* people, in spite of their differences, were basically the same and should be treated equally. Make students aware of their basic similarities with this special class booklet. Using the pattern on page 156, duplicate pages for the booklet on white construction paper. To create the first page, cut out and program one copy *We are all alike because....* After a discussion about ways in which all people are similar, distribute a copy of the pattern to each student. Have each student cut out his copy and then write his name and a completion for the sentence. Have him decorate the outline to resemble himself using construction paper and fabric scraps, yarn lengths, crayons, and/or markers.

To assemble, tape the pages together to create an accordion-folded booklet. To showcase your booklet, unfold and display it along a chalk ledge or windowsill.

Pattern

Use with "One And The Same" on page 155.

Penguins On Parade

Dressed in tuxedo attire is a fascinating bird that refuses to cross into the Northern Hemisphere. But don't let that stop you! Just head south with the following activities, reproducible booklet, and patterns for an unforgettable learning experience.

ideas contributed by Linda D. Rourke

They Like It Cold!

Millions of penguins make their homes in the cold waters of the Southern Hemisphere. From Antarctica to the equator, penguin homes can be found. Because penguins will not cross into warm ocean waters, they are not found in other areas of the world.

Identify the Southern Hemisphere on a world map or globe. Have students locate Antarctica, New Zealand, Australia, South Africa, the Falkland Islands, and the Galapagos Islands—all penguin habitats. Next remind students that penguins prefer water to land. Help students determine that penguins would live along the shores of the above locations.

A Unique Bird

Though penguins are warm-blooded and feathered like other birds, they also have characteristics that make them unique. Enlighten students with the knowledge that penguins do not fly. At least not in the air! Their powerful wings, which they use like flippers, enable penguins to "fly" through the water at rapid speeds. Another unique penguin characteristic is their posture. Penguins stand up straight like people. This is because of the way their legs are attached to their bodies. If they leaned over like other birds, they would fall flat on their faces!

Students will enjoy making their own unique penguins. Each student will need.

construction paper

2" x 12" piece of black
1 1/2" x 6" piece of black
1 1/2" x 6" piece of white
1" x 5" piece of black
1" x 5" piece of white
2" x 3" piece of black
3" x 3" square of orange

other supplies

scissors, glue, hole punch, black crayon

Directions:

1. Roll the 2" x 12" and the 1" x 5" pieces of black into cylinders and glue. Glue the two cylinders together to make the head and body. Crease the lower portion of the body as shown.
2. Round the corners of the 1 1/2" x 6" piece of white; then glue to the front of the body.
3. Fold in half the 1 1/2" x 6" piece of black. Cut out two matching wings.
4. Fold in half the 1" x 5" piece of white. Cut out two matching wings. Glue each cutout atop a black wing.
5. Glue the wings to the body.
6. Fold in half the orange square. Cut out two matching feet. Glue feet to the body.
7. Trim the 2" x 3" piece of black to make a tail. Glue to the body. Crease the tail as shown.
8. Using a hole punch and a scrap of white, make two eyes. Add details with crayon. Glue eyes to head.
9. Cut a beak from a scrap of orange. Glue to head.

Little To Big

Penguins come in a wide range of sizes. The fairy penguin—a little over a foot tall and weighing around two pounds—is the smallest of the 18 penguin species. The emperor penguin—nearly four feet tall and weighing close to 100 pounds—is the largest. Write the names of the penguins on tagboard strips. As a class activity, measure and display the strips on a wall at the actual heights of the penguins. Challenge students to locate similar information about other penguin types. You'll soon have a parade of penguin information!

Penguin Type	Approximate height
Blue	16 inches
Rock-hopper	24 inches
Crested	28 inches
Royal	28 inches
Yellow-eyed	30 inches
Adélie	30 inches
Gentoo	30 inches
Chinstrap	30 inches
King	38 inches

Get Along, Little Penguin!

Trying to keep up with a penguin in the ocean would be next to impossible! They are excellent long-distance swimmers, and their normal swimming speed is equal to the speed of the fastest human runners! But when a penguin comes ashore (which occurs each year), its mobility is greatly hindered by short, stubby legs. In an open area, have each student loosely tie a bandana or strip of cloth around his ankles; then have him stand erect to mimic penguin posture. Challenge students to walk from one side of the room to the other in an effort to better understand the restraints penguins endure. Next inform students that most penguin species walk in their own special way, which is relevant to their size. For example, emperor penguins sway from side to side, while the smaller rock-hoppers hop. Gentoo penguins (which fall between these two penguins in size) trot briskly. Have students attempt these penguin walks, then devise walks of their own. At the end of this activity, students will better understand why penguins choose to "toboggan" (sliding on their stomachs, while pushing with their wings and feet) when there's snow on the ground. It's not easy walking like penguins!

Something Fishy

Each type of penguin has its favorite kind of food. These foods are found at different depths in the ocean. Krill, shrimplike animals, are found near the ocean's surface. Penguins that feed on fish must dive deeper. And the deepest-diving bird of them all, the emperor penguin, searches for squid up to 885 feet beneath the surface of the ocean! How do penguins hold onto their slippery meals? Fleshy barbs cover the tongue and lining of a penguin's mouth. These barbs point backwards down its throat, enabling prey to slip in, but not out! There's no doubt that Pepperidge Farm's Goldfish tiny crackers will enhance penguin-related word problem practice. Provide students with ample amounts of crackers to manipulate atop paper plates. When the math lesson is complete, the manipulatives may be eaten!

Do Penguins Get Cold?

Like man, penguins are warm-blooded and make heat inside their bodies. But unlike man, penguins have insulation that enables them to withstand extremely cold temperatures. A penguin's insulation is several layers thick. A layer of tightly packed feathers covers a penguin's body. Beneath that is a layer of air, and then skin. Under the skin is a thick layer of fat called *blubber.* This insulation keeps a penguin warm in extremely cold temperatures. A penguin's insulation is so efficient that it can get too hot! When this happens, a penguin fluffs up its feathers to let the heat escape, and may even pant to cool off. That's hard to imagine in below zero temperatures! Have students compare how they dress for cold weather to how a penguin is dressed. Through discussion help students deduce that a system of layers is an effective way of retaining body heat. Then bundle up for a few minutes of outdoor play.

Simply Amazing!

Standing in -50°F temperatures for two months without food isn't the type of thing a normal bird would do. But an emperor penguin is not a normal bird! The reproducible booklet entitled "The Amazing Emperor Penguins" tells about the special way emperor penguins incubate their young. Duplicate pages 159 and 160 on white construction paper. Instruct students to cut on the dotted lines only. Have students color the illustrations, then paste the booklet pages in order on 30" x 5 1/2" strips of bulletin board paper. Punch holes where indicated and tie with ribbons. Fold back the top cover and accordion-fold the pages to complete the booklet.

Note To Teacher: Use with "Simply Amazing!" on page 158.

Emperor Penguins

Name ______________________________

4

The father stands with other father penguins.
The mother goes to the sea for food.

5

In two months a fluffy penguin chick hatches.
The mother returns.
The hungry father goes to the sea for food.

6

The mother takes care of the chick.
The father will also help when he returns.

Note To Teacher: Use with "Simply Amazing!" on page 158.

The Tooth Fairy Presents

DENTAL Dynamics

The tooth fairy has been wielding her tiny little wand again. So, if your dental health lessons have lost their zip, try one, or two, or a half-dozen of the tooth fairy's new, improved tips. They're guaranteed to add a magical spark to your dental studies.

ideas contributed by Karen Lambert and Karen Shelton

Dental High Jinks

You don't have to be in the tooth-recovery business to have realized that the uses and appearances of teeth vary greatly in the animal kingdom. There are animals such as some whales, birds, toads, and turtles that have no teeth at all. There are animals—like snakes, bats, lions, and sharks—that are feared because of their awe-inspiring teeth. But the teeth that amaze the tooth fairy the most are those that never stop growing. Did you know elephants' tusks are actually overgrown teeth?

Begin your dental unit with a playful study in "what if…." Have each youngster draw an illustration in which the body of one animal is bestowed with the teeth of another. Then have the youngsters write a sentence or two about the problems or benefits associated with the mismatched teeth.

Tina Toad's tusks are great book holders. And Tina uses them to prop up her makeup mirror.

Pam Crane

Pearly White Results

In this activity, youngsters reveal their dental hygiene habits and then step back to analyze the sparkling results. Provide a tooth-shaped poster board tracer; then have each of your youngsters create a personalized tooth-shaped cutout for this graphing activity. For a gleaming graph, have students cut the tooth shapes from white, luminescent gift wrap or laminated white poster board and decorate the shapes with permanent marker or glitter pens.

As a lead-in to each new dental health concept in your unit, post a related question that will reflect your students' hygiene habits. Each time, program a blank bulletin board grid with student responses to that question concerning dental health habits. Then have each youngster attach his tooth-shaped cutout to the grid to indicate his response. Discuss the results of each graph.

adapted from idea by Ellen Allaire—Gr. 1, Good Hope School, Frederiksted, St. Croix, United States Virgin Islands

Star Performances

This photo opportunity will no doubt have your youngsters excited about plaque control. Whether you decide to capture the moment with snapshots or videotape, load and prepare to shoot. Provide a new toothbrush, some toothpaste, and a disclosing tablet for each youngster. Then have him brush his teeth and chew a disclosing tablet. Amid the grins and giggles, photograph each youngster before he brushes his teeth again and flosses. Then photograph or videotape each youngster's smile once more. Display your photographs on a bulletin board with multicolored star cutouts and the caption "Smile! You've Got Style," or if you chose the videotape option, have your youngsters munch healthy snacks while they watch themselves on television.

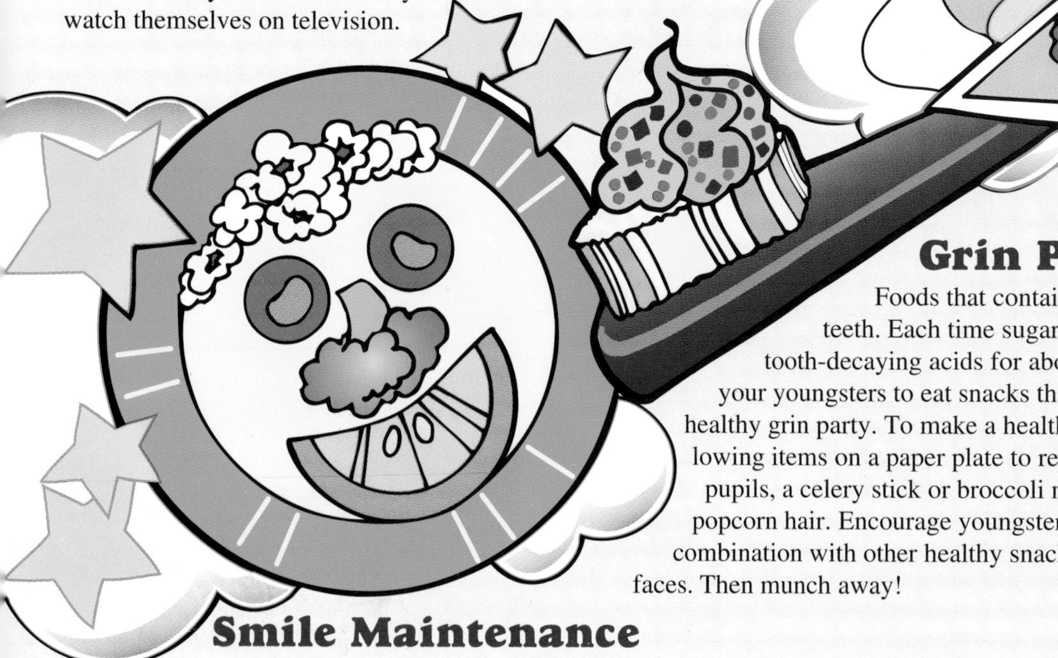

Grin Party

Foods that contain sugar are threats to healthy teeth. Each time sugar is eaten, bacteria in the mouth produce tooth-decaying acids for about 20 minutes. In an effort to persuade your youngsters to eat snacks that are good for their teeth, have a healthy grin party. To make a healthy grin, have each youngster place the following items on a paper plate to resemble a face: sliced carrot eyes with nut pupils, a celery stick or broccoli nose, an apple or orange slice smile, and popcorn hair. Encourage youngsters to rearrange the foods on their plates in combination with other healthy snack choices to create more funny, grinning faces. Then munch away!

Smile Maintenance

Invite a dentist into your classroom to speak to youngsters about the importance of good dental health. After his visit, encourage your youngsters to see a dentist every six months. Duplicate the award on page 164; then color and attach ribbons or crepe paper streamers to the backs. Present a copy of the award to each youngster who has been to the dentist within the last six months. Keep extra copies on hand to present to other youngsters after their dental appointments.

My Dentist And I Are Taking Care Of My Smile!

Loose Tooth Tales

Between the ages of six and eight, the 20 primary teeth begin to fall out to be replaced by 32 permanent teeth. According to the tooth fairy, losing and gaining teeth is a natural subtraction and addition situation. Create a high-interest learning center by programming several tooth-shaped cutouts with tooth-tale story problems containing the names of your students. Program the back of each tooth for self-checking if desired. Store these cutouts in an infant's pillowcase. Place a basket of apples at the center with a note offering an apple to each youngster who completes the center.

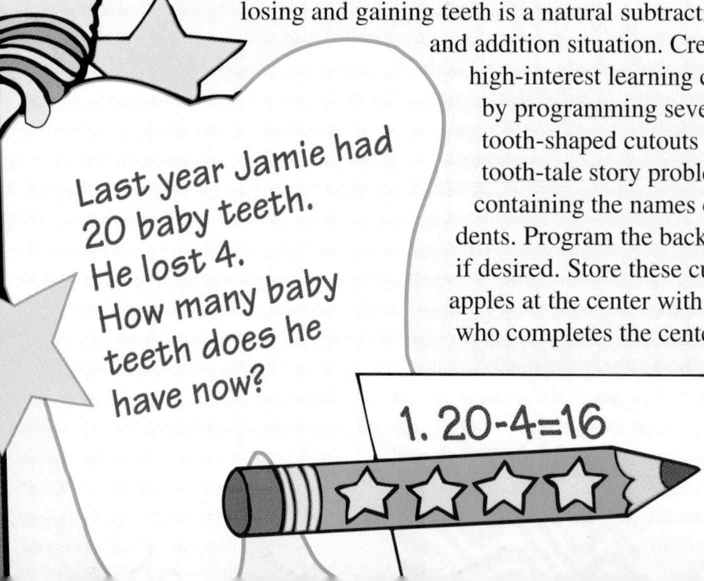

Last year Jamie had 20 baby teeth. He lost 4. How many baby teeth does he have now?

1. 20-4=16

Tooth-shaped cutouts will make other marvelous February centers as well. For any type of matching practice, cut tooth cutouts in half using jigsaw-like cuts. Then program the halves to match.

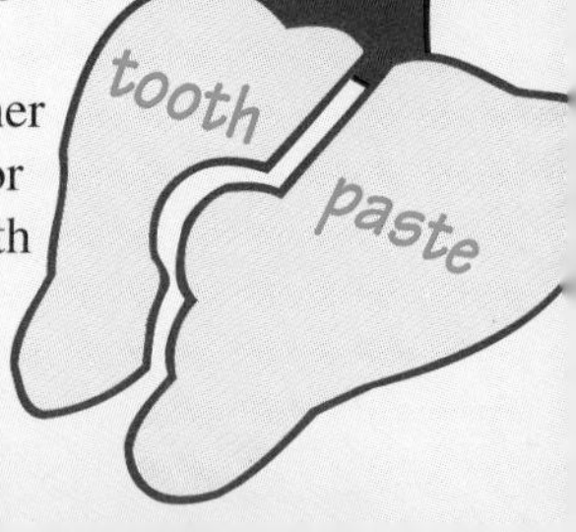

tooth paste

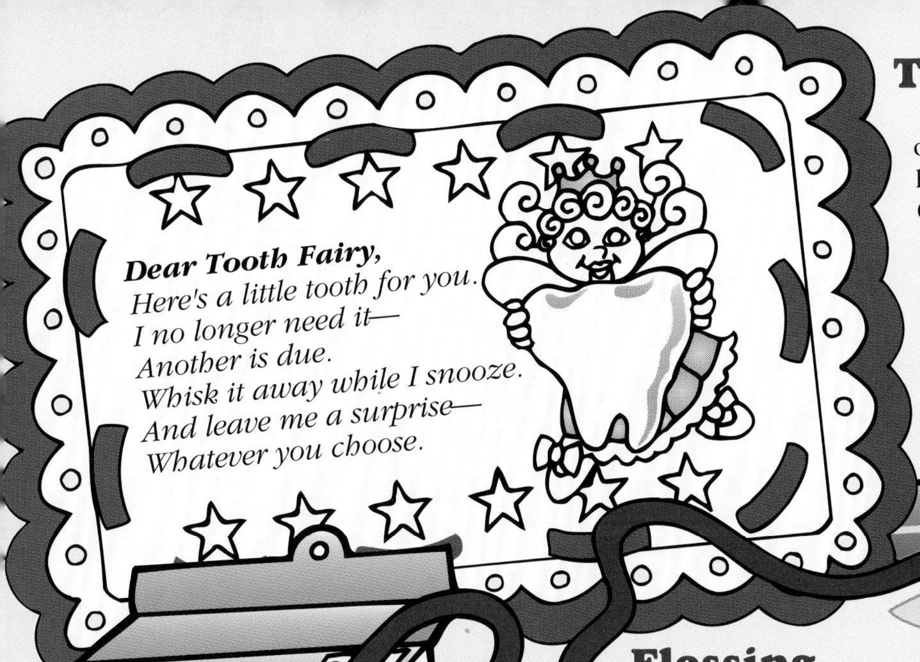
Dear Tooth Fairy,
Here's a little tooth for you.
I no longer need it—
Another is due.
Whisk it away while I snooze.
And leave me a surprise—
Whatever you choose.

Tooth Fairy Pillow

The loss of a tooth is an exciting moment in the life of a youngster. So be prepared to give each tooth the honor it deserves. Duplicate the pattern on page 164. Cut out the design and use a hole puncher to punch a hole at each dot. Glue the front of a small envelope to the back of the pillow pattern. When a child loses a tooth, give him a pillow pattern and a 36" length of ribbon or yarn to thread in and out of the holes to embellish his pillow. Place the tooth inside the envelope for its safe transport home.

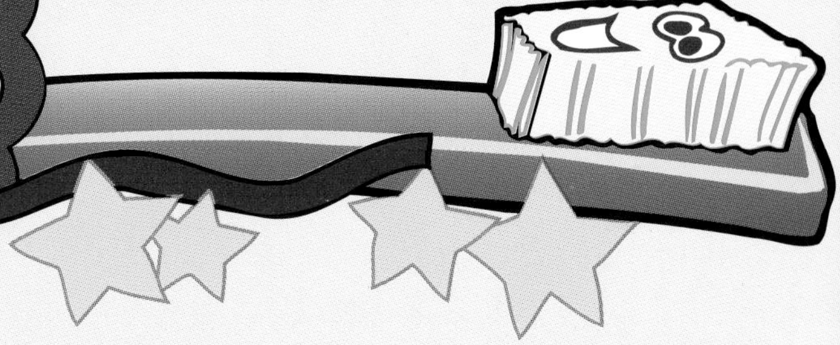

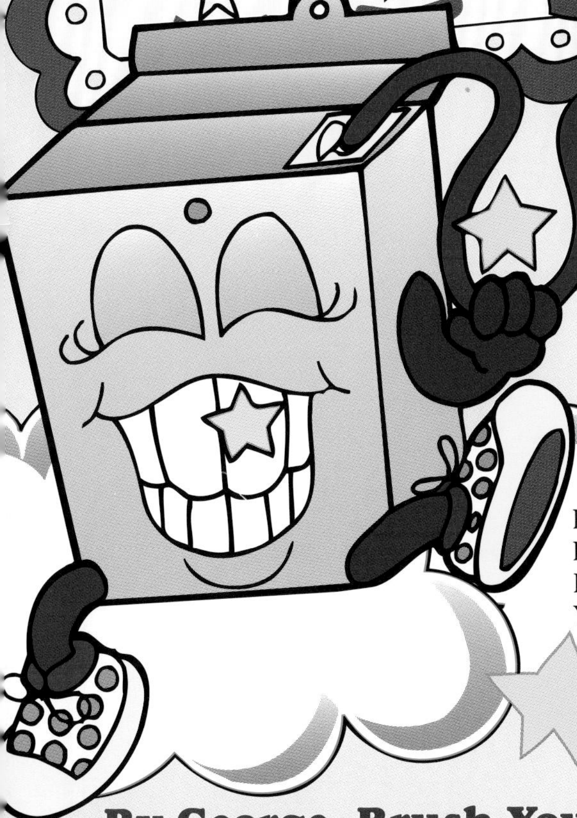

Flossing

If you're having trouble coming up with an upbeat follow-up to your lesson on flossing, then toss your inhibitions aside and give this unusual tactic a try. Have volunteer musicians use pencils, their hands, and their feet to tap, clap, and stomp out a syncopated rhythm for "Row, Row, Row Your Boat." Then have other student volunteers sing the new dental-health version of the song (below). Make sure everyone has an opportunity to get into the act.

Floss, floss, floss your teeth.
Floss them every day.
Plaque, plaque, plaque, be gone.
You're not here to stay!

By George, Brush Your Teeth

Have your youngsters ever noticed that most of George Washington's likenesses show him as unsmiling? He was plagued by defective teeth and later ill-fitting false teeth. His dentures—which were made of ivory and gold—were heavy and fit poorly. If he had had access to the dental technology that we currently enjoy, the one-dollar bill might have shown him flashing his pearly whites instead of projecting such a somber image.

Give each youngster an 18" x 36" sheet of green bulletin board paper, and provide an oval tracer. Have each youngster trace the oval onto the center of his paper and convert the paper into an oversize one-dollar bill—but with a smiling George. Have each youngster attach a contrasting conversation balloon bearing a dental health message near George. Mount your collection of oversize one-dollar bills on a bulletin board with the title "Take Care Of Your Teeth, By George!"

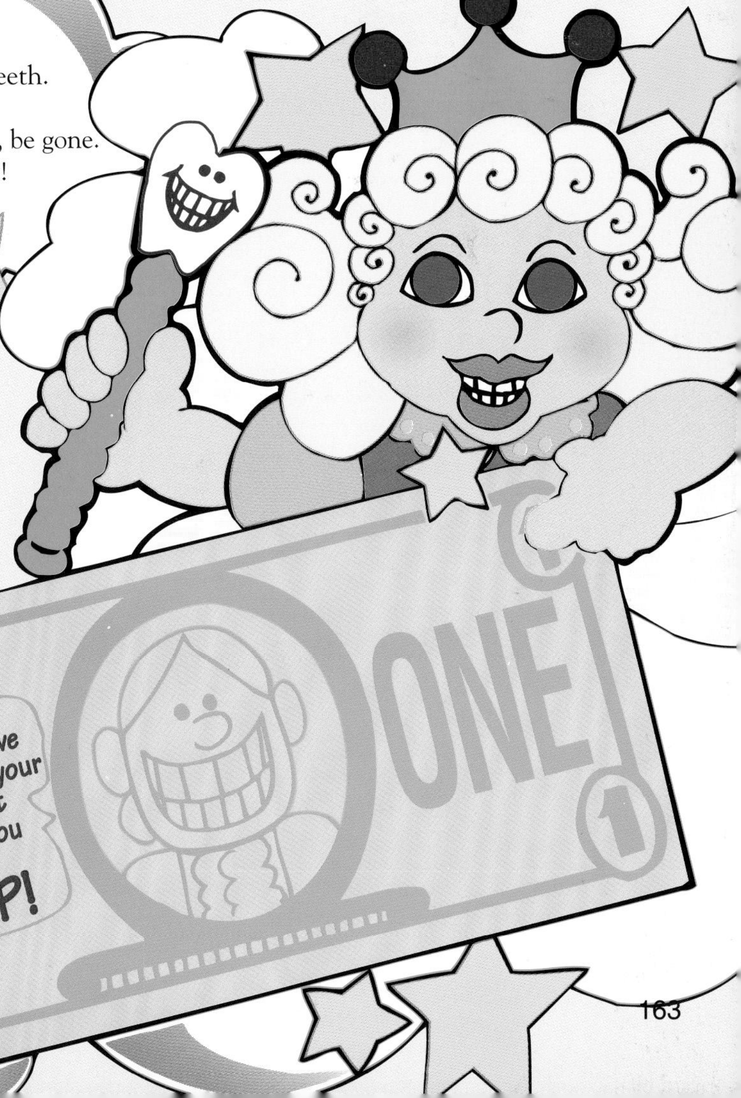
ONE
You don't have to floss all your teeth—just the ones you want to KEEP!

Use this pattern with "Tooth Fairy Pillow" on page 163.

Use this award at the conclusion of your dental health unit.

Use this award with "Smile Maintenance" on page 162.

CELEBRATING BLACK HISTORY MONTH

This February as you celebrate Black History Month, honor the achievements of black women. The following activities and reproducibles introduce a few of these remarkable women and their contributions to our country.

ideas contributed by Linda D. Rourke

A Winning Poet

Introduce students to Gwendolyn Brooks, winner of the 1950 Pulitzer Prize for poetry. Gwendolyn began writing original poetry at a young age. When she was 15, she sent one of her poems to a poet. The poet responded with words of praise and encouragement. He even gave Gwendolyn a few tips. In 1945, Gwendolyn's first book of poetry, *Bronzeville Boys and Girls,* was published. Her second book of poems, *Annie Allen,* won her the Pulitzer Prize.

Gwendolyn's first book of poetry expresses the feelings of children. One poem is about a boy who envies a tree because the tree will never have to move—something he has had to do seven times. Make a list of events that have recently happened to your students; then list their reactions alongside the events. You'll create a poem that your children are sure to enjoy!

You'll Never Believe What Happened
Lost my sweater—oh no!
Made a new friend—lucky me!
Ate a plate of peas—yuck!
Earned a sticker—hooray!
Talked to my grandpa—funny!

The Pioneer Of Black Dance

Katherine Dunham—dancer, choreographer, anthropologist—used her many talents to give the world an important gift. Katherine's love for dance evolved early in life. By age 14, she had organized her own dance group. But it was a trip to the West Indies as a student of anthropology that changed Katherine's life. There she was inspired by the beautiful cultural dances. These dances made her realize she could use the language of dance to teach people about black history and culture, and about themselves. Though Katherine no longer performs today, many of the dances she created are still performed.

Compile a list of feelings such as happy, sad, lonely, frightened, courageous; then, in an open area, challenge students to arrange a series of dance movements to express each feeling. Encourage students to make their own music. Then let the show begin! Wouldn't Katherine be proud?

The Queen Of Soul

Aretha Franklin grew up around beautiful black voices. By the time she had graduated from high school, Aretha knew she wanted to be a professional singer. At age 18, Aretha made a demonstration record for record companies. She also went to a special school to train as a performer. Aretha sang at nightclubs and concerts and made records. But none of the records were best-sellers. It was not until Aretha was allowed to sing "her music" that she became a star. Aretha often accompanies her "soul sound" with her own piano playing.

Aretha once said, "I like life. And I love people. You'll never find me messing with drugs. Life is just too beautiful." Discuss and list the things students feel are beautiful in life. Have each student illustrate one item from the list. Mount the illustrations on a bulletin board entitled "Life Is Beautiful!"

Name ______________________________ Story sequence

A Very Fast Runner

Wilma Rudolph is a real winner! She is a lady who never gives up. Here is her story.

Wilma became very sick when she was a little girl. She had a disease called *polio.* Wilma got better. But she could not walk. So Wilma had to wear a leg brace. Wilma did not like wearing the brace. She wanted to walk on her own. And she really wanted to run. Wilma never gave up. She just kept on trying. Soon Wilma was walking without the brace! Then she was running!

Wilma loved to run. When she had extra time she practiced running. In high school Wilma won many races. Wilma even won an award to go to college. She ran on the college track team. Then, in 1960, Wilma was chosen to run on the Olympic track team! It was there that Wilma proved how great she was. Wilma won three gold medals! No other American woman had ever won three gold medals in track! People called her the world's fastest woman runner.

Read the phrases in each group.
Number the phrases to show the correct order.

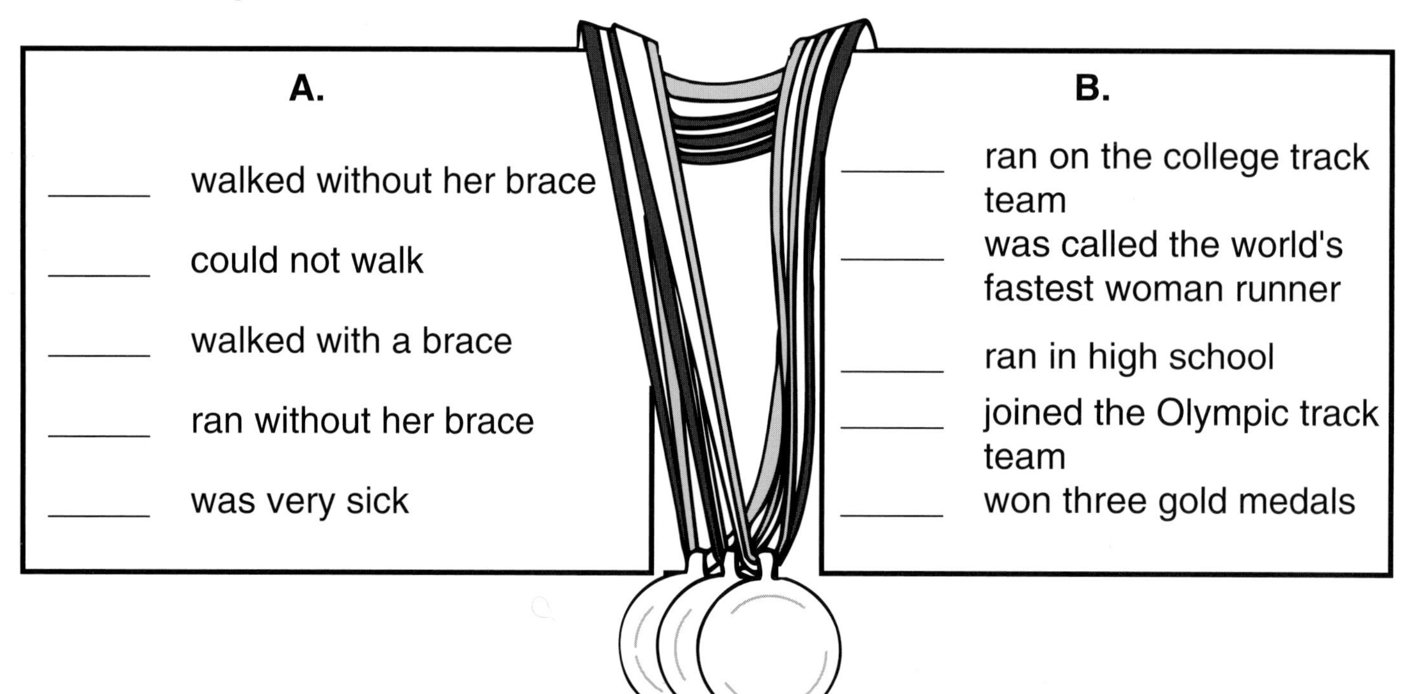

A.

_____ walked without her brace

_____ could not walk

_____ walked with a brace

_____ ran without her brace

_____ was very sick

B.

_____ ran on the college track team

_____ was called the world's fastest woman runner

_____ ran in high school

_____ joined the Olympic track team

_____ won three gold medals

Bonus Box: On the back of this sheet write a sentence telling about something you hope to do one day. Then think about Wilma's story, and write what you think Wilma would tell you to do.

Name ______________________________

What A Lady!

As a little girl, Oprah Winfrey had a dream. She wanted to become an actress. But she never thought her dream could come true. After all, she lived on a pig farm. So how could she become famous?

But Oprah's dream did come true. Today Oprah Winfrey is famous. She is an actress and a model. Oprah has her own talk show, too. And she owns a restaurant. Oprah also bought her own film and TV studio. She is an amazing and talented woman. She likes to do many things. And she isn't afraid to try something new. What do you think Oprah will do next?

Find a word from the story for each description below. Write the words on the lines.

1. scared ______________
2. an animal ______________
3. opposite of few ______________
4. a wish ______________
5. a lady who acts ______________
6. a place to eat ______________
7. very well-known ______________
8. a person who poses ______________
9. small ______________
10. rhymes with harm ______________

Bonus Box: Oprah likes to do many things. On the back of this sheet list three things you like to do.

Kitty's Candy Counter

How sweet it is! Kitty's Candy Counter offers a tantalizing collection of manipulative math activities using conversation hearts, red-hots, and other confectionery delights. It's the perfect opportunity to sweeten up your youngsters' math skills.

ideas contributed by Patsy Higdon

Kitty's Candy Box

Kitty's candy box is sure to satisfy every youngster's sweet tooth. To prepare the box, glue four muffin tin liners in an empty, heart-shaped candy box. Inside the liners, glue four, different-colored, heart cutouts. Glue a matching set of heart cutouts on a tagboard strip; then program each heart (on the strip) with a different value. Place the candy box, the strip of programmed hearts, and a container of candy hearts at a center.

A student counts out ten candy pieces; then he randomly places the pieces in the liners. To determine the total value of his candy, the student uses the programmed strip. (For example, if there are two candies in a liner bearing a pink heart, the student finds the value of the pink heart. Then he lists two candies at that amount on his paper.) He continues in this manner until he has found the individual values of all ten candies. He then adds to determine the candy's total value.

Because the candies can be arranged in many combinations, a student can complete the center numerous times. Now that's a sweet sensation that lasts and lasts!

Flavorful Fractions

Kitty's candies make learning about fractions a sweet treat for students. Give each student eight conversation heart, M&M, or Skittles candy pieces. Have each student determine what fractional part of his set each color represents. (For example, if three of the eight candies are pink, then 3/8 of the set is pink.) Or give each youngster 12 candy pieces and have him arrange his candies to show one-half of his set, then one-third of his set, and then one-fourth of his set. The possibilities for this sweet treat are endless!

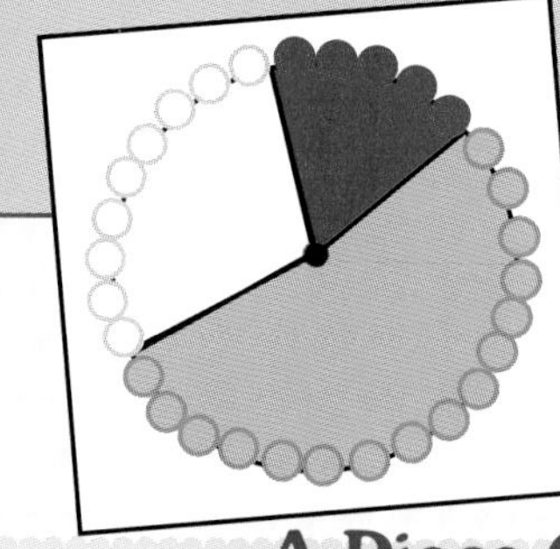

A Piece Of The Pie

Easy-to-create candy pie graphs are Kitty's specialty! For every two students, trace a six-inch circle onto an eight-inch square of tagboard. Indicate the center of the circle with a dot. Also distribute 30 Skittles or holiday M&M's to each student pair. To make a pie graph, a pair first sorts its candies by color; then it glues the candies (by color) atop the perimeter of the circle. When the glue has dried, the two students take turns drawing radii to separate the different colors of candy. The students then color each section of the resulting pie graph to match their corresponding candies. Display the completed graphs and invite students to discuss the similarities and differences among them.

Palatable Patterns

Kitty loves to display her candies in pretty, colorful patterns. Using Ziploc bags filled with assorted candies, challenge youngsters to duplicate candy patterns you've created for them or have them create candy patterns of their own. To preserve their patterns, have youngsters work atop sheets of white construction paper. Then, when a pattern is complete, a student can draw and color a matching candy piece beneath each candy in his pattern. He may then return the candy pieces to the Ziploc bag or create a new pattern atop his paper.

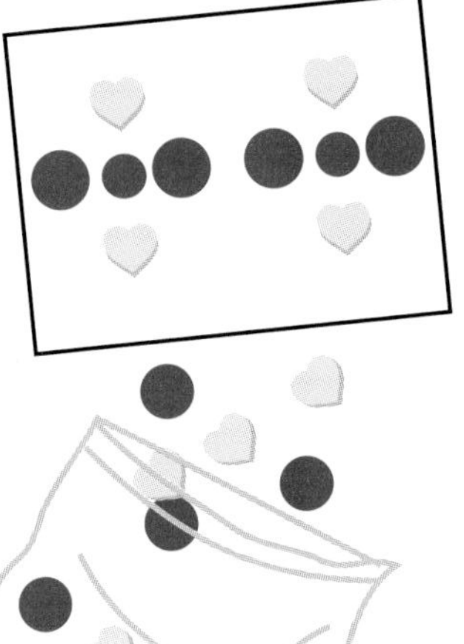

Mmm! Mmm! Measurement

Measurement with Kitty's candies is always mmm-mmm good! Give each student a copy of the worksheet on page 170 and a supply of conversation hearts. Using his candy hearts, have each student measure each length and perimeter to the nearest candy heart. For added fun, have each student estimate the length (or perimeter) before each measurement. To extend the activity, have students repeat the activities using another kind of candy pieces, then compare their results. Ah! Sweet success!

Mouth-watering Multiplication

Turn multiplication practice into a tasty experience! Give each pair of students an eight-inch-square grid (containing 64 one-inch squares) and a supply of candy pieces. Working atop its grid with a specified number of candies, have each student pair form arrays to demonstrate multiplication factors. (For example, the following arrays can be made atop the grid using 12 candy pieces: three rows of four, four rows of three, two rows of six, six rows of two.)

For a fun culminating activity, have each pair color its grid to resemble a checkerboard. Then, using its supply of candy pieces, have the pair play a rousing game of "candy checkers." What's the tasty twist? Students may eat the candy checkers they jump!

Delectable Division

Use Kitty's delicious delights to introduce students to division. Divide students into small groups. Give each group 24 candy pieces and three 9" x 12" sheets of construction paper. Have each group fold one sheet of construction paper in half, then unfold the paper and arrange its candy pieces atop the paper in two equal sets. After discussing the outcome of this activity, have each group fold its second sheet of construction paper into thirds and its remaining sheet into fourths. Then have the groups repeat the activity atop each unfolded paper. For added fun, try each activity using 12 candy pieces.

Sweet Solutions

These problem-solving challenges have sweet solutions! Using 24 conversation hearts, have each student try his hand at solving Kitty's brainteasers!

Kitty's Brainteasers

- Arrange six candies in a triangle. Invert the triangle by moving only two candies.
- Use three different-colored candies. Arrange the candies in as many different combinations as possible.
- Use the candies to create geometric shapes. Can you make a square, a triangle, a rectangle, a circle, a rhombus, a trapezoid, and a hexagon?

Name ____________________

Heart To Heart

Measure from ♥ to ♥.
Use candy hearts.

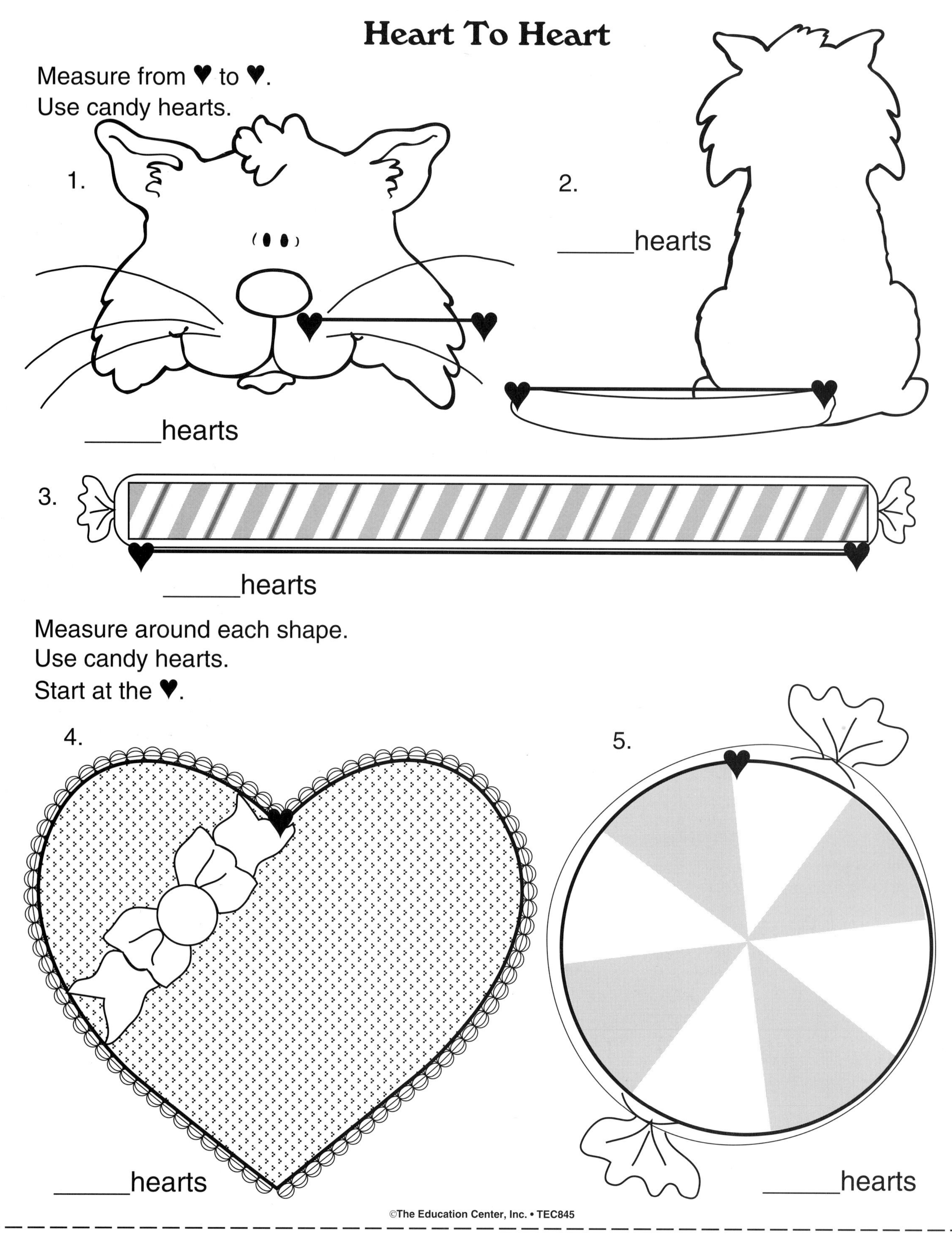

Measure around each shape.
Use candy hearts.
Start at the ♥.

 Note To Teacher: Use with "Mmm! Mmm! Measurement" on page 169.

Name ____________________

One-of-a-Kind Valentines

Use the code.
Color the hearts so
that each one is different.

Color Code

Bows:	red or pink
Stripes:	pink or purple
Dots:	red or purple

 Key p. 192

Name____________________

The "Purr-fect" Valentine

Use a calculator.
Use the numbers in Kitty's heart to complete each math sentence.
Use four **different** numbers in each sentence!

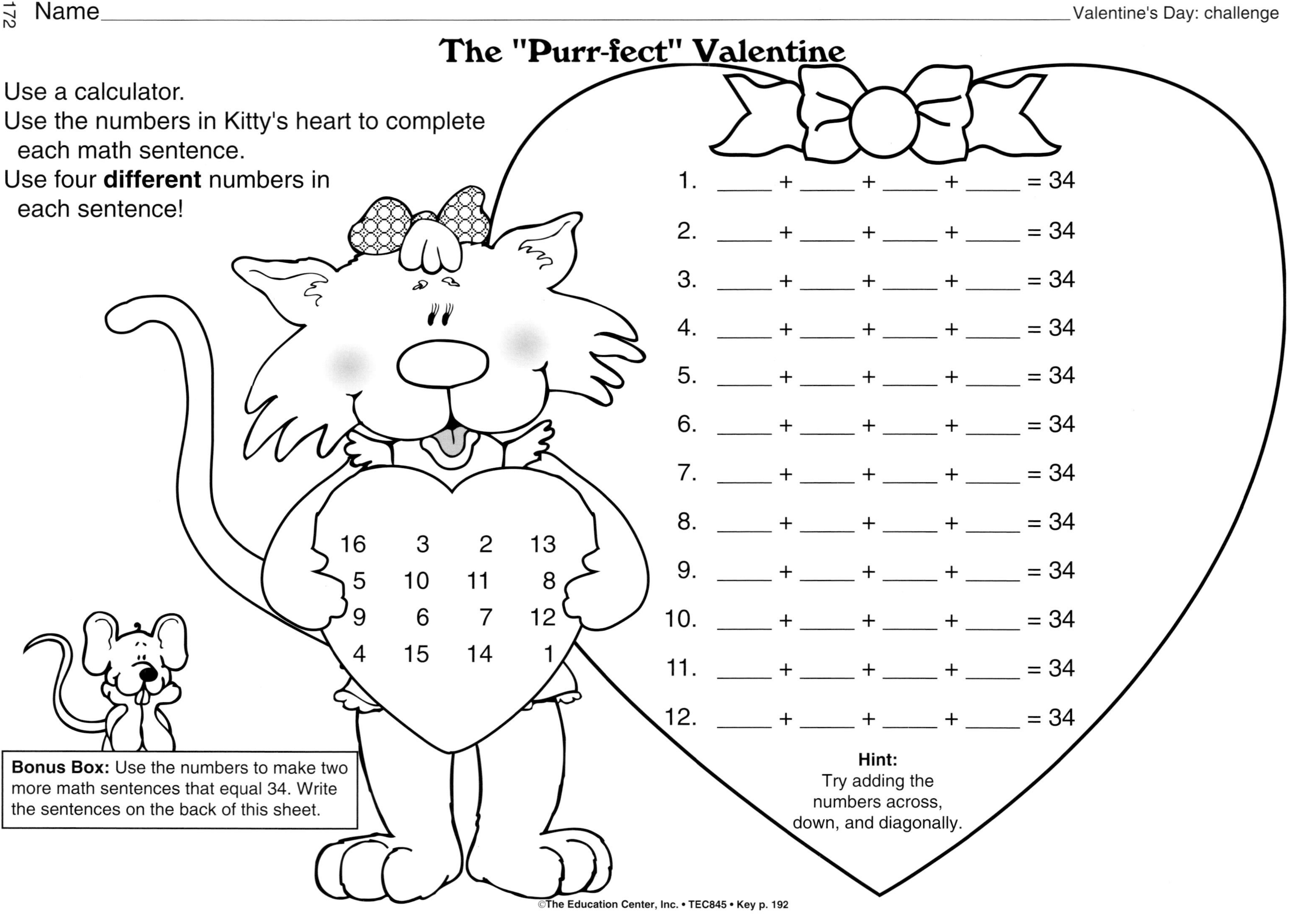

1. ____ + ____ + ____ + ____ = 34
2. ____ + ____ + ____ + ____ = 34
3. ____ + ____ + ____ + ____ = 34
4. ____ + ____ + ____ + ____ = 34
5. ____ + ____ + ____ + ____ = 34
6. ____ + ____ + ____ + ____ = 34
7. ____ + ____ + ____ + ____ = 34
8. ____ + ____ + ____ + ____ = 34
9. ____ + ____ + ____ + ____ = 34
10. ____ + ____ + ____ + ____ = 34
11. ____ + ____ + ____ + ____ = 34
12. ____ + ____ + ____ + ____ = 34

Hint:
Try adding the numbers across, down, and diagonally.

Bonus Box: Use the numbers to make two more math sentences that equal 34. Write the sentences on the back of this sheet.

 Key p. 192

Robbie Robot's Simple Machines

Put students' thinking skills in high gear with Robbie Robot's collection of hands-on activities! Robbie introduces students to the six simple machines—the lever, inclined plane, screw, wedge, wheel and axle, and pulley—as he challenges students to discover how and why they work.

ideas contributed by Bill O'Connor

Activity 1:
Simple Machines To The Rescue
Reducing Friction

You will need:

four, round pencils   a textbook   a tabletop

What to do:

Place a textbook on a table. Move the textbook back and forth across the table a few times. Then lay the pencils, parallel to one another, on the table. Place the textbook atop the pencils; then move it back and forth a few times.

Questions to ask:

- Was it easier to move the book atop the table or atop the pencils?
- Why do you think the pencils make the book easier to move?
- What do we call something that makes work easier?

Robbie's Reasons:

It was easier to move the book atop the pencils because ***friction*** was reduced. Friction is the rubbing of one object or surface against another. Machines make work easier because they reduce the amount of friction that occurs.

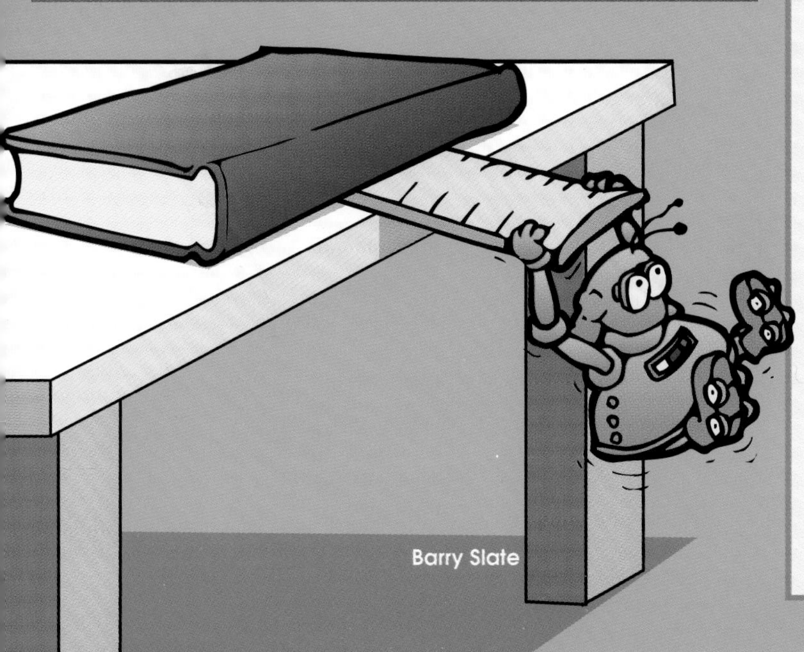

Activity 2:
Robbie's Ruler Trick
The Lever

You will need:

a wooden ruler   a textbook   a tabletop

What to do:

Lay a ruler on a tabletop so that one end extends over the edge. Lay a textbook atop the opposite end of the ruler. Attempt to lift the book by pressing down on the extended part of the ruler. Repeat this procedure several times. Each time, move the book closer to the table's edge (by pulling on the extended part of the ruler) before pressing down. Continue until the book is at the edge of the table.

Questions to ask:

- How was the book lifted? What kind of simple machine was used?
- Was it easier to lift the book with a long or a short lever? Why?
- What are some other levers?

Robbie's Reasons:

A ***lever*** was used to lift the book. A lever is a simple machine. It has a strong, stiff bar which rests on a turning point ***(fulcrum)***. In this experiment, the ruler acts as a lever and the edge of the table acts as a fulcrum. A lever makes it easier to lift a load. The book was easier to lift with a long lever because the fulcrum was closer to the load. Crowbars, bottle openers, and seesaws are also levers.

Activity 3:
Robbie's Race Car Rally
The Inclined Plane

You will need:

five textbooks stacked on a tabletop
a medium-sized toy race car
a medium-sized rubber band
two paper clips
a yardstick

What to do:

Suspend a rubber band from a paper clip; then slide the clip onto one end of a yardstick. Attach the other clip to the race car; then suspend it from the rubber band. Hold the yardstick perpendicular to the tabletop; then lift the yardstick straight up to the top of the stack of books. Record the length of the rubber band. Next reposition the yardstick so it makes a ramp from the tabletop to the top of the book stack. Record the length of the rubber band.

Questions to ask:

- Why was the rubber band more stretched when the perpendicular yardstick was on top of the book stack?
- Which simple machine reduced the stretch of the rubber band?
- What are some other inclined planes?

Robbie's Reasons:

It took more force to lift the car straight up, so the rubber band stretched farther. An ***inclined plane*** decreases the amount of force needed to move something. Because it takes less force to move the race car along an inclined plane, the rubber band is less stretched. Skateboard ramps and slides are inclined planes.

Activity 4:
Robbie's Roll-up
The Screw

You will need:

a right triangle (cut from a nine-inch paper square)
a pencil
tape
a marker
a tabletop

What to do:

Use a marker to outline the diagonal side of the triangle. Hold the triangle perpendicular to the tabletop.

Stop and ask:

- Which simple machine does the triangle look like? *(an inclined plane)*

Then:

Place the triangle facedown on a tabletop. Place the pencil atop one leg of the triangle; then roll the paper around the pencil. Tape the loose end in place.

Questions to ask:

- What simple machine has been made?
- What are some examples of this simple machine?

Robbie's Reasons:

A ***screw*** was made by winding an inclined plane around in a spiral. The base of a light bulb, a spiral staircase, and a corkscrew are screws.

Activity 5:
Robbie's Rap-Tap-Tap
The Wedge

You will need:

a nail
a bolt
a hammer
a block of wood

What to do:

Attempt to hammer the bolt into the block of wood.

Stop and ask:

- Why do you think the bolt can't be hammered into the block of wood?

Then:

Compare the bolt and the nail. Hammer the nail into the block of wood.

Questions to ask:

- Why do you think the nail was easier to hammer into the block of wood?
- Which simple machine made this possible?
- What are some other wedges?

Robbie's Reasons:

The nail was easier to hammer into the wood because it is a ***wedge***. A wedge is two inclined planes joined together to form a sharp edge. Most wedges are used to force things apart. Knives, axes, forks, and needles are types of wedges.

Activity 6:
Round And Round With Robbie
The Wheel And Axle

You will need:

a funnel | a marker | chalk
a ruler

What to do:

Hold the small end of the funnel. Have a student hold the large end. Have the student turn the large end while you try to hold the small end still.

Stop and ask:

- Could the small end be kept still? *(No.)* Why? *(Turning the large end created a very strong force.)*

Then:

Use a marker to make a dot on the large end of the funnel and another one on the small end. Draw an *X* on the floor with chalk. Place the dot on the large end of the funnel atop the *X*. Roll the large end of the funnel one time. Draw an *O* with chalk where it stops. Measure the distance between the *X* and the *O*. Repeat the procedure using the small end of the funnel.

Questions to ask:

- Which end of the funnel traveled the farther distance with one turn?
- Which kind of simple machine makes things easier to turn?
- What are some examples of wheels and axles?

Robbie's Reasons:

The larger end traveled the farther distance. A wheel that turns on a rod is called a ***wheel and axle.*** Less force is needed to turn the wheel and more distance is covered. Turning the axle takes more force and less distance is covered. Doorknobs and pencil sharpeners contain wheels and axles.

Activity 7:
Robbie's Rope Trick
The Pulley

You will need:

two brooms | a length of soft rope

What to do:

Have one student hold a broom parallel to the floor. Have another student hold a broom about 18 inches away from and parallel to the first broom. Tie one end of the rope length to the first broom handle; then loop the rope around both brooms three times. Have a third student slowly pull the loose end of the rope, while the other two students attempt to keep the brooms apart.

Questions to ask:

- Why was it hard to keep the brooms apart?
- What type of simple machine works in a similar way?
- What machines have pulleys?

Robbie's Reasons:

The brooms were hard to keep apart because pulling the rope exerted force on them. Broom handles with a rope looped around them work like a ***pulley***. Pulleys decrease the amount of work needed to lift something. Fishing reels, curtain rods, elevators, and flagpoles have pulleys.

Activity 8:
Robbie Reveals A Secret
Compound Machines

You will need:

a pair of scissors | a punch-type can opener | a hand drill
sheets of paper | clean, empty soup cans | two large blocks of wood

What to do:

Have students examine and use the scissors and paper, the can opener and soup cans, and the hand drill and wood.

Questions to ask:

- Which simple machines are found in scissors?
- Which simple machines are found in a can opener?
- Which simple machines are found in a hand drill?
- What do you call a machine made up of two or more simple machines?
- What are some other examples of compound machines?

Robbie's Reasons:

Scissors contain two levers (the halves of the scissors) and two wedges (the sharp sides of the blades). A can opener contains a lever (the handle) and a wedge (the punch). A hand drill contains a wheel and axle (the handle), a screw (the bit), and two wedges (the tip and the sharp, spiral edges of the bit). A machine made up of two or more simple machines is called a ***compound machine.*** Bicycles and wheelbarrows are other compound machines.

Stuck On Spelling!

Sweeten your youngsters' enthusiasm for spelling with this collection of activities, games, and reproducibles contributed by our "bee-loved" subscribers. Now that's something to "buzz" about!

Magnetic Spelling

Attract students to better spelling skills with this fun tactile activity. Post a spelling list and an assortment of magnetic letters on a metal filing cabinet. A student manipulates the magnetic letters to spell each word on the list. Encourage parents to set up similar centers at home using their filing cabinets or refrigerators.

Sentence Chips

Add a fun twist to an often-dreaded spelling activity. Program one plastic chip to correspond with each numeral on a numbered list of spelling words. Place the chips in a container. Have each student draw five chips from the container. Before returning the chips, the student writes each chip number and its corresponding spelling word on his paper. The student then writes five sentences. Each sentence must feature one of the spelling words he drew.

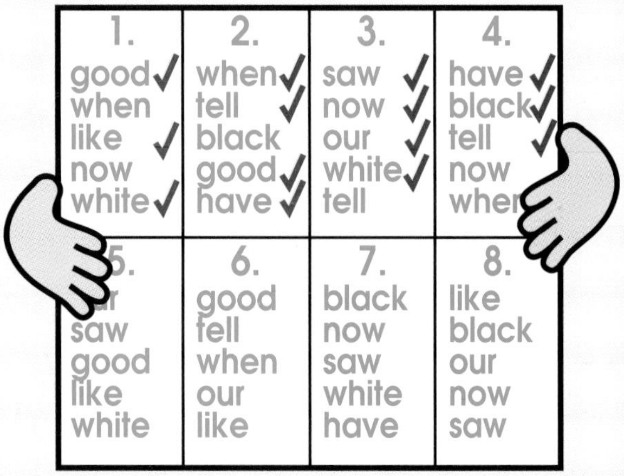

Got It

1.	2.	3.	4.
good ✓ when like ✓ now white ✓	when ✓ tell ✓ black good ✓ have ✓	saw ✓ now ✓ our ✓ white ✓ tell	have ✓ black ✓ tell ✓ now wher
5.	**6.**	**7.**	**8.**
ur saw good like white	good tell when our like	black now saw white have	like black our now saw

Try this fast-paced game to familiarize students with new spelling words. Post the weekly spelling words. Then have each child fold his paper into eighths, number the sections sequentially, and randomly program each section with five words from the list. (Words may be used more than once, but only once in each section.) To play round one, call out the posted words in random order. Students check off the words in the *first* section of their papers as they hear them called. The first student to check off all five words calls out, "Got it!" He must then correctly spell back each word. If all five words are spelled correctly, he becomes the caller for the second round. Play proceeds in the same manner for a total of eight rounds.

As a variation, call out the definitions of each posted word. Or display individual flash cards programmed with phonetic respellings for the listed words.

Scrabble Spelling Tiles

Hang on to that old Scrabble game! Have students arrange the tiles to spell their spelling words for a wonderful hands-on spelling activity.

Hands On Spelling

Tactile learners get a real feel for their spelling words with this activity. Place the wooden or macaroni letters needed to spell each word in individual containers. Number the containers. A student first numbers his paper to match the numbered containers. He then manipulates the letters in each container to spell a word and writes the word on his paper by its corresponding number. Provide an answer key so students can check their spelling accuracy as soon as they have completed the activity.

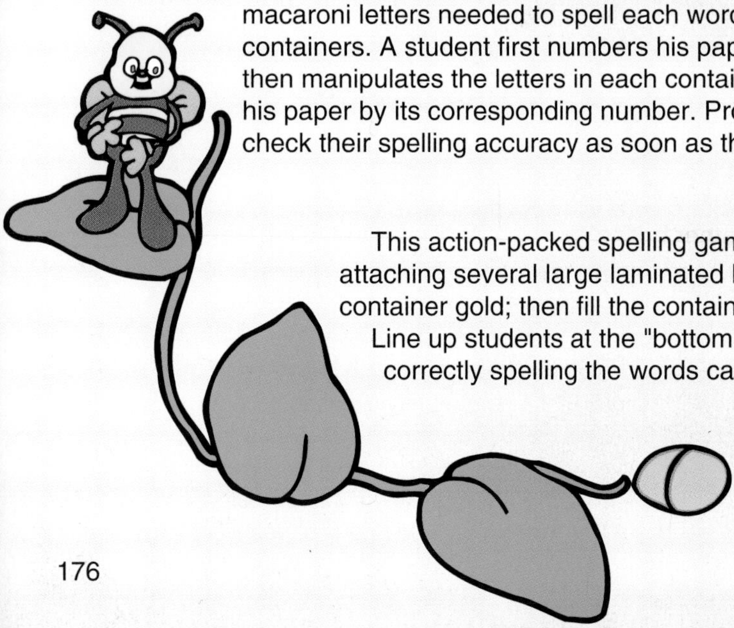

Bean Stalk Spelling

This action-packed spelling game is sure to be a gigantic success. Create a large bean stalk by attaching several large laminated leaf cutouts and a length of green yarn to the floor. Paint a L'eggs container gold; then fill the container with small rewards and place it at the "top" of the stalk.

Line up students at the "bottom" of the stalk. In turn, each student attempts to "climb" the stalk by correctly spelling the words called to him. Each time he spells a word correctly, the student follows the yarn length and steps to the next leaf cutout. If he misspells a word, the student "falls into the hands of the giant" and must go to the back of the line. Each student who spells his way to the "top" of the stalk may take a reward from the golden egg.

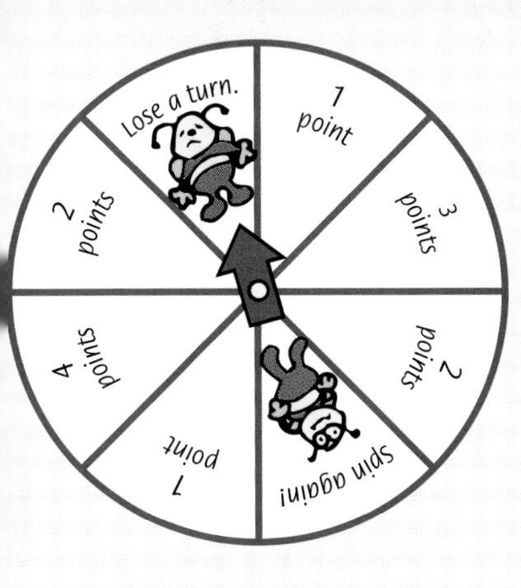

Spin And Spell

This team game motivates students to master their spelling words. Program a large poster-board circle as shown. Use an arrow cutout and a brad to create a spinner. Divide students into two teams. In turn, one student from each team spins the spinner. He either follows the directions indicated or (if the spinner lands on a point value) is given a word to spell. When a word is given, the player must write the word on the chalkboard as the other children write it on individual chalkboards or papers. If he spells the word correctly, his team is awarded the specified number of points. If the word is spelled incorrectly, no points are awarded. Play continues until each child has taken a turn. Reward the team scoring the most points (the winning team) by allowing each member to "pass" on one word during the weekly spelling test.

A Spelling Puzzle

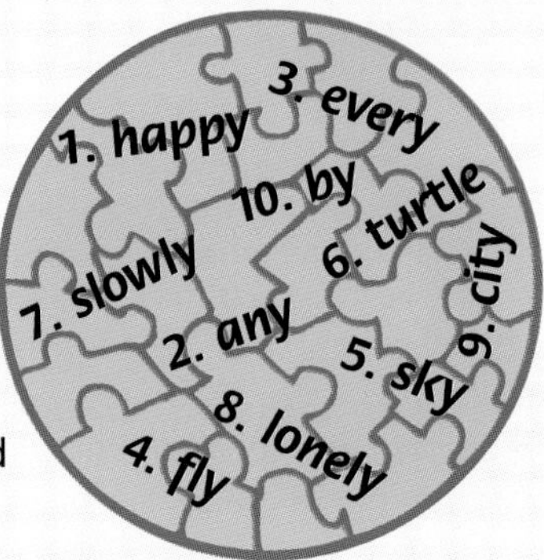

Students piece together their weekly spelling words by completing this center activity. You will need a large-sized paper plate. Program the front of the plate with the weekly spelling words and one "mystery word." Number each word; then cut the plate into puzzle pieces. Store the puzzle pieces in a large Ziploc bag. A student assembles the puzzle, then copies the words on his paper in numerical order. He then identifies the mystery word (on his paper) by circling it before checking his list against a provided answer key.

Word List Recording

Students will quickly tune in to this fun listening activity. In advance prepare a recording of your spelling word list. To do this, say a spelling word, pause for approximately ten seconds, then verbally spell the word. Pause again for approximately ten more seconds before continuing with the next spelling word. Continue in this manner until each word has been called and spelled. Place the recording in a listening station along with pencils and paper. Individually or in small groups, students listen to the tape, write the words on their papers, and immediately check their spellings by listening.

Sporty Spelling

Nerf balls provide a sporty twist to this spelling game. Divide students into two teams. Alternating between the teams, toss a Nerf-type ball to each team member. A team scores one point if a member catches the ball, and another point if the member can correctly spell the spelling word you call. Present pennant cutouts to the members of the winning team.

Spelling Bee

"Bee-dazzle" your youngsters with this spelling game. Program a set of cards with spelling words. Seat children in a circle. Select one child to be the Spelling Bee. Have the Bee choose a word card and proclaim the spelling word on the card as "the stinger" word. As the seated children chant—"Spelling Bee, Spelling Bee, buzzing on a spelling spree. Ha, ha! Hee, hee! You can't sting me!"—the Spelling Bee moves around the circle. When the word *me* is called, the Bee taps the child nearest him on the shoulder. The child who has been "stung" must orally spell "the stinger" word. If the child correctly spells the word, he trades places with the Spelling Bee. If the child misspells the word, the Spelling Bee takes another turn.

Class Spelling Story

Involve the whole hive in this cooperative learning activity. Together brainstorm a story containing one or more spelling words in each sentence. As the story unfolds, write the sentences on the chalkboard. When the story is completed, pair students and assign each pair one sentence from the story. Working together, each student pair must copy and illustrate its assigned sentence on provided paper. Order, then staple, the completed papers between construction paper covers. Place the book in your classroom library. These weekly publications will be at the top of your students' reading list!

Pretest Boost

Take this positive approach for evaluating spelling pretests. At the completion of the test, call out the spelling of each word. On his paper, a student draws colored dots under all the correct letters he has written. He also marks out any extra or incorrect letters and writes in any needed letters (see examples). By studying these marks, students can easily identify the word parts they need to study and be reinforced by the number of "correct" marks on their papers.

Sensory Spelling

Students will swarm to master their spelling words with this sensational activity. Place a sheet of waxed paper atop each child's desk. Position a dollop of finger paint, pudding, whipped topping, shaving cream, or other similarly textured medium atop each child's waxed paper. Have each child spread his "goo" evenly and then use a fingertip to write the called spelling word in his "goo." Enlist a volunteer to orally spell each word after it is called. Each youngster checks his spelling and then smooths out his "goo" and prepares to write another spelling word. It's a spelling experience that's sure to leave a lasting impression.

"Bee-gin" With Bingo

wind	ripe	fire	smile	might
fry	blind	wife	dry	child
wild	prize		high	pipe
slide	bright	child	sky	wind
shine	drive	grind	fire	prize

Start off the week with a motivational game of spelling bingo. Have students complete duplicated bingo cards by randomly copying their spelling words for the week in the blank spaces. Call out the spelling words in random order. If the called word is on a student's card, he covers that space with a bean, plastic chip, or paper marker. The declared winner of the first game becomes the caller for the second game. It's a fun way to familiarize students with their weekly spelling words and takes a minimal amount of preparation time.

Stuck On Studying

Use the versatile contract form on page 180 to help youngsters improve spelling study habits in the classroom or at home. Duplicate student copies. Have each student write his spelling words on the lines and then color a flower every day he studies his words. Or program a copy of the contract with daily spelling assignments, white-out and reprogram the directions to match, and duplicate student copies. A student writes his spelling words on the lines and then colors a flower every day he completes his assigned work. Whichever method you choose, your youngsters' study-habit blues will "bee" gone!

Squirt Bottle Spelling

A squirt of spelling here and there adds up to a refreshing warm-weather spelling activity. Fill a squirt bottle with water and venture outdoors with your students. Have students take turns forming the letters of each spelling word by squirting water on an area of dry pavement. For a fun wintertime spelling activity, mix a few drops of food coloring into the water. Students can create a colorful array of spelling words by squirting the tinted water onto a snow-covered area.

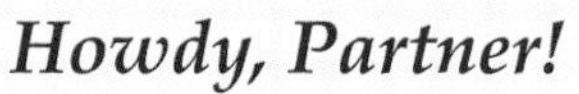

Howdy, Partner!

Corral your young spellers; then assign each a spelling partner for the grading period. Have spelling partners meet each morning for five to ten minutes to practice spelling their weekly words. Use an auditory signal to indicate when "partner spelling" begins and ends, and encourage students to use different methods of study during the week. Just a taste of partner spelling will have your students stuck on studying!

Jell-O Spelling

Here's a honey of a homework idea! Sprinkle powdered Jell-O atop cookie sheets or pieces of waxed paper. A parent calls out a spelling word. His child uses a fingertip to write the word in the powdered Jell-O. If the word is spelled incorrectly, the child smooths out the powder and tries again. Have parents reward correct spellings by allowing their children to lick their fingertips before they call out the next word. Accurate spelling brings sweet success!

Batter Up!

This spelling game is a guaranteed crowd-pleaser! Create a baseball diamond by positioning four bases (or similarly shaped tagboard cutouts) in your classroom. Divide students into two teams. Determine which team will bat first; then, one at a time, have the players from that team step up to home plate. Deliver each batter a "pitch" by calling out a word to be spelled. If the batter spells the word correctly, he advances to first base. If he misspells the word, he is out. A player on first base advances one base each time a teammate correctly spells a word. When a player crosses home plate, he scores one run for his team. Each team continues to bat until six runs or three outs (whichever occurs first) have been earned. Total the runs scored by each team at the end of every inning. The team with the most runs scored at the end of the last inning of play wins.

Word Investigations

Tackle tough spelling words by initiating undercover word investigations. Identify words that are unfamiliar to students or are particularly difficult to spell. Have each student choose one of the identified words, then investigate his word by completing a copy of the worksheet on page 181. Or post one or more challenge spelling words each week. Reward students who investigate the words with a treat, a privilege, or bonus spelling points.

Tic-Tac-Toe Review

Play this version of tic-tac-toe for a fun spelling review and a critical-thinking challenge. Draw a tic-tac-toe grid on the chalkboard. Group students into two teams: an *X* team and an *O* team. Alternating between the teams, call out a word to a player. If the player correctly spells the word, he draws his team's symbol on the displayed grid. If the player misspells the word, the word is given to a player from the opposing team. If this player responds correctly, he draws his team's symbol on the grid; then play resumes with his team. If the alternate speller also misspells the word, announce the correct spelling of the word before resuming play as described above. A team earns one point for each game it wins. If the game is a draw, no points are awarded.

Finger Spelling

Students will enjoy spelling their words using this "secret code." Inform students that finger spelling is a form of sign language used for communication by the hearing impaired. Explain that each letter of the alphabet is represented by a different position of the fingers. Display a poster featuring the American Manual Alphabet. (Ask a special education instructor for assistance in locating such a poster or create your own poster by using an encyclopedia [see Sign Language] or other reference book.) Introduce and practice the finger spelling of each letter of the alphabet. In no time at all, students will be finger spelling their words with ease. It's a great independent, partner, or group spelling activity.

Our thanks to the following contributors to this spelling article: Karen Aden—Special Education, North Hollywood, CA; Karen D. Burkey—Gr. 2, Alexandria, OH; Tonya Byrd—Gr. 2, Shaw AFB, SC; Marsha Cameron—Gr. 3, Cullowhee, NC; Denise Capozzi—Resource Room, Seneca Falls, NY; Anne Croxton—Gr. 2, Richmond, VA; Linda Fonner-Brown—Gr. 2, Ocean City, MD; Julie Gaynor—Grs. 1–3, Baltimore, MD; Nancy Griffin—Gr. 3, Houston, TX; Elaine Gunterman—Gr. 2, New Albany, IN; Diane Hecker—Gr. 2, Phoenix, AZ; Vicky Hofer—Gr. 3, Eudora, KS; Martha Johnson—Chapter I, Bowling Green, KY; Julie Lambert—Gr. 1, Guilford, IN; Mrs. Dale Pelchman—Gr. 1, St. Louis, MO; Laura Porter—Gr. 3, Shannon, MS; Debbie Montsde Oca, Winter Haven, FL; Cathy Muehl—Gr. 2, Punta Gorda, FL; Ann Rowe—Special Education, Omaha, NE; Joyce Smudde—Gr. 2, Freedom, WI; Patricia Tagliarini—Gr. 2, Murphy, NC; Dartha Williamson—Gr. 2, Athens, GA

Name ______________________________

Spelling Is Special

Write your spelling words on the lines.
Color a flower each day you study your words.

1. ______	6. ______	11. ______
2. ______	7. ______	12. ______
3. ______	8. ______	13. ______
4. ______	9. ______	14. ______
5. ______	10. ______	15. ______

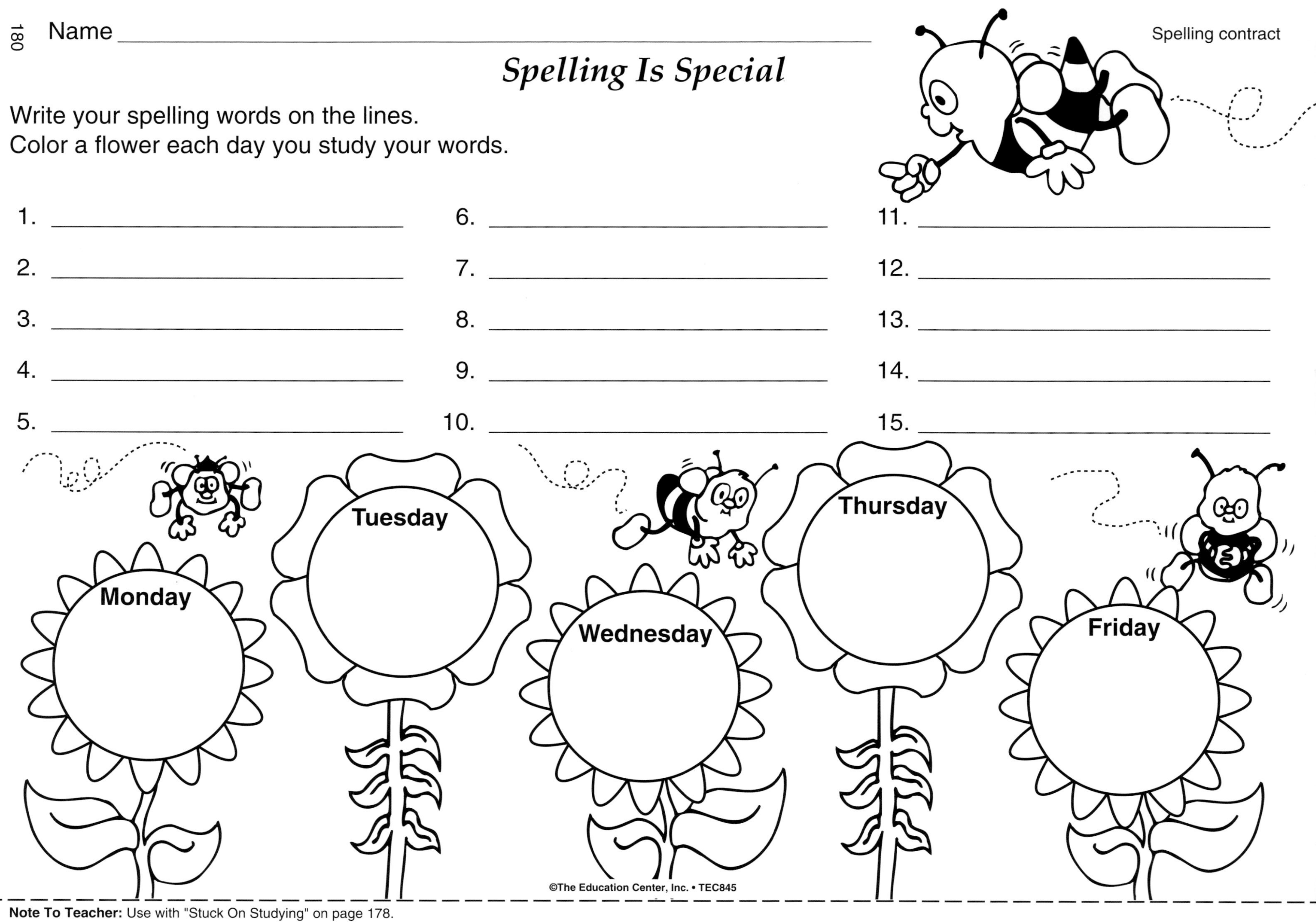

Note To Teacher: Use with "Stuck On Studying" on page 178.

Name ______________________________ Word report

A Word Investigation

Complete the investigation form.

I am investigating the word ______________________.

This word means ____

____.

Here is a way to write this word in a sentence: ______________________

____

____.

Two more things I discovered about this word are ____________________

____

____.

My opinion of this word is ____________________________________

____.

Here is a picture to show what this word means to me.

Bonus Box: Color your picture.

Note To Teacher: Use with "Word Investigations" on page 179.

FROGS!

Leap into the following fun-filled frog activities. There's no time for "pond-ering"—take the plunge!

ideas by Michelle S. Bourlet, Jan Trautman, and Laurie Vent

Finding Out About Frogs

"Ribbit" your youngsters' attention with this eye-catching display! On a bulletin board, mount a large, green frog cutout. Next invite your youngsters to tell everything they know about frogs. List this information on a length of bulletin board paper. When your youngsters are finished, attach the list to the frog's mouth as shown. As new facts are learned, add them to the list.

Frog Habitats

Frogs can live in a variety of places—ponds, swamps, gardens, trees, streams, and deserts. Ask students to describe the places where they have found frogs. List these locations on the chalkboard and explain that these locations are called frog *habitats.* Complete the list by writing any frog habitats that were not mentioned. Next divide students into small groups. Have each group choose a different habitat from the list; then, using markers or crayons, have each group illustrate the habitat that it chose on a length of white bulletin-board paper. Label and display these completed illustrations around the classroom.

At a center, display a collection of books, magazines, and reference books containing information about frogs. Challenge youngsters to draw, color, label, and cut out different kinds of frogs to attach to the appropriate habitats.

Lickety-split!

This froggie center activity is sure to attract lots of attention! Using the patterns on page 184, duplicate a supply of frogs on green construction paper. On red construction paper, duplicate an equal number of tongue patterns. Program the frogs with math problems and the tongues with corresponding answers. Laminate and cut out the shapes. Using an X-acto knife, slit each frog's mouth along the dotted lines. Next carefully insert each programmed tongue into its corresponding frog. Continue to slide each tongue into the frog mouth until the answer is hidden. A student copies and calculates each problem on his paper, then checks his work by pulling out the frog's tongue!

From Eggs To Frogs

Using a variety of illustrated resource books, explore the development of a frog. One excellent resource is *Tadpole And Frog* by Christine Back and Barrie Watts (Silver Burdett Company, 1986). Then follow up your research with this hands-on activity.

Using the wheel pattern on page 184, duplicate one white and one green construction-paper wheel for each youngster. To make a picture wheel, first color the illustrations on the white copy of the wheel. Next cut out both wheels. Cut one triangular section from the green wheel; then place the green cutout atop the white wheel so that the programming on both cutouts faces inward. To attach the two cutouts, insert a brad through the center of both. If desired, attach a tissue paper flower atop the resulting "lily pad wheel cover." To make the flower, attach individual squares of white and lavender tissue paper that have been wrapped around the end of a pencil and dipped in glue. When the projects are complete, pair students and let each youngster explain the different stages in a frog's development by using his picture wheel.

Freeze Frog

Take a break from your regular routine to play this modified version of freeze tag. Students will jump at the chance! Designate an area of your playground to be "the pad." Choose one student to be It and instruct all other students to be "frogs." When a frog is tagged outside the pad, he must freeze and remain motionless until he is tapped by a mobile frog. When all of the frogs are frozen or after a predetermined amount of time has passed, select a new It. For added fun, require each It to identify himself as one of the frog's natural enemies.

Paper Plate Frogs

Have youngsters create a pond full of croakers using these directions. To make a frog, use green tempera paint to sponge print the outside of a paper plate. Copy the patterns on page 185 onto green construction paper; then cut out the patterns. Trace a second eye and front leg shape onto a 4" x 9" piece of green construction paper; then cut out the resulting shapes. Decorate the eye cutouts using scraps of white and black construction paper. When the painted plate has thoroughly dried, glue the pieces around the plate as shown. Then, using a black permanent marker, draw a large smile on the frog. If desired, wrap a 1/2" x 6" strip of pink construction paper around a pencil; then remove the strip and attach one end of it to the frog's mouth.

A Froggie Finale

Plan a froggie finale and watch your youngsters jump for joy! During this closing celebration, invite students to share what they found most interesting about frogs, stories or reports that they wrote about frogs, and books featuring frog (and/or toad) characters that they read. For refreshments, serve each youngster a celery stick that has been filled with peanut butter and adorned with raisins (flies on a log) and a frog float. To make a float, partially fill a paper cup with 7-Up; then float a scoop of lime sherbet in the liquid. Decorate the scoop of sherbet with two chocolate chip "eyes."

Patterns

Use frog and tongue patterns with "Lickety-split!" on page 182.

Use wheel pattern with "From Eggs To Frogs" on page 183.

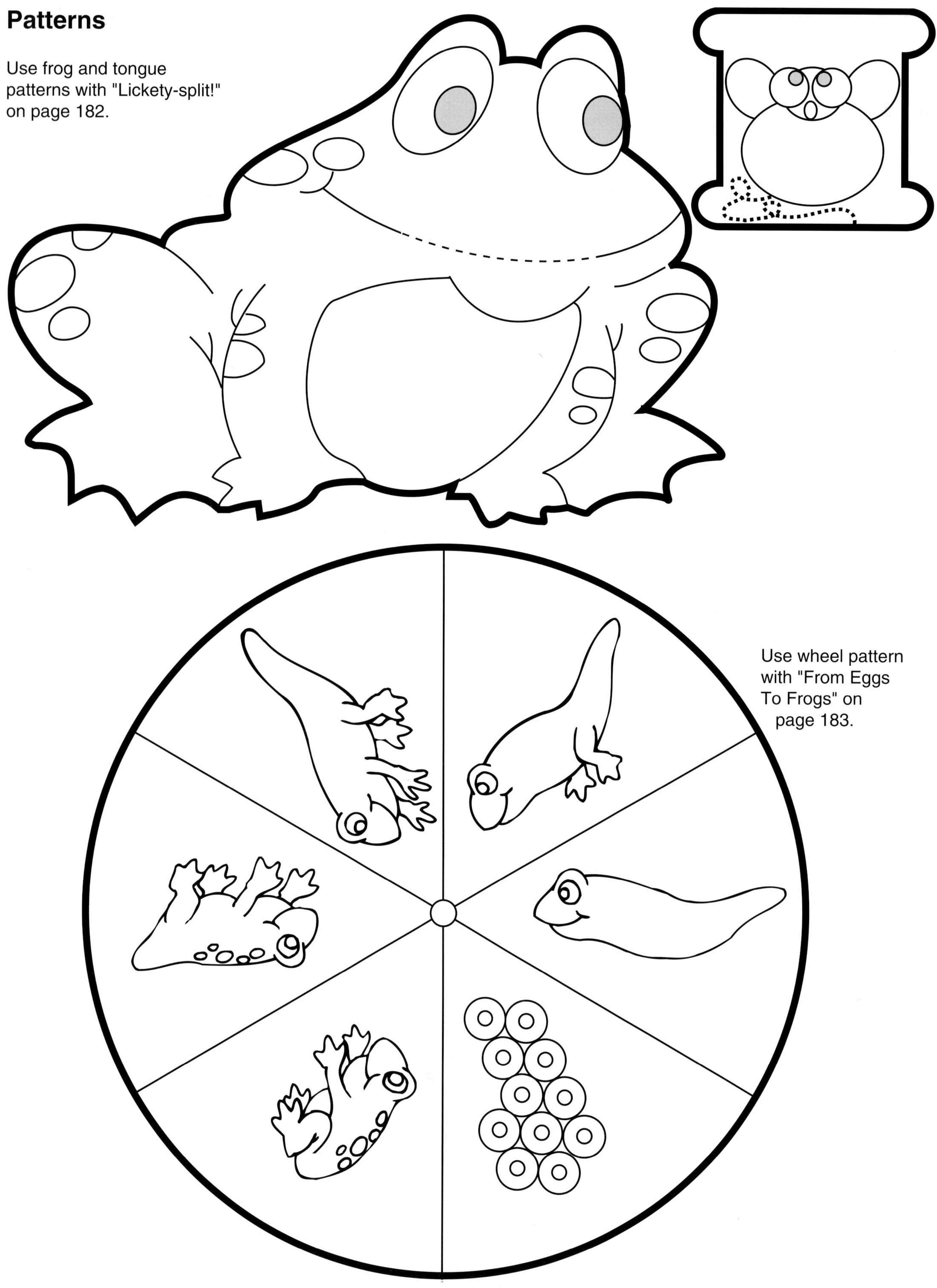

Patterns

Use with "Paper Plate Frogs" on page 183.

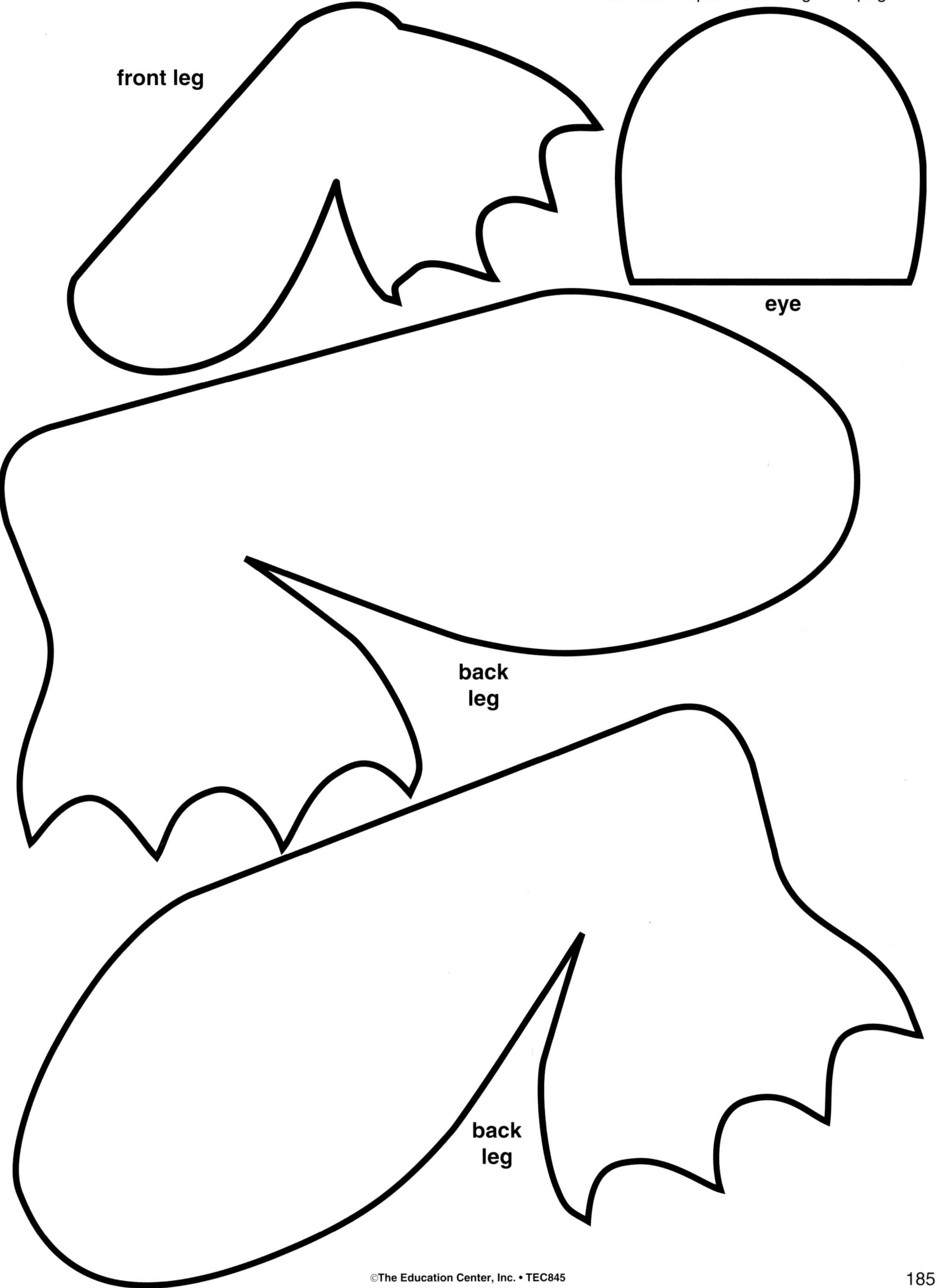

Bon Voyage!

Teacher-tested Activities For The End Of The Year

Prepare your "crew" for summer departure with this collection of fun-filled activities and reproducibles. You'll have "all hands on deck" until the final bell sounds!

Spotlighting The Crew

Each crew member will have his day of glory when you follow this end-of-the-year plan. Label a paper strip for each student; then place the strips in a decorated container. To determine a starting date for the plan, count back (from the last day of school) one school day for each student. Each day select one strip from the container. Have this student be your personal helper for the day and award him other special privileges, if desired. On designated paper, have each of his classmates write two or more positive sentences about him. Compile these papers between construction paper covers. At the end of the day, present this booklet of positive comments to the honored crew member. What a day!

Reading Rocks

This year send your students home with reading rocks! Have each student personalize a small rock by decorating it with paint, construction-paper and fabric scraps, glitter, and other art supplies. Encourage students to keep their rocks "healthy" during the summer by reading to them each day. These eye-catching gems are fun reminders for students to keep their reading skills polished!

Year End Read-in

Host a daylong read-in during the last week of school. Ask each student to bring magazines and books, a large comfortable pillow, and a nutritious snack for the event. Schedule times for independent reading, a read-aloud session with follow-up activities, and other organized reading events such as partner, small group, and choral readings. It's a fun change of pace and a wonderful opportunity for students to realize the reading progress they've made during the year.

Piece By Piece

Here's a fun activity for the kids that's an end-of-the-year timesaver for you! Pull out all your puzzles and other center-type activities having pieces. Then have students complete the activities. Identify and relocate "extra" pieces; then make note of any missing pieces before storing the activities. Now isn't that a fun and efficient way to organize?

Pam Crane

A Special Keepsake

Treat yourself to a special memento of the past year. Have each student design and color a picture especially for you. Then, on the back of his picture, have the student write a letter in which he shares his thoughts about the past year, his summer plans, or anything else he would like to write. Attach a copy of each child's school picture to his completed page; then compile the pages in a scrapbook. Complete the scrapbook with snapshots taken during the year and other special remembrances. It's a keepsake you'll treasure year after year!

This Year's In The Bag!

Students carry home their belongings and special memories from the past school year in these personalized bags. Have students brainstorm sentence starters that reflect on the past school year (for example: The best thing about second grade was..., The hardest word I learned to spell was..., My favorite book was..., I feel proud about this year because...), and list their suggestions on the board. Then have each student cut six large shapes from construction paper and copy and complete one sentence starter on each. Using crayons or markers, have students decorate their shapes before gluing them to the outer surfaces of large-size grocery bags. Each student then places his belongings inside his completed bag and folds and staples the bag top closed. No doubt about it! The year is in the bag!

End-of-the-Year Introductions

Once student placement for the following year has been completed, have each student write a letter to his teacher for next year. The students are excited to showcase their writing talents and the teachers enjoy the personal messages. The letters also provide the teachers with terrific handwriting samples.

Mini-Lesson Sessions

Unite your creative talents with three co-workers' to launch this fun-filled event. Each teacher prepares materials to teach one 30-minute activity four times. Activities might include an art project, an outdoor relay, a manipulative math activity, and a sing-along. On the day of the event, each teacher divides her students into four groups (A, B, C, and D). Have each group meet in one classroom; then let the teaching begin! At the end of 30 minutes, rotate each group to its next activity along a predetermined route. Students enjoy the activities and the chance to work with new classmates and teachers. And teachers have minimal preparation. Adjust the lengths of the sessions and the number of participating teachers to suit your needs. Happy teaching!

Awesome Autographs

Add a fun twist to your end-of-the-year autograph party with T-shirts and fabric paint. Each student (and you!) needs a solid-colored T-shirt and a tube of fabric paint for the occasion. Have each student use his paint to sign his classmates' T-shirts. When dry, have everyone sport their autographed shirts for an end-of-the-year snapshot. Present reprints of the snapshot for fun end-of-the-year gifts!

A Fairy-Tale Finale

Involving students in a study of fairy tales is a fun way to end the school year. Introduce students to different versions of three or four well-known tales such as *Jack And The Beanstalk*, *The Three Billy Goats Gruff*, and *The Three Little Pigs*. Have students complete an assortment of activities relating to each tale; then have each student select the tale he would like to present to his classmates. Working as part of a group, each student helps write a script and create costumes before rehearsing his chosen fairy-tale production. Videotape each group performing its tale during the final days of school. On the last day, serve popcorn and beverages; then sit back and premiere your "star-studded" fairy-tale video!

Summertime Suggestions

These handy lists of summertime suggestions can be lifesavers to students and their parents. As a group, brainstorm a list of summer activities. Write each child's contribution on the chalkboard; then label it with his initials. Continue until each child has one or more contributions listed. Transcribe the initialed list; then make student copies. For a personalized touch, have older students copy and initial their own suggestions on a lined ditto master; then duplicate student copies. Whichever method you choose, the lists are certain to be well received.

Stepping Up

Involve your entire teaching staff in this one-hour activity. Have each teacher prepare one hour of activities appropriate for her grade level. Then have each class of students "step up" to the next grade level for one hour of instruction. Emphasize to students that they are getting a "preview" of the upcoming school year and that the teachers they visit may or may not be their teachers next fall. The students in the highest grade level may "step down" and give the teachers of the lowest grade level a hand with end-of-the-year tasks. Students enjoy the visits and their memories may help eliminate beginning-of-the-year jitters.

Summer Reading List

This year rely on your most valuable reading source to create a summer reading list. First have each child list a predetermined number of favorite book titles. Then, as a class activity, decide upon three or four book classifications (such as *funny stories, scary stories, true stories*), and categorize the suggested book titles. Type the final results and duplicate student copies. During the last days of school, invite each student to tell his classmates why they should read the book titles he recommended. Have students indicate the titles on their lists which particularly interest them.

Sizable Memorabilia

Culminate your school year with this large-group activity. In advance, trace and cut the shape of each student's name from tagboard. Arrange students in a circle on the floor. Each student needs crayons or markers and his corresponding name cutout. Begin the activity by having each student pass his cutout to the student on his right. On this shape, each student writes a positive comment about the owner of the cutout and signs his name. At the end of two minutes, have students repeat the procedure by passing the cutouts to the persons on their right. Continue in this manner until the students' original cutouts are returned. For added fun, play music during each two-minute writing session. The start of the music signals students to begin writing. When the music stops, students pass the cutouts to the right. Have each student sign and date the back of his cutout at the completion of the activity.

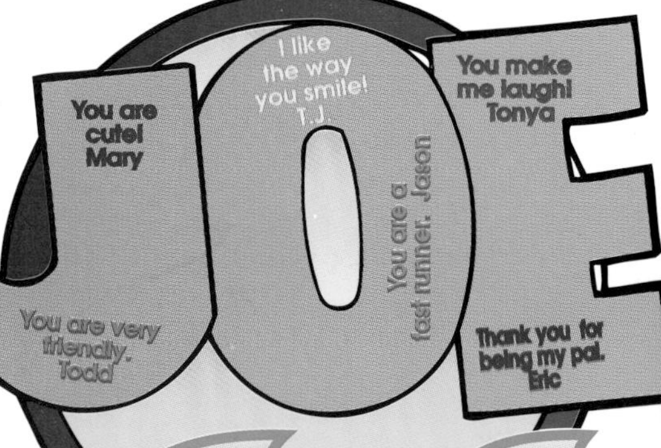

A Proofreaders' Club

Maintain high-quality work during the last days of school with this incentive club. Attach a copy of "Here's The Proof" (patterns on page 190) to the top of each student's desk. Each student colors one box on his form when he remembers to proofread and correct (if necessary) his assignment prior to turning it in. When all the boxes on a student's form are colored, present him with a completed copy of the certificate on page 190. You'll have top-notch student work and ample help completing a variety of end-of-the-year tasks such as correcting, sorting, and distributing student papers!

A Showcase Of Talents

Plan to showcase your students' talents during an end-of-the-year talent show. Students may choose to perform, write narration, direct, create artwork, or contribute to the show in other ways. Begin your preparations in advance, and plan to rehearse each week until the final performance. Have students write invitations to their parents and/or neighboring classrooms and prepare refreshments if desired. At the end of the show, honor each student by recognizing his contribution and presenting him with a certificate of participation.

And That's A Promise!

This activity invites first-grade students to boast about their past school year. And the resulting booklet is fun to share with the upcoming class. Have each student copy, complete, and illustrate the following sentence: I know you will like first grade because.... Compile the completed pages between two construction paper covers which each student has signed. Then have each student share his booklet page with a visiting class of kindergartners. The kindergartners will love hearing about first grade from the children's point of view, and the first-grade youngsters will love sharing their expertise!

Ending The Year With A Bang!

This eye-catching display guarantees that the last week of school will be filled with surprises. Label each of five paper strips with an end-of-the-year surprise such as lunch outdoors, a popcorn party, or a video. Place each strip inside a balloon; then inflate the balloons. On a bulletin board, display a character cutout holding five balloon strings. Entitle the display "Let's End The Year With A Bang!" Attach the inflated balloons to the ends of the strings. Pop a balloon each morning of the last five school days and enjoy the resulting surprise that day. Pop goes the year!

Our thanks to the following contributors who contributed to the original unit: Diane Afferton—Gr. 3, Morrisville, PA; Susan Blume—ESE Teacher, Grs. K–6, Chattahoochee, FL; Mary Dinneen—Gr. 2, Bristol, CT; Nancy Dunaway—Gr. 1, Forrest City, AR; Lori Falknor—Gr. 1, Houston, TX; Pam Free—Gr. 2, Blue Springs, MO; Dianne Giggey—Gr. 1, Pensacola, FL; Jo Glazener—Gr. 2, Grand Prairie, TX; Sheri Groelsema—Gr. 2, Ontario, CA; Kenneth T. Helms—Gr. 3, Greensboro, NC; Marian Johnson—Gr. 2, McPherson, KS; Pam Kauth—Gr. 2, Stoughton, WI; Linda Leach—Gr. 1, Chatham, IL; Mary E. Leary—Gr. 2, Buffalo, NY; Jennifer Morici—Gr. 2, Bristol, PA; Tamra Oliver—Gr. 2, Blacksburg, VA; Donna Ransdell—Substitute Teacher, Grs. K–5, El Cajon, CA; Virginia Riordan—Gr. 2, Ansonia, CT; Annette C. Sheldon, Denville, NJ; Mrs. Jerroll D. Shires—Gr. 3, Gladstone, OR; Vickie Simpson—Gr. 1, Big Rapids, MI; Catherine R. Smith-DuGay—Emotionally Handicapped, Tampa, FL; Babs Sullivan—Gr. 2, Fort Wayne, IN; Julie Wieters—Gr. 1, Richardson, TX

Pam Crane

Use with "A Proofreaders' Club" on page 189.

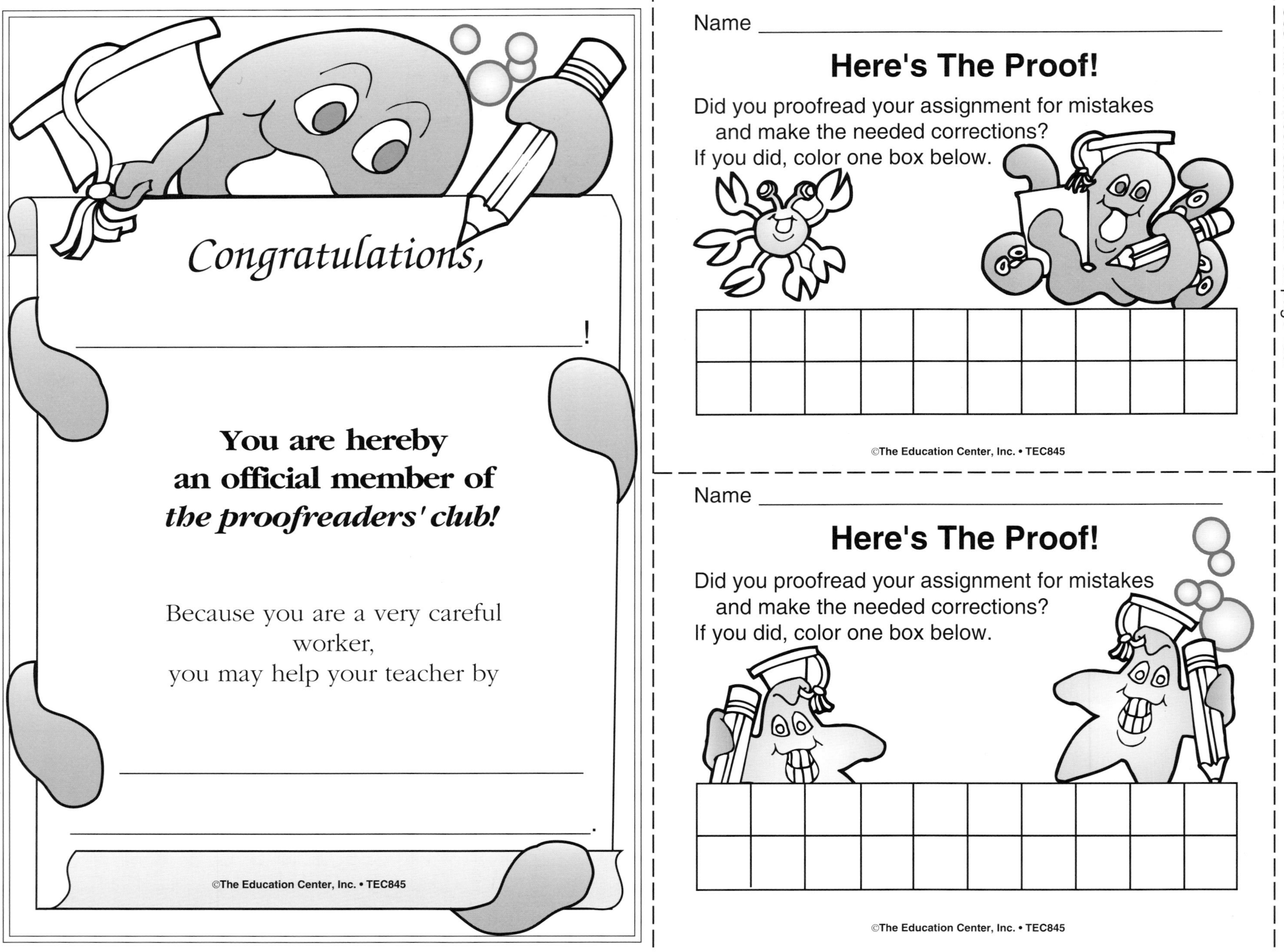

Answer Key

Page 116

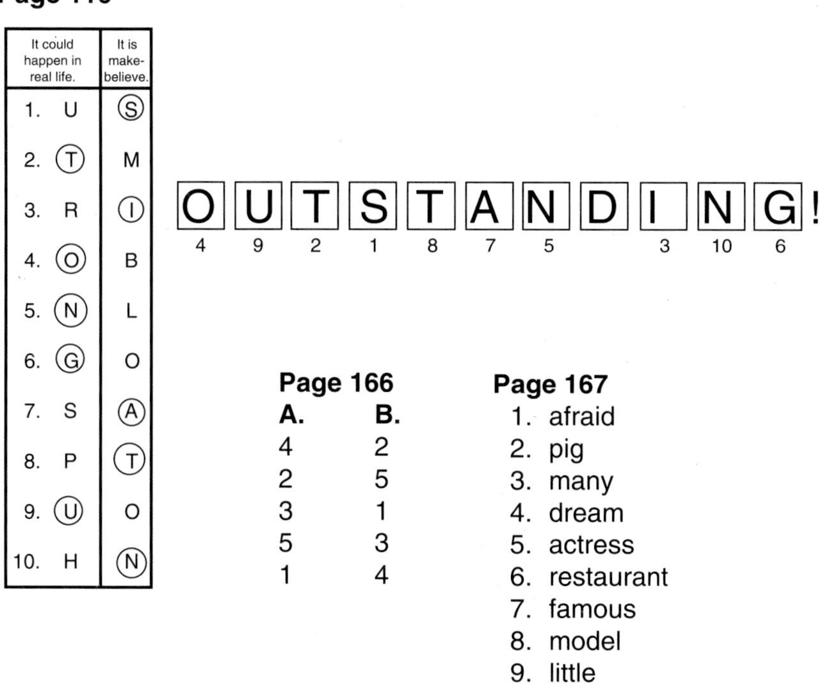

It could happen in real life.	It is make-believe.
1. U	(S)
2. (T)	M
3. R	(I)
4. (O)	B
5. (N)	L
6. (G)	O
7. S	(A)
8. P	(T)
9. (U)	O
10. H	(N)

O U T S T A N D I N G!

4 9 2 1 8 7 5 3 10 6

Page 166

A.	B.
4	2
2	5
3	1
5	3
1	4

Page 167

1. afraid
2. pig
3. many
4. dream
5. actress
6. restaurant
7. famous
8. model
9. little
10. farm

Page 117

Mr. Popper put his paintbrushes away.
Captain Cook arrived.
Greta arrived to keep Captain Cook company.
The penguins grew too big for the refrigerator.
The house filled with snow!
There are now 12 penguins to feed.
Mr. Popper decided to train the penguins.
The penguins performed in Stillwater.
Mr. Popper and his penguins spent a week in jail.
Mr. Popper and his penguins left for the North Pole.

Page 135

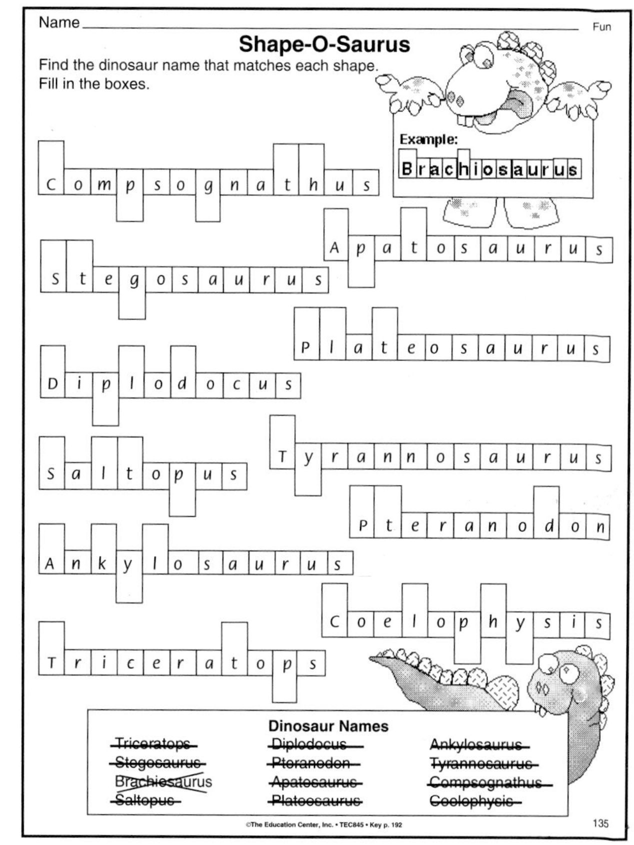

Page 171

The following color combinations are possible:

Bows	Stripes	Dots
red	pink	red
red	pink	purple
red	purple	red
red	purple	purple
pink	pink	red
pink	pink	purple
pink	purple	red
pink	purple	purple

Page 172

The following 16 combinations are possible:

1. 16 + 3 + 2 + 13 = 34
2. 5 + 10 + 11 + 8 = 34
3. 9 + 6 + 7 + 12 = 34
4. 4 + 15 + 14 + 1 = 34
5. 16 + 5 + 9 + 4 = 34
6. 3 + 10 + 6 + 15 = 34
7. 2 + 11 + 7 + 14 = 34
8. 13 + 8 + 12 + 1 = 34
9. 16 + 10 + 7 + 1 = 34
10. 4 + 6 + 11 + 13 = 34
11. 16 + 13 + 1 + 4 = 34
12. 10 + 11 + 6 + 7 = 34
13. 9 + 3 + 8 + 14 = 34
14. 5 + 2 + 12 + 15 = 34
15. 9 + 5 + 8 + 12 = 34
16. 3 + 2 + 15 + 14 = 34

©The Education Center, Inc. • TEC845